MW01115818

ESSAYS IN CONTEMPORARY SOCIOLOGY

SECOND EDITION

Daniel Giverny

ISBN: KDP 9798854669221 (paperback)

4

Table of Content

Chapter One: Sociology and History

Sociology is intimately tied to history. One may not know this if one takes a casual view of how it is taught at most universities in America today. One may not know this if one takes a casual view of the major academic journals in the discipline – the American Journal of Sociology and the American Sociological Review. In these many universities and journals, sociology is rendered into some academic discipline that is oriented toward the systematic, if not scientific, study of the patterns and patternings of social relations amongst individuals and groups. While this definition is in its most general sense somewhat accurate, it fails to appreciate the central role of history in this story. In this book, we begin with a slightly altered definition: Sociology is the systemic and historical study of the patterns and patternings of social relations amongst individuals and groups.

It is rather curious that a chasm has emerged in American sociology between sociology and history. It is curious in that what are identified as some if not most of the more important founding figures of sociology all stressed the need to focus on historical matters. This was certainly and obviously true when considering Max Weber and Karl Marx, but it was also true when considered another founding figure: Emile Durkheim. While Durkheim's scholarship is often seen as not historical, he himself has noted the centrality of history to sociology.

A primary contention of this book is that sociology is and should be understood as inextricably connected to history. The relationship between sociology and history exists in two distinct yet interconnected ways. First, the object of study for sociology is or should be historical. In contrast to much American sociology today which focuses on understanding social dynamics in the present (or more accurately in the eternal present – as there is no conceptual reference to history or time in such studies), the object of study in sociology is or should be a study of the systematic social formations that have arisen in history and that affect the course of history. Thus, sociology may study the political organization of a society and how this organization changes in history and how this changes history. Or one may study the place of religion in sociology and how a religion in a society has arisen and how the religion influences the course of history in that society. A third example: bureaucracies. The important, seminal German sociologist Max Weber (1864-1920), focused a great deal of his attention on bureaucracies, large formal organizations – how they are organized, what historical conditions are conducive to their growth and spread, the impact of the growing dominance of bureaucracies on the modern world, etc.

A second way that sociology relates to history is in terms of the historical development of the field of sociology itself. An interesting parallel exists between the stages of historical development in sociology and the stages of historical changes in American society at large. We can identify four stages – of history and of sociology. The first stage, spanning roughly 1800 through the 1920s, was birthed by **the Enlightenment** (or The Age of Reason). The Enlightenment was an all important period in Western and in world history from 1600 through the late 1700s. It was a period in which philosophers and scientists and other thinkers appeared across Western Europe arguing for new ways of thinking and new ways of being. These scholars looked at their worlds and looked at the intellectual anchors of their worlds, most notably the themes of tradition and religion, and saw these things as having been very harmful to societies. Tradition and religion shackled science; it demanded that science conform to faith rather than to the reasoned assessment of objective facts. Galileo was persecuted in the early seventeenth century for daring to present scientific evidence that the earth revolved around the sun rather than the other way around which was standard Roman Catholic doctrine. Tradition and religion were the bases of the political, social, and economic orders of Europe for more than a thousand years. The nobility and the Catholic Church benefited greatly from this order while the masses largely did not. The Enlightenment philosophers argued for a new set of principles to replace tradition and religion. They argued that a new set of principles was needed to understand and to order their worlds – both the natural and the social worlds. They championed reason (hence the term The Age of Reason). If we were to use reason and rationality systematically to understand and to organize our worlds, they argued, we would have a better, more prosperous, more just world. Reason should replace tradition and religion as the governing principles. This gave way to the dramatic changes of the Enlightenment: modern science was born; modern political and economic systems were born – modern democracy and capitalism -- most notably through the two great revolutions at the end of the eighteen century – the American Revolution (1776) and the French Revolution (1789).

Reason was not the only central theme of the Enlightenment. The elevation of the individual as a moral object, as a philosophical object, as an object of scientific inquiry, and simultaneously as a subject, was also vitally important to many of the Enlightenment philosophers, from Descartes, to Locke, to Kant. Arguably, we would not have the modern human sciences, at least not in the form that we now see these – from psychology to sociology – if it was not for the acceptance of the overarching ideas related to the individual espoused by these scholars. In addition, it was not only the themes of reason and the individual that lay at the foundation of the Enlightenment, but it was also the incredible optimism of these men (and almost all were indeed men). Our philosophers and scientists were deeply convinced that if societies systematically applied the principles of the Enlightenment to understanding and to organizing their worlds, then the world would be a more just, more prosperous world. The march of Reason is ineluctable, and it is good, or so the Enlightenment figures would have it.

The First Stage – 1800-1930

The Enlightenment gave birth to the first stage of modern history relevant to sociology. Coming out of the seventeen hundreds a new world was born – in Europe and in the United States. From 1800 through the 1920s, change becomes the constant. Industrialization, urbanization, rationalization, secularization – though in the United States the claim of secularization needs to be qualified, appearing as it did in some quarters and not in others, all contributed to a world expanding and changing, a world becoming more prosperous, a world in which technology and science and capitalism become more and more central.

At the time of the American Revolution, the United States was overwhelmingly a rural society. The vast majority of Americans lived on farms or in small towns. By 1900, all this changed. Most Americans by that time, were living in or near cities, and the cities were growing tremendously in size and in number. Philadelphia, New York, Boston, and later Chicago, and others, grew from a few hundred thousand people in 1800 (Chicago did not even exist at the time), to massive urban centers with millions of people by 1900.

It is the last part of this stage, in the period from 1890 to 1920 or so, that I wish to draw the readers' attention because this is the period where modern sociology in America was born. This period is often called by social and cultural historians the Progressive Era. In addition to all of the changes noted earlier, this period is also characterized by a number of other centrally important ones. Most notably the era is defined by the movement of massive numbers of people. Specifically, this was the era of a massive immigration stream largely from Southern and Eastern Europe into the major cities on the Eastern seaboard, and it was a period of huge internal migration of African Americans fleeing the oppressions and persecutions in the Jim Crow South and moving to the major cities in the north with the hopes of a better future.

A few more words need to be said about each of these movements. First, one needs to appreciate the size of the European immigration stream into the United States at this time. America has experienced several large immigration streams in history. It is experiencing one right now. The present immigration stream is largely from Latin America, and specifically from Mexico. It is somewhat comparable in size, at least proportionately, to the immigration stream of the Progressive Era. The immigration stream of the Progressive Era was very significant for American history. It has been estimated that one out of every four New Yorkers in the early 1900s could not speak English. The composition of this immigration stream was of particular consequence. Overwhelmingly, the immigrants coming to America at this time were from Southern and Eastern Europe – from Italy, Poland, Russia, etc. Of note, the vast majority were Roman Catholics and Jews, though the size of the latter was significantly smaller than the former.

This profoundly altered the ethnic and religious make-up of the United States. The dominant ethic group for much of American history were the WASPS – the White Anglo-Saxon Protestants, i.e. Protestants who came from Great Britain. America was dominated by WASPs from the colonial period through the 1950s or so, at which time, the descendants of Catholics and Jews from the immigration stream of the Progressive Era, came to alter this dominance. WASPs dominated all facets of power. They controlled the American political system, the economic system, the cultural system. Whether it was in the judiciary, or the legislature, or in corporate board rooms, WASPS controlled all levers of power. For example, Prior to the election of the Roman Catholic, Irish-American John F Kennedy as President in 1960, all presidents were Protestants, and even in 1960 there was great public discussion about this issue. America was defined by Protestants in their image.

In the late 1800s and early 1900s, a strong Nativist movement existed. That is, there was a strong sentiment amongst many WASPs that America was their country and that they should prevent Catholics and Jews from immigrating. This Nativism is classically captured in the radical activities of the Klu Klux Klan, the John Birch Society, and other similar racist and white nationalist organizations.

And yet, the expanding industrial capitalism that was America during the Progressive Era needed workers. The immigrants served the bill. But the huge numbers of foreigners flooding into the major cities were of concern to the ruling classes. Catholics and Jews from Southern and Eastern Europe were foreign in so many ways. They were different, and as we see below, were seen by many Americans with contempt. The immigration flood gates were all but closed as a result in the early 1920s with Congress passing a series of laws, including the Immigration Act of 1921, which all but shut the door to significant further immigration.

At the same time as Catholics and Jews were flooding into America, black Americans were fleeing the rural Jim Crow South and heading into the cities. The growing number and percentages of black people in the major northern cities, from Philadelphia to New York and beyond were significant. Prior to the late 1900s, the size and percentage of black residents of the major northern cities was relatively small. This all begins to change in the Progressive Era, as black Americans moved to the cities in hopes of getting jobs in the booming factories and industrial economies of the north. By force and by choice, black Americans in the large northern cities were put together in ghettos, which remain to this day.

Like the Catholics and Jews coming into the cities at this time, Black Americans were subjected to racist animus and distain. But the degree of hatred toward black Americans was not on the same register as the WASPs disgust with the white ethnics, i.e. the Catholics and Jews. It was far more significant. As a result, Catholics and Jews could and did get the jobs in the booming industrial economy, but Blacks were largely shut out. Whether it was in the fire departments of the major cities, often controlled by white ethnic groups (such as the Irish-Americans) or in the factories, Blacks were largely excluded from much of the economy, in large measure by newly arriving white ethnics together with the WASPs already present.

This period is called **the Progressive Era**. The term largely refers to the developments in laws, and politics, and particularly within policies related to the human services, e.g. medicine, social work, psychology, etc. that occurred at this time. It refers to a new social and cultural ethos that arose largely amongst the dominant WASPs in response to all of the many changes noted above occurring in the late nineteenth and early twentieth century, most notably the changing demographic composition of America, and specifically within the changing American cities.

At the heart of progressivism, lied the belief that science fused with humanistic compassion could be employed by the state – either the federal or state governments – to address the social ills of the day. Progressives saw the state as an active entity that should be used to contain and control the excesses of capitalism, whether these excesses were the incredible concentration of wealth in the hands of the wealthy class or were the poverty and misery of the poorer classes. Behind and beneath this patina, however, lies a more central dynamic of progressivism: How is WASP America going to maintain itself as a WASP nation in the face of the immigration streams noted earlier?

It was within this context that the social work profession emerged. Social work as a profession was started largely by middle class WASP women as well as protestant ministers who sought to aid the poor and the immigrant and to teach them the values and proper ways of being Americans, i.e. being proper WASPs. The settlement house movement, a major aspect of the founding of social work, embodies this, where middle class women social workers would develop these houses in poorer neighborhoods to model and to teach proper ways of conforming to America.

Of note, the progressives – whether in social work or in politics or elsewhere – were most certainly not revolutionaries. They, by and large, did not see capitalism or democratic capitalism as fundamentally flawed and needing to be overthrown. Instead, they believed in the goodness of capitalism; they merely wanted to check its excesses. They wished to reform not overthrow capitalism. (Indeed, many progressive reformers saw their efforts as a way to combat the perceived evils of the seductions of communism – which was a growing force in Europe, as an alternative to the limits or perceived failures of capitalism.) Relatedly, and importantly, the progressives routinely eschewed thinking about the social, as either the cause of problems or as solutions, and instead focused on the individual and immediate social relations. It was the individual person that needed adjustment or that needed help. It was not large-scale systematic forces of society that needed to change to provide this adjustment or help. As such, psychological orientations emerged as a dominant focus. This was a time when psychiatry emerged as a tool to be employed outside of the asylums. Community mental health was emerging as an area of interest. Social work was at the time beholden to psychiatry.

This focus on the individual, rather than on the social, has a long history in America, and this history continues through the present. (Reflect upon how public discourse today occurs related to issues such as crime or mental illness. The focus is not on a discussion of the social conditions that might be producing such things. Instead, the focus is on individual psychology.) And yet while progressive reformers largely identified the individual as the object of concern and as the object of intervention and treatment, a different approach emerges, which is, at least in some ways as we will see, contrary to the focus on the psychology of the individual. Here we have the birth of sociology, a science ostensibly focused on understanding the changing social world by focusing on the organization of social relations, e.g. by focusing on what is happening between or among people, rather than by focusing on the individual itself.

Modern sociology has its roots deep in the Enlightenment (The Age of Reason). August Comte (1798-1857) is generally recognized to be the first modern sociologist. Comte was a French scholar and philosopher, a student of the influential political philosopher Saint-Simon. Embracing fully the principles of the Enlightenment, Comte argued that a science of society, a "social physics," which we now call sociology, should be developed. He believed that there was one and only one way of doing science. Thus, the approach – the methods and epistemologies – of all scientific fields, from chemistry and physics, to biology, psychology, and sociology, all should use the same philosophical approach. That is, they all should embrace the fundamental claims of science. They all should make causal claims about the way the world (naturally) works by objectively observing empirical facts and by observing the ways that one fact or one set of facts causes another set of facts to arise. The intent in science is to discover the natural and timeless laws governing the natural world. In this view, the world – including the social world – is like one big mechanical clock. Comte called this philosophical foundation positivism, and he believed that sociology should embrace positivism, just like all the other sciences have done.

But American sociology did not emerge as an established academic discipline for another fifty years or so. It only began to emerge in the late 1800s. The first major center of sociology in America was at the University of Chicago. In the late 1800s and early 1900s, sociology became established there and within a few decades, sociology was being introduce at many of the major research universities in the country. (The same was happening in Europe, but the form of sociology emerging there was different, as we note below.) At the University of Chicago, men such as Robert Parks, Anthony Burgess, and many more, created a way of doing sociology that became known as the Chicago School of sociology. Progressive sensibilities rippled through much of their work. They sought to create a science of sociology, and their focus was largely on the city, and in this case on Chicago. Urban sociology was central to their project. They also sought to develop a scientific understanding of the workings of the city and most notably they sought to understand how the organization of social relations was impacted by these workings. Specifically, one of the notable types of research conducted by the members of the Chicago School was urban ethnographies – qualitative studies of individuals and groups living in the city. Researchers from the universities would in these studies spend considerable time amongst a group of people – often poorer individuals and groups -- living in the center of the city. The researchers would observe and interact with these people and try to make sociological sense of these observations.

One of the more important intellectual influences on the Chicago School was the philosophy of George Herbert Mead

(1863-1931). Mead taught at the University of Chicago for many years, from 1894 until his death. He was one of several American philosophers in the eighteen and early nineteen hundreds who developed a type of philosophy called pragmatism. The most notable pragmatists were William James, C.S. Pierce, John Dewey, and George Herbert Mead. In general, pragmatism is a uniquely American philosophical perspective that says that if one wishes to understand and explain human behavior, and the human condition more generally, that one must begin with the assumption that people are practical, problem solvers. We assign meanings to our world and act upon our worlds based upon those meanings. Mead took these ideas further and developed a form of social psychology that sees the individual and the social world as fluid and emergent with social actors doing things to solve practical problems in front of them and to affirm their understanding of themselves and their worlds. The social world is a fluid and ever-changing place, and the individual self is constantly creating and recreating itself – creating an understanding of "who am I?" -- through social interactions. While Mead was in the Philosophy Department he had a significant impact upon the sociologists – the latter turned Mead's ideas into a sociological theory called symbolic interactionism, which was influential upon the Chicago School and continues to be an important theoretical tradition in American sociology today.

Of particular note here is the focus on individuals and on immediate social relations rather than upon the organization of the entire society. Symbolic interactionism is considered today to be a micro-approach to sociology rather than a macro approach. The former is much like a form of psychology – but importantly a *social* psychology -- while the latter is oriented toward understanding the large scale forces, such as the organization of the economy or of culture to account for social behaviors. This micro orientation, with a focus on social interactions, fits neatly with progressive era sensibilities.

The Second Stage: 1930-1965

The 1920s is sometimes called the "roaring twenties." It was the time of prohibition, where alcohol was illegal to buy, to sell, to consume, in America. It was a time of speakeasies – where people drank alcohol illegally and flaunted that law. It was a time of a growing economy. In general, the average wages were rising, and the wealth of the country grew. Urbanization and industrialization plowed on. All of this dramatically changed with the Great Depression. The stock market crashed in 1929 and the economy collapsed. Unemployment rose to twenty five percent and those who had jobs saw their wages cut and cut. The capitalist economy was not working. Herbert Hoover, the President at the time of the crash embraced the free market. If we just allow the free market to work, he said, we would naturally pull ourselves out of this economic downturn. But this did not happen. The market did not correct itself. The Depression continued and it got worse. The entire decade of the 1930s was mired in this horrible situation. And it was not only America that was suffering. The Depression was a world-wide phenomenon, hitting Europe particularly hard.

The Democrat Franklin Delano Roosevelt was elected president in 1932, and then re-elected again and again in 1936 and 1940. Roosevelt enacted numerous and large federal public programs to address the calamity of the Depression. He created social security – a public insurance program to protect the elderly and poor. He created various federal public works programs. He funded countless social programs meant to both alleviate the miseries of the Depression on the masses and to stimulate the economy. His impact on the role of government is American life was profound. He greatly expanded the role of the federal government in the economic and in the social spheres. By most accounts, his policies helped to get American through and past the Depression (though it is not uncommon now for conservative or arch-conservative economists, often employed by the wealthy in right-wing thinktanks, today to claim that Roosevelt's policies actually prolonged and did not resolve the problems of the Depression).

It was during the 1930s, during the Depression, that fascism took over much of Europe. Mussolini, the Italian dictator, rose to power in the mid-1920s. But in Germany, Hitler was elected to power in 1933, partly as a result of the German voters' experiences of the Depression, which hit Germany particularly hard. Hitler's Nazi Party received almost forty percent of the vote. Germany had, and still has, a multi-party democratic system. As such, to gain power one party often has to negotiate with another to share power. This is what occurred in Germany in 1933 when the mainstream conservative party, which was historically the largest party, did not have the votes to rule by themselves. As a result, they reached out to the radical right Nazi party and agreed to give Hitler power, with the mistaken belief that they could control him.) Hitler soon coalesced his power and by 1934-5, democracy no longer existed in Germany. (And many other countries in Europe also abandoned democracy in favor of one or another form of fascism.)

The Great Depression largely ended with World War Two, 1939-1945. The War pitted the allied powers – The United States, England, and the Soviet Union – against the axis powers – the fascist regimes of Central and Southern Europe – Germany, Italy, as well as Japan in the Pacific, etc. The War started when the ultra-nationalist Hitler demanded that all of the lands in central Europe in which Germans lived should be part of a greater Germany. He took over Austria, then Bohemia (a German speaking part of the Czech Republic.) The allied powers did nothing meaningful in response. They did not oppose his actions, and some claimed that they could still work with him. Then Hitler invaded Poland and World War Two began. Hitler, of course, embraced a radical racist right wing philosophy, one which led to the Holocaust and the extermination of not only six million Jews, but millions and millions of others – the mentally and physically disabled, gays and lesbians, communists, etc. All told, around fifty million people died in World War Two (with the Soviet Union suffering the most deaths).

After the Great Depression and after the horrors of World War Two, the United States was the only major democratic, capitalist country left intact. In Eastern Europe, the Soviet Union, a communist country, shared the victory with, but paid a far higher cost than, the United States. The decades after World War Two were described as the Cold War, an international ideological conflict between the two powers: the democratic, capitalist United States and the communist Soviet Union. It was not a shooting war, but the fear that at any moment the conflict could erupt into an actual war was constant. This was a significant and tense period in which both sides became nuclear powers, and in which the contest of ideologies and power spread across the world in various proxy wars, such as the Viet Nam war.

Within the United States, from 1945 through 1960 or so, a patina of order and prosperity existed. The economy expanded through this time, more and more Americans became wealthier. Many of the second and third generation of white ethnics – Catholics and Jews, whose parents and grandparents immigrated to America in the early years of the century, experienced upward mobility, due largely to the expanding economy. The cohesion of the dominant ethnic group in traditional America, the WASPS, was weakening. And the fundamental character of the dominant group in America was expanding. The new dominant group was now emerging as "whites." It now included white ethnic Catholics and Jews.

The images of social cohesion, order and prosperity that saturated the dominant ideology of the time can readily be seen and understood through the widespread use of the newly emerging technologies of radio, television, and the movies. One thinks here of the western television shows, such as Gunsmoke, or the 1950s shows like Father Knows Best. This was well before the cacophony of voices and images seen today through the internet, social media, and cable. Then there was a somewhat unified ideological message seen by the masses of Americans. (There were after all only three television networks in the 1960s.) Almost all echoing the same themes – of unity, prosperity, goodness.

All of this belies the actual reality of the post-War decades. Massive inequalities continued. Black people continued under the yoke of oppression. Women knew their place, as the old and by now satiric phrase was used. (While women got the right to vote in 1920, in practical realities they continued to live as second class citizens; similarly, while Black people technically were supposed to be allowed to vote, in realities, particularly in the Jim Crow South, they were prevented from doing so.) The discontents with the order were real, though largely hidden from popular view. The patina of order and happiness saturated the dominant and popular mindset. It was not until the 1960s when we see this discord appear in popular consciousness and popular practices. We will come back to this below.

Importantly, higher education in America greatly expanded from the late 1800s through the 1960s. The number of universities, the number of graduate schools, the numbers of people receiving college degrees and advanced degrees, such as Ph.D.'s, greatly expanded throughout this period. And with this, sociology as an academic discipline became established across the country. Undergraduate majors in sociology were now offered as were doctorates in sociology.

The American sociology of this period reflects, embodies, and reinforced the sensibilities noted above. Specifically, the dominant approach in American sociology from the 1930s through the 1960s was called **structural functionalism**, and the main figure associated with the development and spread of this approach was Talcott Parsons (1902-1979), who was a professor at Harvard University. Parsons received his graduate training in Germany and largely was responsible for introducing and championing the ideas of two important early European sociologists: the French scholar Emile Durkheim (1858-1917) and the German scholar Max Weber. Parsons developed the approach called structural functionalism by fusing the ideas of Weber and Durkheim (along with the ideas of the conservative Italian economist Vilfred Pareto).

At the heart of structural functionalism is the idea of model building. To understand the social world, to understand society, one should create an abstract model of that world. Toward this end, Parsons drew heavily upon the ideas of Durkheim. Durkheim drew often on biological models or biological metaphors to understand the workings of the social world: Society is like the human body he often suggested. Just like the human body is a unified whole with specialized parts that exist to maintain a healthy whole, so to society is structured in the same way. The heart exists – for evolutionary reasons – because it functions to pump the blood in the circulatory system. The lungs exist because they have a useful function to maintaining the healthy body; the lungs process oxygen. In the same way, a structural functionalist would look at the various parts of society, and if these parts maintained themselves for long periods, then they must serve a function to help to maintain the stability or health of the social order. The family, for example, structural functionalists would say exists in all societies. It therefore must have a function or functions. Among other things, the family provides support and protection; it socializes children, etc. Similarly, a functionalist might say that religion exists, as such it must serve a function. For example, religions, at least in traditional societies, provides a moral glue for a society. Importantly, for functionalists the biological metaphor of health and equilibrium or balance was central. The body has a natural tendency to maintain its health. It heals, for example. It also maintains an equilibrium or balance. The body, for example, maintains an average, i.e. normal, bod temperature of 98.6, but when the body gets sick one might get a fever and the temperature will rise. So too we have a normal and steady heartrate, but if one runs around the block the heart rate goes up, only to return to normal once the body stops running. The same for society: Societies can be healthy, and they can be sick, and they have a natural tendency to maintain balance and health.

Parsons took Durkheim's ideas and expanded greatly upon them. One of the central parts of Parsons' model building was his conceptual development of systems. The body is a system; society is a system. But there are many, many other systems: families, politics, law, education, the natural environment, the liver, religion, etc. Society is a system that is comprised of other systems, which are in term comprised of other systems. Parsons' sets about trying to identify the common features of all systems. This is the heart of his model. We need not go into details here about the specifics of the models. Suffice to say that he said that all systems needed several things if they are to survive and to operate normally. For example, all systems need resources of one sort or another. The human body, as a system, to survive needs things like food and water as resources. The economy needs money as its resources, etc. The point here, again, is that he creates these models to understand how the real social world operates.

Parsons developed an elaborated and sophisticated model of society that was anchored in functionalism. Importantly, his approach became the unquestionable dominant approach in America through this historical stage – the 1930s through the mid-1960s. Many of his graduate students went on the chair important sociology departments in major research universities across the country.

One perhaps can see the parallels between the form of sociology championed by Parsons and the structural functionalists, and the times within which it dominated, specifically post-World War Two America. These times, it may be recalled, were dominated by a WASP cultural sensibility which was becoming infused with non-Protestant white elements. (It is perhaps worth noting that Parsons himself was very much a WASP.) The image of both the sociological theory and the dominant ideology of the times was one of order and optimism. America was seen as a good, moral place, as a place that is anchored in optimism. America was deemed healthy and whole and was rightfully ordered.

This is not to deny that these forms of thinking did not recognize problems of the day, for example inequalities and racial oppressions. But the nature of the dominant cultural ethos was that there was a place for everyone in this wholesome America – this good, just, prosperous America. At its heart, was an appeal, a demand really, that the discontent surrender their opposition to the dominant moral order, which was ordered, good and functional. All was well with America in the post-World War Two era, or at least this was the image propagated by the dominant classes and by the sociologists of the time.

The Third Stage – 1965-2016

The myth of goodness and order that pervaded the halls of power in the post-World War Two decades came crashing down in the 1960s. To understand this, we need to first appreciate the importance of the extent of the political realignment that occurred in America in the 1950s and in the 1960s, specifically in relation to geography and race. From the end of the Civil War through the 1950s, the white American South was overwhelmingly supportive of the Democratic Party. Basically, if you were a white Southerner, you were a Democrat. In effect, the Democratic Party of the South was a thoroughly racist party. Black Southerners were overwhelmingly Republican, a sensibility going back to the Republican President Abraham Lincoln. In the North in the post war era, the base of the Republican Party was the traditional WASP. But the Democratic Party had a foothold, starting in the early 1900s, in the working classes in the industrial North, and specifically in the white ethnic (Catholic and Jewish) working classes. As such, while the Democratic Party in the South had a monopoly on power (reflecting the lack of a meaningful democracy), in the North there were contested elections between the Republicans and the Democrats, and the two parties traded places in power throughout the time.

All of this changes with the emergence of the Civil Rights movement. The Civil Rights Movement which began in the 1950s and continued through the 1960s had a profound impact upon America – an impact that continues through the present. Both the mainstream Civil Rights movement led by the Reverend Martin Luther King and a host of other and the more radical wings of the movement embodied in the ideas and actions of people such as Malcolm X laid the foundation for major changes in America – changes which today one could argue are to be found as much in the culture and consciousness of Americans as in the practical realities of racial lives in America today.

Here I wish to note the profound change the Civil Rights movement had on political alignments in the United States. It was accompanied by a massive political realignment. From the 1950s through the 1970s, a dramatic political realignment occurred. By the 1980s, the white South was overwhelmingly Republican, and the black South was overwhelmingly Democrat. In the North, the two parties continued to maintain somewhat parity, with one or the other party being in power at any one time. In the North, black Americans were also overwhelmingly Democratic, and in this period, the white ethnic working class was still Democratic.

The important political realignment emerged in the 1950s and 1960s, in no small part because of the Civil Rights movement and the accompanying and significant changes in American culture and social relations that occurred at that time. The Civil Rights movement emerged in part because of the political contexts of the time. This context provided a political opportunity to exist, where none did so before (see McAdam 1999), for Black Americans to assert themselves and demand equality. For example, the national Democratic Party in the early 1960s, had to appeal the northern Democratic vote – which at the time consisted largely of white ethnics and black Americans – while at the same time courting the favors of the traditional Southern Democratic (and racist) base. Thus, for example we seen President Lyndon Johnson, a Democrat from Texas quoting from Martin Luther King (though Johnson is also quoted as having said a number of racist and/or cynical things about race in private). Johnson's Great Society programs, which were a series of social welfare programs much in the spirit of Roosevelt's New Deal forty years earlier, captures the political opportunities that were available in the early 1960s for "liberal" policies that countered the Jim Crow racist sensibilities so prevalent.

The political realignment and the Civil Rights movements came with numerous other events from the 1960s that profoundly shaped or re-shaped American society. This period is generally seen as a "liberal" decade. It was a time of the emergence or revitalization of numerous social movements, many of which drew inspiration if not more from the Civil Rights movement. The student protest movements of the 1960s perhaps are some of the more well known. From Berkeley to Columbia University, students were protesting anything from racial oppressions to gender inequalities, to environmentalism, to gay rights, to policies directly related to their own education, such as requirements to graduate, etc. Of all of the issues of the time, the Viet Nam war stands as one of the starkest. Ostensibly the United States became involved in the Viet Nam war in the 1950s to fight communism. It did so after France, a former colonial ruler of Viet Nam, withdrew. The Vietnamese in the north were fighting arguably as much for national independent and against colonialism as they were for communism. In the 1960s Americans were being drafted into the army to fight in Viet Nam. On campuses across the country – but notably in the north and west, there were numerous protests against the war and other policies of the United States government. (The United States was defeated by Viet Nam in the early 1970s and it withdrew. Over fifty thousand Americans were killed in the war and hundreds of thousands of Vietnamese lost their lives.)

The 1960s were a tumultuous period, led largely by the young and by black Americans fighting to change the existing political, social, and cultural order. Numerous liberal social policies and laws were enacted and put into place. For example, the Civil Rights Act of 1964 was passed that among other things sought to have the federal government supervise elections in the South the ensure that black Southerners could vote and could have their vote counted. It was another nail in the coffin of Jim Crow. There were in this period examples of federal oversight over corporations, from environmental regulation to worker safety regulations. It was indeed a liberal, though decidedly not a radical, period in American history.

The liberal sensibilities of the times – and it bears noting that polling at the time suggests that much of the more liberal sensibilities were not shared by the majority of Americans at the time but were nevertheless accorded a central place of importance for various reasons which we cannot engage with here – continued though somewhat abated through the 1970s and into the 1980s. And many of the particular changes that emerged in the 1960s have continued through the present. One only need to think about "identity politics," e.g. champion the rights of the LGBT+ community, or of women, or of minority groups today, to recognize the enduring legacy of the 1960s. Indeed, one might be tempted to say that America has increasingly become more liberal, at least on cultural issues, since the 1960s, for example on matters of race or lgbtq+ issues. And within the popular cultural arena, arguably it has. Similarly, it has within certain localized sectors of society, such as big cities and universities. But the power of this liberal expansion pales in comparison to the increasing growth of the power of conservativism through this era.

The overall period under question – from 1965-2016 – is defined not by liberalism but by the increasingly radical reaction to and against liberalism. By the 1980s and 1990, conservativism was growing bigger and more influential (in part due to the political realignments noted above) and most importantly it was becoming more and more conservative, though even by the end of this period it still maintained some semblance of the traditional Republican Party conservativism of decades earlier. We will examine this further below. But one more topic needs to be considered first.

To understand the growing political and cultural conservative reaction during this period, one must appreciate two things. The first is demographic. Specifically, the cultural gap between rural and urban America. By population, America, like all industrial and post-industrial societies, is an urban society. The vast majority of Americans live in or near cities, and the majority live in or near major cities. Moreover, it is clear that the attitudes, beliefs, and practices of people living in rural areas are very different from those living in cities. Urban people tend to be less religious, more tolerant, generally more liberal than rural people. Polling consistently shows this, as does other sociological data sources. This is reflected over the last fifty years through polling on a range of issues concerning the "culture wars," from religion to abortion to gay rights, etc. A second, more important thing that needs to be appreciated here is the organization of the political system of the United States. The system is structured to give greater weight to the rural residents than it does it urban residents. That is, the Constitution disproportionately gives more power to rural people than it does to urban people. The vote of a rural person from South Dakota has more power, more weight, than the vote of some living in New York City.

To understand this, we need to turn toward an understanding of the foundations of the American political system. This is anchored in the structure of the government, going back to the founding of the republic. Some conservatives today like to say that America is not and was not created as a democracy. These people often quote James Madison from *the Federalist Papers* to make the claim. *The Federalist Papers* were a series of essays published in a newspaper written by Madison, John Jay, and Alexander Hamilton which were meant to convince the public to agree on the newly drafted, proposed Constitution, which was subsequently adopted. In one section, Madison, says clearly that America is not and should not be a democracy. (See Chapter Twelve for an extended discussion.) He embraced the idea of a republic, that is, the idea of a representative democracy. He believed that the elected representatives would have the temperament, the demeanor, to act in objective ways for the betterment of the society.

Toward this end, Madison embraced the elevated position of the U.S. Senate, which could be considered the "upper house" in relation to the U.S. Congress (the House of Representatives), which could be considered the "lower house." The Congress is and was comprised of seats reflecting the population of states. Thus, states with larger populations had and have more seats in Congress than states with smaller population. California has far more Congressional seats than does Wyoming. But the Senate was and is configured differently. It is not configured by population, but by state. Thus, each state has two senators. California has two senators, but so too does North Dakota, even though the latter only has a tiny fraction of the population of the former. When one looks at the Senate, one can see that people who live in rural, less populated states have far more political power in the U.S. government than people living in urban, populated states because of the composition of the Senate. (The majority of the Senate, when the Republican Party rules, represents only a small percentage of Americans – those from rural America.) The political system favors rural America, at the expense of reflecting the democratic will of the American people.

The distortions that come about as a result of these things are reflected time and again in laws, policies, and practices. One only need to consider the composition of the Supreme Court to realize this. Members get appointed to the Court as a result of the U.S. Senate vote, and as the Senate is structurally more conservative, the U.S has gotten more conservative Justices on the Court. (While this has historically been the case, the situation has been greatly exacerbated in recent years. This is a topic we revisit below.) A second example is equally if not more significant. This is the way that American presidential elections are held. The president of the United States is not elected by the popular vote of Americans, as one might think should happen in a democracy. Instead, the president is elected by the electoral college. This is a device created by the founding fathers in part out of fear, noted above, of the passions of the mob, and in part out of a concern that larger states would overwhelm smaller states if the popular vote was to be used to elect presidents.

The **electoral college** is comprised of the total number of U.S. House of Representative seats plus the total number of U.S. Senate seats. The House, as we noted, is determined by population. The Senate is not. It is determined by state. The two parties – Democrats and Republicans -- select people who will act as members of the electoral college should their candidate win the popular vote in their particular states, and traditionally (and by law in many states), the members of the electoral college vote in ways that reflect the majority presidential vote in their state. Thus, if the people of North Dakota vote in a presidential election for the Republican candidate, the person designated by the North Dakota Republican party will serve on the electoral college and will vote for the Republican candidate.

As a result, we have seen in the last several decades several instances in which the President of the United States was elected to office even though he did not receive the majority of votes in the country. And in recent decades it has been the Democratic candidate who has won the popular vote while losing the election. There is little reason to believe this trend will be reversed anytime in the near future. Again, this electoral process skews presidential elections in favor of rural, conservative, and disproportionately white voters and disfavors urban and liberal voters. (We will return to this situation below.)

Another issue centrally important to the times in which we live, and centrally important to an understanding of sociology, concerns the state of the American universities during the period of 1965-2016. We return here to the universities to note again one other very significant effect of the 1960s – that is in its impact upon the universities. From the late 1800s through the 1970s, American higher education was the engine that propelled the ascendance of the United States. The economic growth of the twentieth century was largely due to American higher education. But it was not simply economics. America's cultural and social landscape was greatly influenced by higher education as well. America was the envy of the world, and higher education was widely respected amongst Americans. Americans saw higher education as a positive force in society. They believed, if nothing else, that a college degree was a key toward upward mobility and prosperity. But the character and status of the university begins to change in the closing decades of the twentieth century, and today, as I argue below, they are adrift like many contemporary American institutions.

We can begin our discussion here by focusing on the core undergraduate curriculum. It is arguably the case that the college educated in the earlier period, from 1890 through the 1950s, served as the foundation of the middle and upper classes ,and that a unified middle and upper class, anchored in the ethnic groups of WASPS and later whites ethnics, contributed to the maintenance of social order and stability in the country. The ideological cohesion produced through the intellectual socialization of these groups contributed to a unity and coherence (at least ideologically) in the country. At the heart of this socialization within the universities was **the Great Books tradition**. At the core of undergraduate education through this earlier period lay the set of liberal arts requirements that all or almost all undergraduates had to take across the country. In addition to language requirements for all undergraduates – at first Latin or Greek, then later any of the major European languages, e.g. French, German, etc., students had to take a number of courses related to Western civilization, reading and learning about the classics from the Ancient Greeks to the modern world. The classics of the Western intellectual tradition were required, From the Iliad and the Odyssey to Shakespeare, from the great Enlightenment philosophers of Locke, Descartes and all the rest, to the classics of American literature such as Melville's Moby Dick and the writings of Thoreau, students were required to learn a shared, core body of knowledge. As everyone from the upper classes were taught the same things, it suggested that they would share world views and ways of looking at the world.

But this all begins to change in the 1960s. The Great Books tradition was eliminated from most American universities by the 1980s. What was left were a set of general education requirements that varied from one university to another, and that by and large did not require many if any of the classic books. (Students today often graduate from college without ever having read Thoreau, or worse without ever having learned about Thoreau.) This tradition was eliminated largely as the result of relentless academic criticisms of the curriculum, particularly emanating from liberal scholars (as well as the student protests often supported by young academics). Critics argued that the tradition ignored and by implication denigrated the important contributions to the modern world and to American society by people of color, by people other than white, male, Europeans or European Americans. Similarly, the tradition ignored women. And it implicitly favored the upper classes and the upper classes' world views, while ignoring the realities and views of the great masses, particularly from the poorer classes. Historians, for example, began to argue for a "history from below". That is, some historians complained that traditional histories focused on the activities and lives and ideas of the rich and powerful and ignored the lives of the poorer and dis-empowered groups. These historians advocated for historical studies of the common and poor people's experiences throughout history and the important roles they played rather than the traditional focus on the rich and powerful. There was also a liberal theme of refocusing higher education toward contributing not to the perpetuation of the upper and middle classes through socialization into the Great Books tradition, but toward using higher education to advance the historical democratic project. As such, what was the point of learning Latin? How is it useful to address the issues of the day?

As a result, universities by the late 1900s no longer required students to read Thoreau or Chaucer or to learn Latin (or to read the Bible). The Great Books tradition was all but dead, or at best badly wounded. But this trend did not go unanswered. A number of widely read conservative criticisms of the demise of the Great Books tradition appeared. Perhaps the most widely read was Allan Bloom's *The Closing of the American Mind: How Higher Education Has Failed Democracy and Impoverished the Souls of Today's Students* (1987). Bloom lamented what he saw happening to higher education in America, largely as the result of the rejection of the Great Books tradition. He roundly criticized many of the new academic majors and departments, such as African American studies and gender studies, and complained that the social sciences were fostering a harmful relativism – particularly a harmful moral relativism – amongst students. The new curriculum was away in an ethos of anything goes and the belief that there are no certainties and no rights in the world. He was particularly disdainful of how much the ideas of the great German sociologist Max Weber had gained traction within the social sciences during this period.

Yet despite these criticisms, and despite the rise and growth of conservativism throughout the halls of power in America in the closing decades of the twentieth century, the universities largely were unmoved by such criticisms. Indeed, as we see below, it is arguably the case that the trends set in motion during this time, e.g. the rejection of the Great Books tradition, the championing of new academic programs such as gender studies, etc., continue through the present.

Sociology throughout this period – 1965-2016 – was intimately tied to all of the above. It was affected by the many changes noted above and it affected many of these changes. It will be recalled that American sociology in the post-World War Two era was dominated by the model of structural functionalism. The discipline was largely unified behind this approach (though some may argue this claim is an exaggeration, pointing out the existence of various approaches, most notably symbolic interactionism). This unity and coherence broke down in the closing decades of the twentieth century. Structural functionalism was roundly criticized in the 1960s and 1970s on numerous grounds. Many noted problems of logic, i.e. circular reasoning, embedded in the approach. For example, a structural functionalist might say that the nuclear family exists because it serves a function for maintaining the stability of society. And how does one know that this function is why it exists as it does? Because it exists! But there were other problems as well. One of these was the criticism that structural functionalism claims to be an objective and unbiased scientific approach to sociology, but when one looks closely one sees that it is in fact a biased and politically conservative approach. It assumes that the way the social world is, is the way the world ought to be. It assumes, for example, that inequalities are necessary and beneficial to the order and harmony of society. As such, any attempts to address inequalities or to reduce them are deemed by the structural functionalists as dysfunctional or harmful to society.

The destruction of the hegemony of structural functionalism in sociology was accompanied by the emergence or re-emergence of a multitude of approaches. An alternative to this approach can be found in symbolic interactionism. This was noted earlier in our discussions of the first important center of sociology in America: The Chicago School, anchored at the University of Chicago. The relative influence of this School upon American sociology in general abated during the 1930s through the 1950s, but remerged strongly in the 1950s and 1960s as the Second Chicago School. Scholars such as Howard Becker, Erving Goffman, Joe Gusfield, and many, many more are associated with this School. At that time, symbolic interactionism became central to their project. Symbolic interactionism, it will be recalled, is a form of social psychology. It is a micro perspective that says in order to understand social behaviors one must focus on how individuals are interacting with each other and how individuals assign meanings to their worlds in this process. The concept of self and the fluidity of social realities are also central to this approach. Symbolic interactionism also fosters a social constructionist view of the world, i.e. a view that says that people act based upon their understandings of the world, and not upon the actual facts of the world. We construct our understandings of the world and act based upon these constructions.

Numerous scholars emerged championing the interactionist perspective, many of these focused on the fields of deviance and social control. The ideas of labeling theory and social constructionism emerge through this tradition. Labeling theory is an explanation for deviance behavior that claims that individuals have sense of self and this sense of who they are is created and recreated through social interactions. Thus, if people call me stupid over and over again, under the right (or wrong!) circumstances, I might start to believe I am stupid, and if I do so, then I will act in ways to conform to and to confirm my self-concept, i.e. "I am stupid." Social constructionism is related to this, but it focuses not on the individual who is being labeled, but on the people doing the labeling. Our world, this perspective says, is constructed. It is not simply there. We define our situation and act accordingly. For example, a social constructionist might say that a person who is defined as mentally ill is not mentally ill until some professional assigns the label of mentally ill to the person.

Symbolic interactionism was not the only perspective to gain strength during this period. Numerous other ways of thinking about the social world and doing sociology emerged. Most notably, a range of critical and highly critical approaches emerged through the 1960s and 1970s. Perhaps most notably was the introduction of the ideas of Karl Marx in the American academy, in the American university. Marx was the nineteenth century radical theorist and revolutionary who developed a theory of history. At the heart of his theory was the claim that capitalism was an oppressive system, and one that would be overthrown. Communism would and should replace it. In the twentieth century there were a number of significant communist revolutions, inspired by Marx, around the world. Most notably the Russian Revolution of 1917-1919, led by Vladimir Lenin, led to the creation of the communist state of the Soviet Union (which ultimately collapsed in 1989) and China, which had a communist revolution led by Mao Zedong in 1948-49. China continues to proclaim itself to be a communist society to this day (but in reality, its economy is a form of state capitalism). Perhaps the most notorious example of a country today proclaiming to following the ideas of Marx is the oppressive, nightmare state of North Korea.

In contrast to the United States, Marxist ideas were very much a part of mainstream political culture in much of Europe for much of the twentieth century, and Marx's ideas were also embedded with many of the universities in Europe. In French universities in the mid-1900s, in particular, Marxism was particularly widespread. This is radically different from the situation in the United States. In the United States, Marx was self-consciously absent in the universities before the 1960s and was reviled in political culture through that time. (One might briefly note the McCarthy era here – a period in the 1950s where Senator McCarthy and his supporters conducted witch hunts to supposedly exposure communists in America who were secretly hiding their beliefs and aspirations. The McCarthy era ruined the lives on many, many people.) As such, sociology programs in the United States all but ignored or dismissed or denigrated Marxism through the 1940s and 1950s.

But young scholars and graduate students in sociology in the 1960s began to read Marx and Marx inspired writings and came to introduce these into the academy. By the 1980s, Marx and Marxism was an established part of American sociology. Marx was by then, and continued to be, seen by most sociologists as one of the three main "classical" sociological theorists, along with Max Weber and Emile Durkheim (though Marx himself was not a sociologist; he was a philosopher and revolutionary). None of this should suggest that many or most sociologists in the closing decades of the twentieth century were Marxists. Indeed, the vast majority were not Marxist. But most sociologists did come to believe that Marx had something of value to say regarding sociological analysis.

To be clear, and to repeat, it is not that most or even many American sociologists became Marxists in this period. Instead, some came to believe that Marx had something of value to say. As a result numerous forms of Marxist inspired and influenced form of sociological thinking arose. One of the more noteworthy of these was the ideas of the Frankfurt School. The Frankfurt School refers to a group of German, and largely Jewish, scholars who first came together at the University of Frankfurt in the 1920s and 1930s. They included social thinkers such as Theodor Adorno, Marx Horkheimer, and Herbert Marcuse. These scholars were Marxists, but not traditional Marxists. They drew extensively upon other thinkers such as Max Weber, Sigmund Freud, and the rich German philosophical traditions of the nineteenth centuries and grafted these onto Marx. At the very least, they were not traditional Marxists. They were, on the other hand, harshly critical of capitalism, and they focused mostly upon what they saw as the ways that capitalism was oppressive to culture, to consciousness, to social relations. They focused largely on the harmful effects of science and scientistic thinking, on the harmful mechanical modes of being resulting from the widespread use of technologies, and on the empty pleasures of consumerism. All of these combined rendered individuals empty consuming machines who thought they were free and happy. This allows capitalism to continue, but at what price?

The Frankfurt School was not the only critical approach embraced by American sociologists in this period. The flood gates were opened to an increasing array of highly critical approaches in sociology. These often focused on such things as race and gender and inequalities and power.

The newly emerging diversity of sociological approaches in the late twentieth century resulted in three distinct but overlapping approaches to sociology during this period. Most sociological orientations from this period fall into one or more of these three approaches: The scientistic, the interpretive, and the critical. **The scientistic (some use the term "positivistic" here) approaches** embrace the idea that sociology is our should aspire to be scientific just like any other scientific field, such as physics, biology, or chemistry. There is only one proper way of doing science and all scientific disciplines should follow the same set of principles and same research methods. The scientistic approach argues that sociologists should objectively and in an unbiased manner look at social facts in the world and look for causal relationships amongst the social facts. This is what scientists do. But for sociology the issue becomes a bit more complicated and a bit different from the other sciences. That is, while chemistry and physics and all of the other natural sciences seek to discover the laws of nature by employing the steps just noted – objectively looking at facts and seeking to discover causal relations amongst these – most sociologists by and large recognize today that there are no timeless natural laws governing the social world. The point then for scientistic sociology is not to discover any such natural laws but instead to engage in research which could definitely account for and explain particular social realities using the principles noted herein. That is, sociologists using scientism study a social condition and using research claim that the condition occurs because of this or that reason, all the while relying upon empirical facts to make the claims.

The second perspective is the interpretivistic one. This perspective may or may not draw upon these same scientistic principles, but at its heart the interpretivistic perspective is different. At the heart of the interpretivistic approach lies the concept of meaning. The task of the sociologist, this perspective says, is to understand the meanings of social behavior, particularly the meanings assigned by the actors themselves. When someone enters a new situation, for example, walking into a classroom for the first time, on some level or another, the person tries to make sense out of the situation. The person is forced to assign meaning to the situation. The person, on one level or another, asks him or herself, "What is the meaning of this situation?" The point is that we act based upon the meanings we assign to our worlds. As such, the task of the sociologist is to understand these meanings – what they are and how we assign them. But meanings cannot often be assessed through scientistic approaches. To determine the meanings, the sociologist is required to make interpretations, much like an art professor in explaining the meanings of the art of Picasso makes interpretations about these meanings.

The third important perspective in sociology for the period under question, i.e. 1965-2016, is the critical perspective. It was noted earlier that the critical perspective was new to sociology. Prior to the 1950s and 1960s, it did not exist in American sociology. To begin, we should note that the critical perspective is not one single approach. It is not simply Marxism. It instead consists of many different approaches – many non- or anti-Marxist, all tied together loosely under the umbrella of critical approaches. Moreover, it is important to recognize that the critical perspective was never throughout the period a dominant approach in sociology. It was indeed a rather small, but significant part of sociology.

As noted, Marx entered the American academy in the 1960s and with it a whole range of critical approaches. Numerous Marxist inspired approaches emerged and were embraced, from the Marxist traditions of the Italian Marxist Antonio Gramsci to the neo-Marxist traditions of the Frankfurt Schools. But critical approaches extended far beyond Marxism. In this period, new critical approaches emerged in feminist scholarship – and critical gender studies including such things as queer studies -- and in approaches to race. In addition, critical globalization and colonialization approaches emerged, as well as newly developed sociological approaches to the environment. In short, a whole host of critical sociological approaches emerged.

Importantly, many of these critical approaches did not simply champion new topics of studies – women, black people, gays, and lesbians, etc. They also called for new ways of thinking and doing sociology. Some claimed that sociologists needed to develop new epistemologies, new theories of knowledge and practices. Some argued that sociology could not and should not model itself upon the sciences of physics and chemistry and the like and instead should abandon the fundamental claims of scientism. Many saw sociology as a vehicle to foster to social change rather than a vehicle to produce objective knowledge of the social world. Relatedly, many critical approaches were influenced by radical epistemological philosophies and philosophies of language which challenged the idea that there was one and only one form of legitimate knowledge and that language could objectively reflect a reality out there.

This leads many of the critical approaches to see the centrality of power in their analysis. This also opens up numerous troubling issues for the viability of sociology as a social science. As we see in coming chapters, critical approaches have been increasingly contested by powerful forces – political, social, and cultural – outside of academia that have significant impact upon academia.

One last important feature of sociology during this period needs to be noted here. This concerns the internal organization of the discipline of sociology. As with any profession, once it is organized a status or prestige hierarchy emerges within the discipline. This prestige hierarchy was clearly present by the 1940s in sociology, at a time when structural functionalism dominated the profession. But in the second half of the century, this hierarchy took a different shape. We can distinguish between the sociology that was being done at the elite research universities -- from Berkeley, to Michigan, to Harvard and the University of Chicago – and the sociology that was being advanced at the non-elite and often non-research based colleges and universities, such as public, regional universities. From the 1940s through the present the core of the discipline, reflected at the elite universities, embraced scientism and largely eschewed critical forms of sociology while at the non-elite universities and colleges interpretive and critical approaches were more often embraced.

This gap is clearly seen in the academic sociology journals over the last seventy years. The two most dominant and elite journals in sociology are the American Sociological Review and the American Journal of Sociology. One needs only take a glance at these journals to see that scientism is embraced and that critical sociology is eschewed. The vast majority of articles appearing in these journals are committed to advanced statistical analysis of one or another aspect of social reality. On the other hand, when one looks at the myriad of other research journals in sociology, i.e. the non-elite journals, one finds some articles using advanced statistical analysis, but one also sees many interpretive and critical articles as well.

The gap between the two – between the elites and the non-elites – crystalized from the 1960s through the early 2000s. And yet, as we intimated earlier and as we will see again, this creates problems for the perceived legitimacy of sociology in the contemporary era. The hope that scientistic sociology could contribute to the public welfare, for example, was at its height in the 1950s and 1960s, when policy makers and judges and others looked to sociology to provide scientific understandings of issues of the day, such as issues related to racial segregation and education in the 1950s (see the Coleman Report). The critical impulses of sociology emerging in the 1960s also were seen as legitimate, at least in some corners of society outside of sociology. But all this has changed, scientism at its heart is soul-less. It provides no basis of values. Moreover, because scientism provides no basis for discovering natural "laws" governing social behavior and social organization – which stands in stark contrast to mainstream sciences such as chemistry, physics and biology that do set about to discover the laws governing the natural worlds – it leads its audiences to question the import of the endeavor. At the same time, the non-elite critical and interpretive perspectives have become the target of the wrath of the growing radical conservativism found in America which began in the late 1900s.

The Current Stage - 2016-now

American society is currently in a state of crisis. As we are living in this period, it is hard to understand clearly and unequivocally what is happening. Distance always fosters the greater possibility of clearer and more objective understandings. Nevertheless, the facts of the world today are clear enough to say that a crisis exists and that at least some of the causes of this crisis are evident.

I would like to go beyond the claim that American society is in a state of crisis: American society does not now exist. There are two Americas roughly defined by the political chasm between red America – largely rural, anchored in the South and geographically consisting of much of the main central part of the geography of the United States, and blue America – largely urban, anchored in the Northeast and in the far west.

To say that America does not exist begs the *sociological* question: What does the word society mean? Is a society nothing more than the same thing as a country? Is it defined by geography, or by legalities? Is it defined by formal membership or by something else? Moreover, one must ask whether one is a member of a society even if one does not believe or act in ways that reflect an acknowledgement or commitment to this thing called society. At its heart, society, as I define it here, is anchored in the concepts of identity and morality. Each of these concepts needs to be explained. There are multiple types of identity. There are personal, situational, and social forms of identity. Personal identities are anchored in those biographical features of one's own particular life that makes each one of us unique. You identify with the unique circumstances of your life – the place you were born and raised, your family, your neighborhood, etc. Situational identities are associated with social roles. One might, for example, identify oneself as a student, or as a brother or sister, or as a worker at Starbucks. These are roles. Social identities are based upon group affiliation. You may be a member of a particular racial or ethnic group, a man or a woman, gay or straight. You may be a Republican or a Democrat, a Christian or Jew or atheist. The list of group affiliations is long.

But identities are not stagnant. They are fluid, and the calculus of their formation changes in history. Five hundred years ago, in Europe and for that matter anywhere else, identities were embedded within the social fabric of the group. An eighteen year old did not have to ask, who am I? or, what am I going to do with my life? He or she knew that he was a peasant or a prince. He or she knew he or she was Catholic or Jewish or what have you. Who one was and what one was to do with one's life was structured into one's life experiences. An eighteen year old women who was the daughter of a poor farmer in rural France in the year 1200 did not have to ask or wonder about who she was or what she was to do. She knew implicitly who she was. Such questions about identity are modern ones. Individual personal, situated, and social identities now are disembedded. Modernity has lifted out the individual from the fabric of social life. How many college age young people do not ask such questions? Who am I? What am I going to do with my life? Am I gay or straight? Catholic or Protestant, a believer or an atheist? And on and on. All three bases of identity have been profoundly changed in the modern era. A destabilization of identities has occurred. We return to this theme in later chapters. For now, suffice to say that while the disembeddedness can be traced back several hundred years, its salience has appeared in full in recent years.

With the disembedded identities, and with the historical conditions that produced an ever greater psychological need (see coming chapters), people are pressed to embrace an identity that is transcendent, one that is not subject to the whims of times; one that is mythically permanent. As such, people grab onto and embrace the social identity. The "us" becomes the most important thing, even if it is fictitious. The shakiness of situated and personal identities in the contemporary era led people to latch on to social identities in the hopes this will give anchor to the confusions of the times. But the very nature of social identities is transient. The fact is that one is born in a particular house within a particular family. One is born into a personal identity, which does not change. But one may convert to Islam or to Christianity, social identities, and perhaps in light of the times and in light of the nature of social identities, this embrace becomes that much firmer.

This brings us back to American society. One of the curious things occurring in America today is the elevated sense of us. But oddly the us experienced by white rural men in Oklahoma or Texas is fundamentally different than the us experienced by a black person living in Harlem. It is a mythic umbrella to proclaim us, and why myths can endure for long times – just think of religions – when myths are confronted with opposing realities, they are strained could produce fundamental social changes. When people worship the flag, and profess patriotism, are they actually worshipping the same sacred thing, the same secular god? Or are they in fact worshipping two different gods?

Among the many important themes shaping the present, three stand out: the impact of the internet and social media; the consolidation of radical conservative power; and the massive tensions and oppositions in America today. We can look at each of these in turn. To begin, we should note these did not emerge in 2016. They emerged in earlier decades. As such, one might ask whether it is justified to identify these changes with the contemporary era. As I argued above, and as I argue throughout this book, the world of today is distinctly different than the world of a few short years ago, much as the world of Germany was distinctly different in 1928 and in 1937. There is no single thing that could quantitatively be argued that distinguishes the present from the recent past. Instead, it is a sensibility, an ineffable difference: real but not quantifiable. America is not what it was in the recent past.

Let us start with the internet and social media. These things of course have been around now for decades. Arguably, the social effects of them have gradually increased, and arguably their effects are greater today than in the past. It is tempting to invoke the well-worn criticisms of the internet and social media. People – from scholars to film directors – have been warning about the harmful effect of technologies seemingly forever. Critics have particularly warned about the harms to the social and political orders, to social relations and to self. Whether it is movie Terminator or 2001 Space Odyssey or Huxley's novel Brave New World, commentators have expressed concerns, many of which have been taken up subtle or not by social scientists. But the impact of technology, of the internet and social media, upon the social world is far more complex than a simple assessment of them being either harmful or helpful.

The spread of the internet and social media likely have and are having effects on society that both are beneficial and harmful. And it is arguably the case that these two opposing sorts of effects – however amorphous and hard to define – are creating social ambiguities, ambiguities that create a field ripe for conquest by ideologists bent on one or another agenda. In this case, these ambiguities aid the increasing power of radical conservative forces in America today. One can identify two factors that relate here. The first is morality. Democracy itself destroys moral consensus, as its nature – at least as conceived and practiced in modern times – is such that it fosters moral relativism. If a majority wins on an issue, this does not mean this majority is morally right. The majority or minority might come to believe, as Tocqueville warned, that the position of the majority is in fact the morally right position, but this possibility seems not to have been realized in the contemporary era, at least not for the two sides in conflict – red and blue America. Curiously, both sides seem committed to the belief that their side is morally correct and the other is morally bankrupt (though it needs to be emphasized here that in blue America the ironic certainty of moral relativism prevails). Democracy fosters an odd relativism – a relativism within blue America and a relativism between red and blue America. This moral relativism, again, creates voids that are yearning to be filled, at least if one seeks the claim of being part of an American society.

Similarly, the internet and social media are destabilizing identity even more so than it has been. We discussed identity above (and will revisit this in later chapters). Here suffice to say that the disembedding of identity in the modern era has been compounded in the contemporary era. All together these things create voids of meanings that cry out to be filled.

Much like the internet and social media first arose several decades ago and have expanded in scope and influence so much so in recent years as to warrant the claim that the period we are now in is significantly different from the one of decades ago, so too the scope and power of the radical conservatives of the Republican Party and their supporters has likewise grown. Moreover, the ideological and practical powers of the radical conservatives have come to be a major influence if not a dominating force in many significant institutions in American society. In politics, in the judiciary and legislative branches, in business, in the military, in religious organizations, in the police forces, even in the universities – contrary to public imagery, in the media, and in other major institutions, radical conservatives have come to dominate. In effect, there has been a consolidation of the radical conservative powers over American society. While there is a patina of political impartiality or even "liberal" sensibilities ostensibly still governing these institutions, the reality is that at best any sort of commitment to democracy and "liberalism" (in the Enlightenment sense) has been dwarfed by the radical right wing sensibilities of the ruling members of these institutions. It will not take much to change the fundamental character of any of these specific institutions and consequentially the fundamental character of American society. Think, for a moment, about the military or the police. There is significant if not overwhelming presence of radical conservativism amongst the rank and file and more importantly amongst the leadership of these institutions.

All of this is captured and embodied in the phenomenon of Donald Trump. We need not get bogged down here in a discussion of whether he created or fostered the radical conservativism that has taken over the Republican Party or whether he merely reflects the sentiments of a large section of the country. I assume here that we should think it is mostly the latter. Whether in terms of policies and positions or in terms of personal leadership style, he has taken the Republican Party into a new direction. Many, including myself, believe that he embodies a number of frightening fascist tendencies (see Chapter Thirteen), tendencies that pose a direct threat to American democracy. One need only refer to the massive delusion or lie that Trump continues to propagate regarding the 2020 presidential election. He claims that Biden did not really win the election and that Trump's win in that election was stolen from him. To be clear: Biden easily won that free and fair election. Biden received around seven million more votes than did Trump and in the electoral college Biden easily defeated Trump. And yet to this day, in 2022, around half of Republicans repeatedly claim that Biden did not win the election. Let us also not forget or diminish the importance of the Trump inspired, if not led, insurrection on January 6, 2020.

This of course is only one of the countless delusions and lies spouted by Trump and his supporters in the Republican party. One need not here recount any of the others. Suffice to say, that it is very threatening to the maintenance of a democracy when huge sectors of the population choose to deny or ignore realities; when huge sections choose to deny or ignore facts upon facts upon facts. (Democracy cannot be sustained if large and influential parts of the populace maintain fundamental beliefs about reality that are not true.)

The last major theme of the contemporary era that we may consider here follows from the above. I am referring here to the major tensions and conflicts in American society. The tensions and conflicts between Red states America and Blue states American arguably has not been as high as it currently is since the Civil War. Many commentators wish to deny this reality; many wish to believe that the divisions in America today are not that significant, or that such divisions have been a longstanding part of America and as such are not something to be concerned about. These commentators are wrong.

And what of sociology in the contemporary era? Sociology as a discipline has not self-consciously responded in any sort of systematic way to the major and dire changes afoot in contemporary America. Instead, it has continued along the trajectory defined by the earlier period – 1965-2016 – discussed earlier. And yet, sociology today is either explicitly ignored by society today or its legitimacy is implicitly denied by powerful forces. We can say a few words here about each of these, and in coming chapters we explore each of these in greater depth. First, the ignoring of sociology. It is striking to me as a sociologist that so many of the major issues of the day can and should be thought of through the lens of sociology but instead are not. Often, they are thought of through the lens of individualistic psychology or through one or another inane quasi-intellectual formulation (typically generated by the radical right wing "think tanks" and media outlets). For example, as I am writing this, there is much discussion in popular American culture about gun violence. Over the last several months – really over the last many years -- there have been numerous cases of outrageous gun violence in America that have been widely reported. A young, white racist man legally bought an AR-15 machine gun and went to a grocery store in a black neighborhood. He then killed ten innocent black customers. Soon after, a young man in Uvalde, Texas legally bought an AR-15 and went to the local grade school and massacred twenty one people, mostly young children sitting in class. Then a week or so later, in Philadelphia another mass shooting on a very busy street occurred. Several young black men engaged in a shootout which resulted in the deaths of three people and the injuries of many others. In a suburb of Chicago, a young man bought a number of guns and proceeded to kill seven people and wound many others at a Fourth of July parade. One could recount these stories again and again.

What is interesting here is how public and political discourse is shaped in response to these endless murders. Notably, there is often talk of the need for more mental health services. There is routinely a focus on the individual and on psychology as a way of understanding and responding to such things. Never is there a discussion of how sociology might inform either an understanding of the causes or possible solutions to these nightmares. Why is this? In a later chapter we address this issue. But here it is worth noting that it would appear that American society, at least the media and politicians and the cultural leaders of the society, believe that sociology has no value here in aiding in understanding or in responding to these crises. And yet, mass shootings – mass shootings of all stripes, political, "senseless," personal, etc. – can best be understood sociologically.

One of the reasons for this denial perhaps is related to the second issue posed above: sociology is implicitly denied. I am thinking here of such things as "cancel culture" and the radical Republican obsession with fighting what it calls Critical Race Theory (CRT), particularly with this obsession to rid schools of CRT. CRT is a legal theory developed largely by minority lawyers beginning in the 1970s. At its heart, CRT argues that the legal system systematically works against black people. A systematic racial bias is embedded in laws. More broadly, CRT put forth the claim that "We are all racists," whether we know it or not and whether we wish to admit it or not. Racism, the argument goes, is embedded in the daily workings of society, and in the case of CRT, within laws. CRT itself – as a sophisticated theory of law – is never taught in k-12 schools in the United States and is only taught within universities within relevant courses (e.g. sociology of race and ethnicity, etc.). Nevertheless, radical Republicans have latched on to the idea that we are all racists and have rebelled against CRT. For these radical Republicans, CRT is merely a proxy for the more fundamental claim that we are all racist.

The point here is that claims such as those raised by CRT which argue that there are systematic social forces operating in the world that are not self-consciously motivating forces in individual lives but are at the same time impactful upon social behaviors is ultimately a denial of sociology itself. Yet there is by now a very long history of research documenting the effects of systematic forces in the world, without the need to invoke individual psychology as an explanation. One thinks here of the notable research on suicide by Emile Durkheim, the important French sociologist writing over one hundred years ago. In his work Suicide, Durkheim demonstrates that suicide rates vary systematically from group to group and from time to time. Thus, from his research he found that Protestants commit more suicide than Catholics, and single men commit more suicide than married men with children, etc. Durkheim gather a great deal of evidence and claimed that suicide rates vary based upon two sociological factors: moral regulation and social integration. Moral regulation concerns the social environment. And morality, for Durkheim, consists of shared evaluations and judgments about good and bad, proper and improper, etc. A well regulated moral environment is one in which what happens is what is expected to happen. But a moral environment that is too well regulated or too little regulated produces confusions and high suicide rates. It bears noting that one of the points of Durkheim's work on suicide was to demonstrate that he could explain a seemingly psychological phenomenon – suicide – without relying upon psychology. Sociology, he argues, is distinct from psychology.

The radical Republican rejection of CRT echoes a rejection of the fundamental claim of Durkheim: patterns of social behavior exist in the world that can and perhaps should be explained by sociology rather than by psychology. As a result, we see a denial of sociology.

The lack of external support for the sociological project, as described above, might suggest that the sociology community engage in a bit of introspection about what the nature of sociology in contemporary America ought to be. But this has not really occurred. Instead, the internal workings of sociology today have continued the patterns established in the late 1900 and early 2000s. That is, there continues to be three main approaches to sociology: the scientistic, the interpretive, and the critical, with the critical still a small segment. (Though in light of historical circumstances, discussed above, even though the critical is small it is seen by powerful external groups as more impactful than it is and this has allowed external critics to dismiss or ignore or to attack sociology today.) In addition, the internal hierarchy of sociology as noted earlier – with the elites in the discipline enshrouded in scientism and the interpretive and critical found more often on the sidelines – continues to be the operating mode of the discipline.

Chapter Two – Darwin, Science, and The Limits of Rationality

The important German sociologist Marx Weber saw rationality and associated concepts such as rational action and rationalization as centrally important to understand the modern world. In Chapter Eight we discuss in detail these concepts as well as the associated ideas of science and technology, which each are based on forms of rationality. In this chapter we briefly discuss the role played by rationality in the contemporary world. As Weber noted, rationality is a dominant governing principle of our world today, and this is a modern and unique phenomena in history. It has only been since the Enlightenment (1600-1800) that this has occurred. Weber was interested in understanding this historical process – why it happened where it did, what are the implication for social order and stability, and what does a future world dominated by rationality look like.

In this chapter we present an overview of rationality and how it has and how it is shaping our world. We revisit some of Weber's ideas and add some of our own. This chapter is dominated by two over-arching themes. The first is the idea that people in a society tend to share a mind-set, a way of looking at the world. (In German sociology, there is a term to describe this shared mind-set: *weltanschauung*. This refers to this overarching world-view shared by a people.) Their consciousness is shaped in particular ways such that they can effectively be members of the society, such that they can understand and communicate with others in society. Moreover, people in different societies have different mind-sets, different forms of consciousness, different ways of looking at the world. In this chapter, we explore the implications of having the mind-set of the modern world, one dominated by rationality. The second dominant theme of this chapter is a focus on the complications that arise when a peoples' consciousness is so dominated by rationality. Here we look at the implications -- some quite negative and harmful -- of the conquest of rationality.

We also examine the limits of rationality, specifically focusing on the idea of scientific racism. Scientific racism is the ideas of using science, based on rationality, to demonstrate the genetic and biological inferiority of one or another race and the genetic and biological superiority of another race. In the Western tradition over the last two hundred years, white scientific racists have used science to claim that white people are genetically superior, and that black people are genetically inferior.

(The reader might wonder whether the claim that rationality has taken over is accurate. Afterall, one look at America today shows there is a massive rejection of rationality and science, from the denial of the safety and efficacy of the COVID-19 vaccines to the denial of global warming. This interesting rejection of rationality is addressed in Chapter Eight. It is argued that the very conquest of rationality ironically has contributed to its rejection in these instances.)

The Limits and Consequences of Rationality

Weber argued that the dominant feature of the modern world was that rationality was taking over. We are experiencing rationalization, the historic process by which this is occurring. He dissects these concepts and identifies several different types of rationality. For Weber, he was particularly interested in understanding instrumental rational action and how modern social settings are increasingly being organized in ways that nurture or require this type of action. Instrumental rational action is simply logical behavior that is unconcerned with any value considerations. It is lining up means and ends (goals) in a logical manner without considering values (see Chapter Eight). It is the logic of a machine.

Weber was concerned about the consequences for the social world when instrumental rational action takes over. He calls this historical process rationalization. If and when people are forced to think and act in this instrumental rational way, then they become like machines, devoid of emotion, morality, values. This can produce horrible consequences (see Chapter Eight). It is not that Weber did not recognize the usefulness and goodness of a society dominate by instrumental rational action. Afterall, modern science and bureaucracies and businesses are all built upon this idea. But he was concerned that if rationalization occurs, then people might not be able to recognize its limitations and pitfalls.

Unpacking the History of Instrumental Rational Action

To understand how rationality works and to understand the contemporary, modern mindset that is arguably saturated with a way of seeing and being in the world that is based upon instrumental rationality, we should look more closely at the actual logic of this way of being and we should look to history to understand how this logic has come about. A discussion of the ideas of Isaac Newton and Charles Darwin here nicely captures some of the foundational building blocks of contemporary consciousness.

Isaac Newton (1643-1724) was a centrally important British physicist who established the main laws of physics (at least until some of these were challenged and revised by Einstein in the twentieth century and still later by more contemporary theories such as string theory and chaos theory). Here we can focus on his laws of motion, specifically the first law: a body remains at rest unless a force is imposed upon it to move it, and a body remains in motion unless and until a force is imposed upon it to change its motion. Our concern for Newton's law of motion is not one of physics, but of sociology. That is, Newton's law creates an image of the world as a mechanical thing, operating on its own, independent of human involvement. This is a powerful and seductive image of the world, one that has been advanced by numerous Enlightenment figures from Leibniz to Condorcet, and is one that continues through the present, for example in the writings of E.O. Wilson (see his book *Consilience* (1999)). When I think of such things, my mind wanders to the idea of "natural philosophy" that was rather common in the eighteenth century, which stands in contrast to the mechanical image of the world. Much of natural philosophy was inspired by the Enlightenment traditions noted above. But natural philosophy, which can be thought of as the science of nature and evolution in its incipient, pre-Darwinian, modern form, was more anchored in the ideas of interconnectedness: Nature was a dynamic force constantly interacting and changing with its environment. The environment could shape nature, could shape the genetics, if you will, of the animal and plant worlds. (This is reflected in the ideas of Lamarckian theory, e.g. the inheritance of acquired characteristics.)

Newton's law of physics is a bit different. It removed the dynamic interplay between one thing and another. It creates a powerful image of the world that tells us the world is utterly independent from us, humans. It operates mechanically, and humans are incidental to its workings. The abstracting, this disembedding, was coalesced further through the philosophers of the Enlightenment, from Locke to Kant. Kant, for example, establishes the difference between appearances and realities, between noumena and phenomena, as a cornerstone of his philosophy of epistemology. This is an approach that has been widely adopted by so many in the modern world.

In short, these traditions, most neatly reflected in Newton's laws, conceptually remove humans from the world. The world, the essence of the world, becomes detached, removed, independent from and indifferent to, human concerns. This form of thinking, encapsuled in Newton's laws, has come to dominate our worlds. But it was not until Darwin's evolutionary theory that this form of thinking and being came to be put into the services of the human sciences, e.g. sociology, psychology, economics, political science, etc. Charles Darwin (1809-1882) was a British scientist credited with establishing the modern theory of evolution on empirical and scientific grounds. This is perhaps most famously captured in his book On The Origin of the Species in which he demonstrates his claims of evolution, anchored in such things as the natural selection and the survival of the fittest. The theory today is all but universally accepted in the scientific community as well as within much of public consciousness. It serves as a foundational orientation in much of biological science today. (It is a fantasy or myth to claim that it is actually contested today in scientific circles. It is not.)

Darwin's theory basically says that life evolves due to genetic variations. Sometimes two parents who are each six feet tall have children that grow up to be six feet tall, but sometimes a child to such parents will be six foot six inches, and sometimes he or she will be five foot four inches tall. There is variation in nature, in genetic inheritance. But more often than not, on average most such children will be nearer to six feet than farther away. The question then concerns which variation is best adapted to its environment? Which variation will allow the species to survive? A deer that inherits genes that do not allow it to run fast, or that make it sickly, will more likely be eaten by the lion chasing the herd. As such the deer's genes will not get passed on. The genes of the faster, healthier, or smarter deer who survived will get passed on. Survival of the fittest. This is the essence of Darwin's theory. The persons with inherited traits that most allow for the individual and species to survive will endure; the persons with those traits that are not useful for survival will less likely survive. This explains how humans evolved from lesser primates. It explains why giraffes have long necks, and why some birds have some types of beaks while others have different beaks.

To understand the significance of this approach more clearly, particularly for the social sciences, we should contrast it with the competing scientific approach in the 1800s. This is the Lamarckian perspective, named after Jean-Baptiste Lamarck (1744-1829), a French scientist. The Lamarckian perspective can be summed up in the well-known phrase, **"the inheritance of acquired characteristics."** This is the argument that if something happens to an individual organism during its lifetime that affects its biological constitution, then this newly acquired trait will be genetically passed on to its offspring. If I worked in a factory and lost my left arm in an accident, then a Lamarckian might say that my child will be born without a left arm. As such, genes in this formulation are malleable, changeable. (Though it bears noting that neither Lamarck nor Darwin knew about genes when they developed their theories.) The environment impacts genetic composition, and this is inherited.

By the late 1800s, Darwin's theory defeated Lamarckian theory and went on to become the exclusive, dominant foundation of modern genetics and modern biological sciences. Of interest here is how much the Darwinian approach fits neatly with a Newtonian form of thinking, and how the fusion helps understand modern social scientific thinking – in the public as well as in the academy. In both Newton and Darwin, we see nature mechanically operating. The genes are hard-wired and passively do what they do. There is no agency here. Genes cannot make choices. (It should be noted that some recent scholarship challenges this simplistic accounting of Darwin's approach. Riskin (2018) writes that this accounting is actually a simplified distortion of Darwin's actually writings. This simplified distortion was not what Darwin actually wrote, but what his legacy later became. In reality, Darwin did not completely reject Lamarckian ideas. He did accord genes with some sense of agency. But his legacy omits this.)

Darwin provided a bridge between biology and the social sciences, and it is this bridge that is central to understanding sociology and the social world today. (Technically, one could rightfully argue that it was Gregor Mendel (1822-1884), the German scientist who laid out the modern understanding of genetics, that was the true historical bridge. But we will stay with Darwin here.)

In theory, if one embraces the Newton mindset coupled with an acceptance of Darwinian evolution, one should submit (surrender really) to the demands of the underlying principles. A scientist should assume that the part of the world that is scientifically knowable, as opposed to the realm of religion, mysticism, etc., is subject to empirical investigation. The scientist as an objective observer who commits to going wherever the facts lead in his or her quest to scientifically understand the workings of the world will discover eternal truths about the world, albeit truths that are recognized as tentative and subject to revision or change based upon future research. The scientist, in this reasoning, can and should be allowed to study anything he or she wishes, provided the scientist adheres to the basic cannons of scientific investigation – such as an embrace of objectivity, a reliance upon facts and their causal relations, etc., and provided he or she adheres to the mind-set anchored in the thinking of the likes of Newton or Darwin.

And yet science does not operate in a vacuum. It never has and never will. It operates within specifical social and historical circumstance. These social and historical environments bear down and shape the workings of science. One can think of another great scientist in history here to illustrate this: Galileo. Galileo (1564-1642) created a telescope and proved Copernicus' helio-centric theory of the solar system. In Galileo's time, the dominant scientific theory of the solar system was the geo-centric theory, a theory that claimed the earth was the center of the solar system and all the planets and the sun revolved around the earth. Copernicus was a Polish astronomer who argued that the helio-centric theory was actually correct. Galileo did not merely argue that Copernicus was right, he scientifically demonstrated it through observing the planets and the moon circling around the planets. He published his findings and promptly was arrested by the Catholic Church for heresy. Here the negative impact of the social and political forces on science is clear. Science today – particularly the hard sciences such as chemistry or physics – has, at least in theory, embraced the position that it should not be allowed to be influenced by any external political or social force, or any external force of any kind. At the least, the scientist can prevent his or her work from being distorted by social and historical circumstance if he or she simply, rationally adheres to the basic principles of the scientific endeavor. The logic of Darwin, Newton, scientism, etc. pushes for the belief that science must avoid being impacted by the social and historical circumstance. It must be done in a pure and objective way.

Discrimination and Racism

In this section, we describe scientific racism and its relationship to rationality. In a later chapter, we describe more fully the concept of scientific racism and its implications, here we focus specifically upon the historical production of this concept and its contemporary uses. To start, we need to unpack the concept of racism. In public discourse today the concept of racism has become quite confused and confusing. This confusion adds to the difficulties of any attempt to appropriately response to it. There are two intersecting problems in the contemporary usage of the term racism. One set concerns the confusion of the term racism with the term discrimination. The other is the confusion of sociological forces with individual, unconscious forces at the root of racism. We tackle each of these in turn.

First, racism and discrimination. If we do not clearly conceptually distinguish these terms, we will not get anywhere towards an accurate understanding of contemporary American society. **Racism** is a belief that one or another racial group is inferior to another racial group. Traditionally in Western history, it is the belief that white people are superior to black people and/or to other non-white racial groups. While racism is a belief, **discrimination** is a practice, a social behavior. Discrimination is treating members of one racial groups unfairly and unequally due to the membership in that racial group. If a white person refuses to hire a qualified black person for a job because the person is black, then this is discrimination (based upon a racist belief).

There are different types of racism and discrimination. The types of racism can be distinguished from one another by the basis or location of the source of the claimed racial differences between groups. One type of racism is biologically based. If one claims that there are socially significant biological differences between races and these differences account for differences in such things as average incomes or wealth of the different groups, or in things like criminal behaviors, then one embracing a form of biological racism. Such claims revert to the science of such things as evolution or IQ and their putative genetic foundations. For example, biological racism might claim that the reason that the average income of white people is higher than that of black people is because income levels are related to intelligence and intelligence is genetically determined, and average intelligence varies from one racial group to another. Such thinking is the core of scientific racism for the last two hundred years.

A different form of racism lies in culture. Culture-based racism claims that the explanations for such things as differences in income and crime can be found in the belief system, the morality and values, the cultural practices of racial groups. As such, culture based racism might say the reason for economic inequalities between races in America and for high crime rates amongst black Americans, for example, lies in some problems with the culture of the minority group. It is defective in some way. (In the mid-1900s, these culturally based explanations to account for differences between racial groups were quite popular, and were often associated with what came to be called the "culture of poverty" argument. Beginning in the 1960s and continuing through the present, critics of the culture of poverty argument complained that this form of argument was "blaming the victim", i.e. blaming poor people and/or minorities for their own difficulties and importantly it was absolving white people of any responsibility for causing or perpetuating this situation.)

The **culture of poverty** arguments from the mid-1900s, for example, might say that the reason that Latinos and Black

Americans are disproportionately poor is that their value system is not in line with the WASP value system. The value system of such minority groups might embrace a form of fatalism or resignation believing that nothing they do can change their lot in life. Relatedly, such arguments claim there is a sense in these groups that forces external to themselves dictates what happens to them rather than forces within themselves. Similarly, a lack of a sense of deferred gratification is produced in these communities such that when they receive any income rather than saving it, they spend it on frivolous consumptions. A whole host of other cultural characteristics have been used to make similar arguments.

Discrimination also takes various forms. Two in particular can be mentioned here: individual discrimination and institutional discrimination. **Individual discrimination** is self-evident: When a person of one race treats a person of a different race unfairly and unequally. If a white person refused to rent his house to a black person because the person is black, then this is individual discrimination. Institutional discrimination is distinct from this. **Institutional discrimination** is when the normal workings of institutions produce discriminatory outcomes. Institutional discrimination can be intentional or non-intentional. Intentional institutional discrimination is when members of a dominant racial group – white people in America – create institutional practices that knowingly discriminate against minority groups. This is perhaps most glaringly seen in the various Jim Crow laws in the South passed by white people from 1875 through the 1950s to maintain inequalities. Creating literacy taxes and poll taxes and other legal devices to prevent black people from voting in the South are examples.

Non-intentional institutional discrimination is when institutions produce unfair outcomes for members of one or another racial group even though the institutions were not self-consciously designed to do so. For example, the policy "of last hired, first fired" that is used by many companies and government agencies seems very fair. If a company or agency has to fire an employee because of economic cutbacks to the company or agency, then the fair thing to do is to fire the most recently hired employee. Seems fair. But is it? The police and fire departments of major U.S. cities through the first half of the 1900s were almost exclusively white. As a result of the Civil Rights movement and other factors cities began to hire black people and other minorities into these departments. But when the city governments had to lay off some police and fireman due to budget constrictions, it was the most recently hired black employees who were terminated. Another example: some fire departments used to require applicants to take written tests as part of the application to become firemen. This had been a long standing practice. But when black people started applying for these jobs, after the Civil Rights movement, they were scoring lower on average than white people and as such they were not getting the jobs. You might ask, what is wrong with this process? It seems fair. And yet, when one looks at the skills needed to effectively perform the job of fireman and when one compares these with the test questions, one sees little to no correlation between the two. One could easily be a good or better fireman even if one scored lower on the tests. The point is that the tests did not measure any relevant abilities needed to do the job as fireman. But again, these tests were not created or intended to be used to discriminate against black people or other minorities. Nevertheless, the outcome was discriminatory. One could cite countless other similar types of examples here.

In public discourse today as well as within academic discourse, inspired by the movement Black Lives Matter and other things, there is much discussion of what is variable called "systematic racism," or "systemic racism," or "color-blind racism," or "unconscious racism." While particular formulations may vary, at the heart of these ideas are several distinct concepts which are fused in ways that are unhelpful and which confuse the intellectual discourse rather than clarify it. The confusion lies in part due to the failure to adequately distinguish between the social and the individual or psychological level, and it lies on the confusions related to the unconscious. The confusion also lies in the blurring of the distinction between the concept of discrimination and racism. When these confusions are not clarified, as they currently are not in contemporary discourse, it opens the door for activities either in support of or in opposition to championing racial equality from not advancing. And it opens the door for policies and activities related to these issues to be based not upon reasoned discourse but upon irrational passions.

The essence of these concepts, however distinct they all may be from each other, is that inequalities among races can be explained by systematic forces that operate without the conscious intent of individuals who act in discriminatory ways. By systematic, I mean social patternings of behaviors that produce and reproduce inequalities through discriminatory practices. As such, here we use the term systematic discrimination to describe the issue at hand. (Importantly, we must not the distinction between systematic discrimination and systematic racism. The idea of systematic racism is confused for some of the same reasons noted above for the other terms. Basically, it suggests a shared belief system not consciously realized by its adherents. As such, it invokes the idea of the unconscious, a concept not amendable to scientific – either social science or the hard sciences -- examination.)

Systematic discrimination is related to non-intentional institutional discrimination, but is distinct. It is different in that systematic discrimination refers to more global and less specific forms of discriminatory practices whereas institutional discrimination refers to the specific workings of specific institutions, as suggested earlier. Systematic discrimination is connected to a long line of thinking in sociology: There are patternings of social behavior that produce outcomes that are advantageous to some groups and disadvantageous to others.

This idea of the social patternings of behavior has a long history in sociology and indeed it could be argued that this is the essence of sociology. Social life is patterned. Street crime is more prevalent in poorer neighborhoods. Divorce rates systematically rise and fall. Political revolutions occur when certain sets of factors are present. Bureaucracies tend to produce certain types of behaviors. One could site countless examples of the realities of social processes that are patterned. Notably, these are patterned and can be understood independently from psychology. One does not have to invoke psychology to understand these.

This was one of the points made by the important early French sociologist Emile Durkheim. In his work titled Suicide, he demonstrated that suicide rates rise and fall depending upon such social factors as social integration and moral regulation. These factors are external to individuals and produce systematic results. Social integration refers to social connections individuals have. Thus, a person who is married with several children is more integrated than a person who is single. Moral regulation refers to the relationship of expectations and outcomes. A well regulated moral environment is one in which what a group of people expects to happen actually happens. For Durkheim, too much or too little of integration or regulation produces high suicide rates. He gathered data of suicide rates in Europe to make his case. Again, the point here is that systematic patternings of the social world can be understood independently of individual psychology.

There are patternings of social relations that also produce and reproduce racial inequalities. More specifically, numerous studies have demonstrated that systemic discrimination exists and explains at least some of these inequalities. For example, an often cited, relatively recent audit study by Devah Pager demonstrates this. Pager (2019) did a study in which she had black and white researchers pretend to be looking for employment. She also added the variable of some being convicted (pretend) of a drug crime and others not having such a conviction. She then created a job resume for all the four. The resumes were identical except for the fake names which indicated race (e.g. some had the name John, for the white applicant; others had the name Jamal, for the black applicant), and except for the criminal record. She then had the researchers submit job applications. Her research showed that the white applicants were far more likely to get the jobs, or at least the job interview, than the black applicant. But even more interesting, she showed that black applicants without a criminal record were less likely to get called for an interview than white applicants with a criminal record. This is a clear instance of systematic discrimination. One cannot deny the realities of these findings without dismissing reality itself.

We have thus far discussed various factors in accounting for racial inequalities – cultural, racism, discrimination, etc. – but there is another, albeit sordid, explanation that often lurks behind the curtain. This is the scientific racist explanation anchored in claims about meaningful biological, e.g. genetic, differences that supposedly account for inequalities. Proponents of biological racist explanations would likely dismiss these other factors as insignificant. (However, biological racism however does not easily explain the various audit studies such as Pager's. Sometimes the racist claim that such instances are not that pervasive, etc. Nevertheless, the biological racist accounts fail to effectively address the result of these studies.)

Rationality and Scientific Racism

Earlier, it was noted that the form of thinking dictated by the embrace of formal rationality views the social, psychological, and objective worlds as operating under the same mechanical principles. Further, this world view sees the world as comprised of discrete entities. This mindset does not readily allow people to understand or to accept such things as the legitimacy of systematic discrimination. Instead, there is an endless push, for example, to isolate the phenomena, to relegate it to individuals rather than to allow it to remain in the social. Hence, the wrongheaded push to explain systematic discrimination in terms of "unconscious" racism, thus rendering the entire discourse muddled and confused.

Another direction taken as the result of embracing a mindset that is mechanical and that sees the world as comprised of autonomous, discrete individual items is toward an embrace of scientific racism, anchored in biology. As noted at the beginning of this chapter, we describe scientific racism in some detail in Chapter Ten. Here I wish to explore and to speculate upon the intersections of rationality, scientific racism, and current circumstances in American societies. To begin, it should be noted that scientific racism in history and in the contemporary world is riddled with deep scientific, moral, and political problems which fundamentally challenge the soundness of the entire approach. We discuss many of these, particularly the scientific claims, elsewhere (see Chapter Ten). Suffice to say numerous scholars have demonstrated that the conceptualizations of scientific racism are wanting (see for example Lewontin, Kamin and Rose 1984) and numerous scholars have demonstrated the basic flaws in the actual science done by scientific racism (see for example Gould 1981). Moreover, it does not even take a detailed analysis to recognize the problems with scientific racism. For example, as I discuss elsewhere, Madison Grant wrote a book titled *The Passing of the Great Race* (1916) in which he warned that the United States was in trouble in the 1920s because it was allowing inferior races into the country. He argued that these newly arriving immigrants were genetically inferior, e.g. less intelligent and less moral, and if they were allowed into the country, they would eventually breed with the strong WASP genetic stock and the country would be greatly weakened. Of note, Grant was not writing about non-white immigrants. He was writing about Southern and Eastern Europeans, e.g. Italians, Polish people, Jews, etc. He believed that Europeans comprised several distinct races and the races from the north and west of Europe – England, Scandinavia, etc. were genetically superior to the races of Southern and Eastern Europe. Of course, one need only replace the words black for Italian and Latinos for Poles and one sees the exact same argument being replicated today by scientific racists.

What about the logic, the rationality, of scientific racists? A racist today perhaps likely would say something to the effect that: "Scientists should be allowed to conduct research and to produce findings about the biological differences and inequalities between races. If this scientific research demonstrates that white people are genetically more intelligent, more moral, etc., then black people, then we should accept these findings. We should allow the freedom to use rationality and science wherever it ends, even if it produces results that may be morally offensive to some." Indeed, if one embraces the pure logic of formal rationality, then should not scientific racists be allowed to do their research? The putative essence of the modern world is one of freedom and rationality and as such all rational, scientific inquiry should be allowed.

Scientific racists accounts and practices were standard fare in America and in Europe from the 1800s through the 1960s, but since that time it has normatively been prohibited in public discourse as well as within the academy to explicitly embrace scientific racism. It is not that scientific racism has not been done or has not been accepted since the 1960s. Rather, there is a strong, very strong, normative pressure to disavow being a racist, and specifically a scientific racist. For example, we see over and over again the authors of scientific racist accounts in recent decades denying they are in fact racist. From Charles Murray to James Wilson, racists deny being so while producing racist accounts. Moreover, many other scientist conducting research that could easily lend itself to scientific racism even if the research itself was not explicitly so also typically reject any charges that they are racist. I am thinking here of evolutionary biologists such as E.O. Wilson and Richard Dawkins. Wilson famously is associated with the theory of sociobiology, which claims that human behaviors by and large are genetically programmed by evolution. A similar thing appears in public discourse where it is normatively prohibited from stating openly and publicly that "I am a racist." For example, many people who fly the confederate flag today or who honor the monuments in the South dedicated to the white Confederate generals routinely proclaim today they are not racist, even though the embrace of such things clearly show otherwise.

One cannot help but thing of the visceral conservative complaints today against "political correctness," which in part is seen as a form of censorship. "People should be allowed to say what they think in public without fear," some conservatives might complain. Implicit in such claims presumably is the ability to proclaim that one is a racist. And yet, the normative power preventing this even in American society today is quite strong.

Thus, there are two dominant themes related to this topic: the ability to openly conduct scientific research studies and the ability to state one's scientific racist beliefs in public without fear of sanction. In effect, it appears we have reached another limit of rationality.

The normative anchors against scientific racism, the bases for working to deny scientific racism a legitimate place in the academy and in public discourse, lies in moral, political, and scientific arguments. Morally, scientific racism is repugnant on its face. It is more than offensive to say that a member of one race is genetically inferior to a member of another. Can you imagine if a scientific racist proclaimed a desire to scientifically study the possibility that Jews are genetically programs to be more greedy and less moral than others? All such topics are morally disgusting, humanly disgusting. Can you imagine if a scientific racist proclaimed a desire to scientifically study the possibility that white people, specifically those descendant from Northern and Western Europe are more aggressive and more selfish than other racial groups? This question is a bit different than the first in that this one is focused upon the deficits of the dominant group – white people. Why is it that in the history of scientific racism those doing the research come from the dominant classes, e.g. whites, and produce findings that show the dominant classes to have better and more admirable traits, by genetics, than others? These questions shade into the political concerns about scientific racism.

Even a casual review of the history of scientific racism – continuing into the present – shows that it has and is being produced by members of the dominant groups and that the findings routinely support the ideologies of the dominant group, i.e. that the dominant group should by nature be dominant.

But the political ramifications of scientific racism are far more pernicious than this. They go to the legitimacy of epistemologies, of theories of knowledge. Specifically, the issue of the relation of truth to power is central here. In the classic view of science, the pursuit of truth through science should be separate from power, from political influence. There should be a wall of separation between truth and power. Truth should not be manipulated to serve the needs or interest of the powerful. This is an essential edict of modern science, and of modern social science.

It is one of the great ironies of today, and it appears to be the natural implosion of the blind embrace of formal rationality, as noted earlier, that the trust that was had in the public mind as well as elsewhere that truth can and should be separated from power, has been deeply eroded in contemporary American society. This is a frightening and alarming development for the future stability of American democracy. We see it in the news media, where media sites such as Fox News emerged to challenge the proclaimed objectivity of mainstream news media. Fox news was and is based upon the claim that the mainstream networks, such as NBC, ABC, etc., proclaim to be objective but in fact have a liberal bias, while Fox claims it is objective in its reporting. As a result, the entire edifice of keeping a wall between truth and power is being assaulted by Fox. It goes well beyond news. Conservative intellectuals have railed against the breakdown of the wall within universities. They complain that political correctness, Marxism, postmodernism, gender studies, etc. have greatly harmed the academy in large part because these forces have themselves broken down the wall between truth and power. When truth is seen as relative and when truth is seen to be a game of power, then the traditional academic project is destroyed. We of course see this very same form of thinking – the belief that there is no wall between truth and power -- in the endless activities of Trump and his Republican supporters.

Rationality and Its Challenges Today

At the beginning of this chapter it was noted that Max Weber was concerned about the social consequences of a modern world that fully embraces rationality, that becomes enslaved to rationality. Yet, in looking at America today it would appear that someone close to the opposite has occurred. That is, instead of people bowing down and blindly accepting rationality, there has been a huge and dangerous reaction against, or rejection of, rationality. This was suggested above with the breakdown of the trust in the possibilities of professionals to be objective and unbiased in their world. But the issue of the rejection of rationality goes beyond this.

In America today, the majority of members of the Republican Party and many others believe things that are not true. They reject basic rational and scientific claims, and instead support beliefs that are not in accord with reality. In addition to the lies or delusions about the 2020 election, many Republicans also reject the COVID-19 vaccines. The COVID-19 vaccines have been demonstrated through scientific research to be safe and effective, yet millions of Americans refuse to get the vaccine (and this refusal contributes to the continued epidemic). Global warming is yet another example. Global warming is real, and humans are destroying the planet. Science is quite clear on this.

Yet if the facts and if science is so clear about such things, we might ask why so many Americans reject these facts. Why do so many Americans today reject science? And what does this say about Weber's thesis of rationalization? Does it refute it? We should start here by noting that the rejection of rationality and science is not total in the minds of the people embracing the falsities noted above. That is, most of these people still go to their medical doctor and largely follow his or her advice. These people largely still fly airplanes (based on technologies, based on science). In most ways, these rejections are selective. They tend to be infused with political and moral sensibilities.

The rejections of rationality we are seeing may at first seem to contradict Weber's claims about rationalization, but upon closer inspection one could argue they in fact support his claims. Most notable, the claim that rationalization, i.e. the conquest of formal rationality, leads to a loss of meaning in modern humans, a loss that cries out to be filled, seems to explain what we are seeing now, just as this same understanding was used by many to explain the rise of fascism and Hitler's Nazi's in the 1920s and 1930s. (It perhaps is relevant here to note the infamous Degenerate Art Exhibit in Nazi Germany in 1937. The Nazis hated modern art. They put on an exhibit displaying modern art to show how this art was degenerate. Degeneracy, at the time, had a precise meaning in biological evolutionary thinking. A human degenerate was an evolutionary throwback to an earlier stage of development. It was an environmental regression, harmful to the genetic stock of a group. Hitler and the fascists saw the modern world being in a state of decade and the way to restore it was to embrace the Nazi model and scientific racism.) Arguably, the emptiness that was created by the rationalization of the world in the industrial capitalism of the modern world in the 1920s, fueled a psychological emptiness that longed to be filled. One could argue that the basic issues associated with rationalization seen in the 1920s and 1930s did not disappear with the defeat of fascism in World War Two, but instead have resurfaced in recent years.

There are more dimensions to this process. Recall that rationalization produces and reinforces a consciousness that is anchored in a fragmented and mechanical understanding of the world. This fits neatly with scientific racism. As such, the embrace of the rejection of rationality does not mean the total rejection of it, but the selective rejection, the rejection of forms of rationality that do not narrowly conform to the fragmented and mechanical mindset.

Moreover, from a sociological perspective one cannot help but think of the current phenomena of huge swaths of the Republican Party rejecting rationality without thinking of the idea of cults. Cults are a form of religious organization often studied by sociologists. (There are several types of religious organizations, cults are one of these: cults, sects, denominations, churches, ecclesia.) We tend to think of cults as small, religiously radical, and fanatical groups that often end with mass suicides. But they need not be. They can be large or very large and do not inevitably lead to mass suicides. The Unification Church (also known as the Moonies) led by Sun Myung Moon, based in South Korea, is often identified as cult. It has millions of members and is quite wealthy. (The recent assignation of the former Japanese Prime Minister Abe was done by a man whose relative became a member of the Unification Church, membership the man blamed for ruining the relative's life. The assassin was upset that Abe spoke at a Unification Church sponsored activity. The Unification Church also owns some American newspapers, such as the Washington Times.)

Cults by their nature tend to believe things that mainstream members of a society would see as delusional or at best bizarre. They are also characterized by the fanatic devotion of their members. Numerous other characteristics could be cited here. The point is that the cult-like quality of the New Republicans followers of Trump should not be ignored or dismissed.

Another religious or quasi-religious quality that can be invoked to help understand this odd phenomena of millions of Americans believing things that are untrue, beliefs which have real and potentially harmful consequences, is that of sacralization. This is a concept discussed in Chapter Eight.

Basically, sacralization is the hypothesis that counteracts the secularization hypothesis. The secularization hypothesis is the claim made by many sociologists that modernity brings about a decline in religion in a population. That is, in modernity fewer people belief in religion and engage in religious practices. That is the hypothesis. Sacralization is the counter to this. It is the process by which people assert their need for a belief in the sacred. As we have seen above, Weber argued that rationalization creates a loss of meaning, which can be accompanied by secularization. But the need for meaning amongst modern humans is there, and arguably enhanced due to the historical condition. In short, religion may change shape. It may appear as things not explicitly religious, but it will remain. There is a need, it is argued here, amongst modern humans to feel, to experience the sacred in their lives.

In a modern, democratic society, it is imagined that the tensions and contradictions of modernity described throughout this chapter can be contained and managed through open, reasoned, public debate. And yet this process is now being seriously threatened by current events. One can only hope that a better understanding of the situation combined with an embrace of open inquiry and a commitment to facts and to reason will successfully combat the ill winds of the irrational that arose in Europe in the 1930s and that are seriously threatening the United States today.

Chapter Three: Sociological Perspectives

The American Sociological Association, the professional association of American sociologists, likes to say that sociology is a science (albeit they qualify this statement greatly). But what does this mean, and is it true? When one thinks of science, one thinks perhaps of chemistry, or biology, or physics. The belief is that all of these scientific fields share a commitment to the scientific enterprise. The assumption is that there is one and only one meaning to the word science; there is one and only one way to do science. Science in this sense is based upon the assumption that the researcher objectively examines causal relations amongst empirical facts – facts which can be seen, measured, or inferred – and draws hypotheses about these causal relations with the aim of establishing truths or the laws of nature, however tentative, about the workings of the world. It is fundamentally a predictive enterprise about nature. This notion of science, what it is, and what it does, has had profound success in the last two hundred years. It has enabled humans to control nature significantly, to aid in health, to develop technologies, to cure and prevent diseases, etc. As a model, this form of science has demonstrated its effectiveness – in biology, chemistry, physics, engineering, etc.

But should this model be used by sociologists? Can it be used by sociologists? And is there only one form or type of science? Is science the only legitimate form of knowledge? Are there others, and which should sociology embrace? If there are others, perhaps we might ask if one or another of these others is more appropriate for sociology? To understand this, we need to recognize that people are not chemicals in a test tube, the stuff of chemistry. People are not predictable atoms, in the fashion of physics. The laws of nature do not apply to social, human being. (However, some scholars such as the evolutionary biologist E.O. Wilson, who championed the idea of sociobiology, say that human behavior is fundamentally programmed by human genetics.) Yet it might be argued that much in the same way that physics and other sciences make their assumptions about predictability there is an unpredictability at the heart of both the natural world and the social world. (Physics has developed something called chaos theory which is built upon this unpredictability.) Statistical probability lies at the heart of all science today. At the very least, all sciences assume there is randomness and chance in nature. If an oak tree is thirty feet tall, does that mean its offspring will be thirty feet? No. It may be a bit taller or a bit shorter, and this may be because of the tree's genetics. Conversely, one can find a similar level of predictability in the social world. For example, as a professor I can predict with great accuracy where students will sit in a class after the first few class meetings. Students, like everyone else, are creatures of habits, and as such creatures they claim a seat and sit in the same seat throughout the semester. Does this suggest that students are not unlike chemicals in a test tube? Is there a "law" governing student behavior? No. Even here, one might note that people make choices; chemicals do not. At the heart of the difference between chemicals in a test tube and human beings is that the latter acts based upon meanings they assigned to the world. Humans interpret their worlds and act upon these interpretations. Rocks, chemicals, and atoms do not do such things.

Sociologists who think of sociology as a science, as a science not very different from other sciences, largely are led to claim that theirs is a science of behaviors – observable social actions, not of thoughts or abstractions. (One cannot after all touch or measure a thought.) As such, the idea of meaning, the idea that one needs to consider how and why people assign meaning to their world, how they understand their worlds, themselves in their worlds, their actions in their worlds, is not relevant. What is relevant is behavior, social behavior.

The issue gets more complicated when we consider that science is in the business of producing knowledge, and there are many, many forms of knowledge besides the knowledge produced by science. Scholars have long recognized that there are distinct forms of knowledge. One only need to look at the knowledge possessed by an art professor and contrast this with the knowledge of a physics professor. The art professor has an expert knowledge of say a Picasso painting; the physics professor may have a scientific knowledge of Boson particles or string theory. The art professor's knowledge is not derived from science, as is conventionally understood, nor could it be. He or she does not subject the Picasso painting to a scientific experiment to understand the painting. Yet he or she *knows* Picasso. But scholars have gone well beyond this in recognizing different forms of knowledge. From the ancient Greeks, such as Aristotle, to the contemporary German sociologist Jurgen Habermas, scholars have identified many different and distinct forms of knowledge. Aristotle, for example, distinguished between theoretical, technical, and practical knowledge. Theoretical knowledge is abstract and reasoned. Technical knowledge is the knowledge of the engineer or scientist who knows the intellectual steps he or she must go through to solve a problem. Practical knowledge is the know-how type of knowledge. If one asks a musician or a basketball player how they did a particular move, they might not be able to tell you, but they know how they did it, they can show you. It is practical knowledge. In the same way, it is one thing to know the rules of the game of chess, it is quite another to know how to play the game of chess.

The questions then are: What type of knowledge should sociologists pursue? Should they pursue scientific knowledge or some other type, and if some other type which type? In fact, many sociologists today do not subscribe to the traditional scientific form of knowledge, that is, the one suggested by the American Sociological Association. Certainly it is the case that the major journals of sociology – specifically the American Journal of Sociology and the American Sociological Review – do indeed embrace the view that sociology is or should be a field that embraces traditional scientific knowledge (excluding of course the pursuit of natural laws, as noted above) – but when one considers the range of sociologists practicing today, one realizes that there are actually several distinct types of knowledge championed by sociology. Not all, and arguably not even most, American sociologists today subscribe to sociology as a traditional scientific enterprise. One can identify four distinct, yet often overlapping, perspectives taken by sociologists today: 1) a scientific; 2) an interpretive approach; 3) a critical approach; and 4) a historical approach. A few words can be said on each of these.

The Scientific Perspective

The **scientific perspective** has been discussed above. One element bears repeating: Of particular importance here is to note the generally accepted difference embraced by sociologists between the form of science employed in scientific fields such as chemistry and physics and that employed by some sociologists. The similarities between the two are their shared commitment to an objective assessment of causal relations among social facts such that explanations and hypotheses can be advanced to explain these relations. A main difference is the commitment to the discovery of laws, natural laws, governing these relations. The natural sciences

– biology, chemistry, physics, has as a prime goal the discovery of the laws governing these relations. In contrast, sociologists have long abandoned this goal. Few if any sociologists would say there are laws, comparable to the laws of the natural world, that govern social behavior.

Perhaps most central to the sociological commitment to the scientific perspective is a belief that the sociologist should and can *objectively* identify, in an unbiased way, social facts and the causal relationship between these. Importantly, most sociologists recognize that it is far more difficult for the sociologist, and the social scientist more generally, to be purely objective in his or her analysis than it is for a biologist or a chemist to be so. What values or biases – moral, ethical, etc., for example, might a chemist give to one chemical agent, say nitrogen, versus another? (In public culture today, the arch-conservatives who have taken over this country have sought to discredit the objectivity of even these sciences. For example, the political assaults on environmental scientists who claim that global warming is a real and serious concern. The reality of global warming has been irrationally challenged for political reasons, or other ill-founded reasons.) In general, objectivity in the natural sciences is not a difficult task. Scientists can put their morality, their religious values, other values, their political sentiments aside and look at the natural world in an objective, unbiased way. In the social sciences, however, it automatically becomes more difficult. Can sociologists, for example, objectively study race or inequality, or is it necessarily the case that the values and biases of the sociologist will inevitably distort, knowingly or not, their findings, thus rendering their work not objective? Some sociologists claim that through professional academic training they can be objective in their analysis of any and all social phenomena. Most sociologists take a more nuanced view and argue that sociologists should be guided by their professional ethics and should commit to strive to be "value free" or objective and unbiased in their analysis while recognizing the possibilities that biases and values can, if not guarded against, seep into the analysis. In short, sociologists should aspire to objectivity, recognizing that it is often not possible to be purely so. Perhaps most importantly, sociologists are trained to be reflective on such matters and as such, their work should and does in reality typically reflect objectively the worlds there are studying.

Many if not most sociologists today subscribe to one or another of the above scientific perspectives, that is, they believe through training they can be objective, or close to it, in their analysis, or believe they can, through their training, strive to be as objective as possible. One of the central elements of professional training of sociologists is and arguably should be for sociologists to learn, to be trained, to seek to identify when their personal biases, values, etc. are influencing or distorting their understandings of the world such that the sociologist could correct these and strive toward an objective accounting of the world. (This professional ethics can perhaps be compared to the professional ethics of other fields, such as medicine. The medical doctor gives his or her professional assessment of a situation and this assessment is based upon an objective assessment of the facts. Similarly, the medical doctor as a professional should treat all patients the same irrespective of whether the doctor views the patient as immoral or somehow unworthy. Sociologists who embrace a scientific perspective strive to do the same in their work. While one should not take the comparison between medicine and sociology too far, the point of the professional ethics guiding the work of both should be noted.)

Interpretive Sociologies

On the other hand, many sociologists today do not believe sociology is or should be a scientific enterprise along the lines of chemistry and physics. Some have advocated an alternative perspective, one rooted in interpretation. The **interpretive perspective** is the second of the major perspectives used by sociologists today. The interpretive perspective assumes that human beings are distinctly different than chemicals or atoms. Humans think; they experience their worlds; they assign meanings, and act upon those meanings; they make choices; they are unpredictable at times; they are social; they use language; they are moral beings, etc. Because of these differences, interpretive sociologists argue that one needs to rely upon a perspective other than science, as traditionally understood, to understand social behavior and social organization. One needs to understand the social processes that shape and inform how and why people assign meanings to the world, and how these things affect their behaviors. One needs to rely upon an interpretive process to understand how the social actors are interpreting their worlds and acting in them based upon their interpretations. After all, the interpretive sociologist might say, can one really understand human behavior without, for example, understanding the whys of the behavior, why social behavior occurs. And understanding why someone does something requires an interpretation of things such as motives and motivations, among other things.

Importantly, there are two distinct versions of interpretive sociology. One of these seeks to graft the interpretive approach onto the scientific one, taking the better elements of both and developing an interpretive science of sociology. This approach calls upon the sociologist to strive to be as objective and unbiased as possible in his or her analysis. It also believes that sociological claims about social realities and causal forces within this reality should be based upon empirical evidence or facts. If a sociologist sees someone chopping wood in their back yard, how does he or she try to explain this as a sociologist using the interpretive science perspective? The chopping of the wood is an empirical fact. But why is the person doing it? How is the sociologist to know? He or she could simply ask the woodcutter why he is chopping the wood. He might say he is doing it for exercise. This statement is another empirical fact. (It is not a fact that the claim is true – as we see below the woodcutter might be chopping for another reason. But it is a fact in that it is a stated claim. Much like a written note about flying elephants is a fact. The note in itself is a fact; it has an objective reality. But what it refers to may not be real.) The sociologist might conclude that the woodcutter is telling the truth and report that he is doing it for exercise. This is the procedure for one type of interpretive sociology as a science. But wait. The woodchopper could be lying or could be mistaken or could be too embarrassed to tell the researcher why he really is chopping the wood. As a researcher in this mode, the sociologist is compelled to seek out as much evidence as possible, with the understanding that the interpretation might change as he or she gets more evidence. For example, the sociologist might speak to the wood chopper's wife, and she might say her husband is chopping wood because the couple just had a fight, and he is getting his anger out. The point is that the interpretive science perspective calls upon the researcher to seek out more and more empirical facts – it is an open-ended process -- and to approach the world in an objective way, recognizing that the researcher's claims about the world can and do change with the discovery of new evidence. As such, this form seeks to fuse elements of the scientific approach with elements of the interpretive approach. This is the traditional mode of interpretive sociology used by most sociologists using interpretive perspectives.

But there is a very different type of interpretive sociology, one that is less commonly used, one that rejects the commitments to science, as conventionally understood. This non-scientific interpretive perspective draws more from the humanities, and perhaps most notably from philosophy, than from the sciences. Think of art history or literature. The art professor can tell you what a Picasso painting means, a literature professor can tell you what Steinbeck's *Grapes of Wrath* means, but neither knows this because they embraced a scientific perspective. It is a different form of knowledge, one that relies upon the interpretations of the researcher. In the same way, some sociologists say that it is not possible to fuse science onto an interpretive approach and as such sociologists should fully embrace a non-scientific interpretive perspective.

Sometimes sociologists embrace a non-scientific interpretive perspective because they believe that it is not possible to scientifically account for social behaviors. After all, can we ever really know why someone does what he or she does? Can we ever really know the motivations of an act? Similarly, can we ever really know what any social reality occurs? Is it possible to make some scientific claim about any of this? The important American literary theorist and rhetorician Kenneth Burke argued that any complete explanation for any social reality entails an answer to five questions: who, what, when, where and why. He argued that the action in a movie, in a theatrical production or in social reality is carried forth by answers to all five of these. He identifies five elements (which he calls the pentad) which answer these question: agent, act, scene, agency, and purpose. A situation, for example, can be explained as the result of the setting. When the tornado pulled Dorothy's house up into the sky in the Wizard of OZ and landed it in the kingdom of Oz, it was the scene and not the agent carrying the action forward. The point for Burke was that an explanation for a social reality can be found in any of the five elements. As such, an explanation is utterly relative. One could explain an event by focusing on one or another of the elements, or upon combining the elements (e.g. act-scene) which Burke called ratios. It is simply up to the researcher or observer to choose which of the ratios he wishes to use to explain the situation. This is highly interpretive, and it is decidedly non-scientific.

This is not the only way of thinking of non-scientific interpretive approaches. It is not the only reason for using non-scientific approaches. Another reason that some scholars use non-scientific interpretive approaches is the claim that the particular object of study does not lend itself to scientific inquiry. Some social realities can more easily be studies in some sort of scientific way than others. One might be able to study scientifically, from an interpretive perspective, a woodcutter, but one study such things as the concepts of society, or civilization or the broad-sweeps of history using such scientific approaches? The once highly influential sociologist Pitirim Sorokin (1889-1968) who immigrated to the United States and was a professor at Harvard for much of his life developed an approach that echoes this interpretive, non-scientific approach (though he would likely argue that he did embrace a commitment to basic scientific principles).Sorokin developed a cyclical theory of history. He said there were three types of societies that have existed throughout history, and these three differed from one another based on the forms of social integration that they produced. The three are ideational, sensate, and idealistic. We need not describe these here. Suffice to note that even with his well-documented histories, his theory was largely anchored in a non-scientific interpretive perspective. (Sorokin's theorizing, and theorizing concerning large-scale societal changes in general, were once quite popular, but today they are not discussed much at all.)

A main problem with the non-scientific interpretive approach is that the basis of legitimacy of the sociology discipline is threatened when this perspective is embraced. That is, sociology as a science, interpretive or otherwise, is legitimated on the claim that sociologists are objective, or strive to be, and that they build interpretations of causal relations in the social world, on the observation of empirical facts. But if these claims are challenged or rejected, what is the basis of legitimacy for sociology? If one makes claims not on the observation of the causal relations of empirical facts but rather on speculative claims about causal relations of facts which cannot be definitively identified and isolated and which cannot be systematically studied, then how can one claim one is being scientific? It becomes no more of an authoritative voice (an authoritative "opinion"?) than those found in the fields of literature or art history. As such, if a non-scientific interpretive sociologist makes a claim about the workings of the social world, one could argue that it is "just the sociologist's opinion." And indeed, it is opinion. But it is not the opinion of the man or woman on the street. It is not the opinion of anyone. It is an expert opinion, a deeply informed opinion. Much as the man or woman on the street could give an opinion about the meaning of a Picasso painting, so too can the art professor. But these opinions, these interpretations, are not of the same order. Most people would recognize the art professor does know much, much more about Picasso than the man or woman on the street and as such his opinion, his interpretations, should be regarded as authoritative. In the same way, non-scientific interpretive sociologists make similar claims.

Critical Perspectives

As an alternative to the scientific and the interpretive perspectives some sociologists embrace a **critical perspective**. The number and percentage of sociologists who embrace a critical perspective is very small compared to these other two, but it has grown since the 1960s. If we define this critical perspective very broadly, we can see that it has arguably been around since the founding of modern sociology, through for example the works of August Comte who saw, in the Enlightenment Era spirit, sociology as a scientific endeavor oriented toward making the world a better place, or through the works of the first major American school of sociology at the University of Chicago, during the Progressive Era (1890-1920), which saw the science of sociology as a means of using science to solve various social problems. Importantly, these types of critical perspectives embrace the fundamentals of science. Their critical orientation did not challenge the underlying scientific perspective, i.e. that sociology as a science should be objective and unbiased in its analysis; that it should focus on identifying empirical facts and determining causal relations amongst these. However, since the 1960s critical sociology has taken much more radical and more diverse forms, informed in part by such diverse theoretical and intellectual traditions as Marxism, post-modernism, feminism, and other assorted recent orientations. As such, there is not one thing called critical sociology. There are many types of critical sociology.

These diverse types of critical sociology can be categorized into two broad camps. (To begin, it is important to realize here that critical perspectives in sociological are more complicated conceptually than the scientific or interpretivistic. Readers are encouraged to recognize the nuances and complexities, whether flawed or sound, in the more sophisticated reasonings of critical perspectives.) The camps differ from each other in terms of the nature of the critical approach. That is, one form of critical sociology is quite compatible with either or both the scientific and interpretivistic approaches, while another is not. The critical approach (really, approaches) that is compatible with the scientific or interpretivistic assumes many if not all of the major conceptual assumptions of the other two approaches. These assumptions are the ones described above, including such things as the striving for objectivity, reliance on empirical facts, looking to explain causal relations between facts, etc. This form of critical sociology basically claims that sociology should be objective or interpretive, in a scientific sense, but at the same time should be oriented toward addressing and solving any of the social problems confronting the world. Thus, critical sociologists might employ conventional research to understand racism or inequality or homelessness with the goal of providing scientific knowledge that could be used by policy makers to address these problems. As such, the only real difference between this form of critical sociology and the scientific or interpretivistic perspectives concerns the explicit selection of the topic of study based upon the value considerations of the researcher. That is, if I was a critical sociologist in this tradition and was raised in a poor household, I might wish to study poverty such that I could help to eradicate it. (This is the perspective taken by the likes of Comte and the Chicago School, noted above). This value commitment in the selection of the topic of study – what Weber calls "value relevance" – is universally accepted as legitimate. The point is that once the topic is selected, this form of critical scholarship says that values should no longer influence the research project, i.e. the researcher should be objective and unbiased in his or her analysis.

The second strand of critical perspectives in sociology is far more controversial and far more complex intellectually. (This is the form of sociology that is the target of so much wrath by arch-conservatives today. Sadly, these critics erroneously see this form of sociology as the dominant or sole form of sociology practiced today when it reality it is neither.) It also comprises a wide range of intellectual orientations. This strand is embraced by only a small percentage of American sociologists today, though the number has grown in recent years. This second strand challenges many of the fundamental claims and assumptions of traditional science. The challenges are largely philosophical in nature, questioning the conventional epistemologies governing conventional science and popular consciousness today. For example, the belief in the pursuit of objectivity and non-bias, which is one of the hallmarks of traditional science, is largely abandoned by these critical scholars. Toward that end, many who embrace this form of critical sociology champion a perspective captured in Marx's famous claim that "Philosophers think about the world, the point is to change it." We could replace the word philosophers here with the word sociologists: "Sociologists think about the world; the point is to change it." It bears noting that most sociologists embracing this second strand of critical sociology are not Marxists. This quote is simply used to illustrate a common thread shared by many of them. For Marx, and for this strand of critical sociology, the very research project itself should be geared toward fostering critical, social change. The very philosophical underpinnings of conventional science are challenged by this approach. For example, some if not many embracing this critical perspective reject the common scientific assumption that objective accountings of the social world are possible. In this light, many see knowledge and research with the context of power. Knowledge, in this perspective, is inextricably tied to power. All knowledge is said to be little more than a tool or instrument of power. Knowledge and power are fused in this thinking; they cannot be separated. Thus, those who have the power determine what is true, and what is determined to be true, do so in ways that foster the interests of one or another group in society. (Marx can be cited again here. Marx once said, "The ruling ideas of every epoch, are the ideas of the ruling class.") As such, sociology is essentially a political endeavor within the game of power, from this critical perspective. Knowledge becomes subservient to power. Sociologists embracing this perspective see knowledge as a vehicle to assert their political interests, rather than to advance knowledge itself. For example, a radical feminist (as opposed perhaps to a liberal or a socialist feminist) embracing this form of critical sociology might seek to use the production of critical knowledge to challenge male domination in society and to advance the interests of women.

The claims and assumptions of this strand of critical sociology are highly controversial, and as I noted above are not widely embraced within sociology, though the number of sociologists embracing these ideas has grown in recent decades. It is highly controversial because it radically reconceptualizes the nature of the sociology enterprise, and the very nature of what knowledge is. Is there an objective, factual social reality, or is all social realty constructed within a context of power? Is all knowledge of the social world essentially biased?

The non-critical approaches in one way or another strive toward an objective accounting of the workings of the social world. It was thought by traditional sociologists that the knowledge produced by the sociologist could be used, or not, by others, by politicians or policy makers, etc. if they wished to do so. But it was not the business of sociology to strive to change the world. This critical approach is controversial because it moves sociology from the realm of science, broadly conceived, to one of ideology (or critics might say propaganda), or political manipulations. This shatters the conventional understanding of the project of sociology and leads to a position that claims "might is right." That is, it rests on the assumption that the powerful dictate what is truth and thus the goal is to strive for power. (This has frightening implications, as I argue in various chapters of this book, and this approach was the hallmark of fascist regimes – such as Hitler and the Nazis, and sadly was a current in the Trump regime and the Republican Party and their assault on truth. These groups continue today in the same mode. But here we are discussing sociology. And in sociology the tendency of those who employ this form of critical sociology are actually on the far left of the political perspective – broadly defined -- rather than the far (fascist) right. Nevertheless, the implication here is that both end up in the same frightening place.)

Perhaps an even more concerning side of this strand of critical sociology is the unwillingness of some scholars who embrace this perspective to acknowledge they are in fact doing so. That is, such scholars sometimes if not often ignore or deny they are fusing their value commitments with their research. When or if these sociologists who embrace the radical form of critical sociology cloak their work under the guise of one or another perspective described above – scientific, interpretivistic, critical in the conventional sense – this produces increased and appropriate skepticism by others, by various audiences, about their true projects, i.e. to use sociology as a political tool. If this perspective was to gain even more traction in sociology than it currently has, it will lead, rightly so, to fundamental credibility problems for the discipline as a form of scientific inquiry.

This is not to deny some of the basic premises of this form of critical sociology. One must recognize that power and knowledge are related. It is merely to call for a more nuanced, more engaged critical appraisal of the critical perspectives than is generally happening today.

The Historical Perspective

Earlier in this chapter, three dimensions to sociological inquiry were noted: perspectives, theories, and methods. Three perspectives have been discussed thus far – the scientific, the interpretive, and the critical. But there is a fourth: the historical perspective. The nature of the **historical perspective** is such that one might wonder if it should best be categorized as either a theory or a method rather than as a perspective. It does not fit neatly into either the three dimensions of sociological inquiry or the idea of perspectives described in this chapter. The historical perspective actually transcends and of these particular categories. As I argued in the first several chapters of this book, sociology began as a historically focused discipline and while this focus has all but disappeared in the American context, I argue that it should be revitalized.

Historical sociology is closely connected to the founding figures and early decades of modern sociology. Most of the nineteenth century sociological thinkers – from August Comte, who is generally regarded as the founder of modern sociology, who in the early 1800s sought to develop science of the history of social evolution – to the great, classical sociological theorists of Karl Marx, Max Weber, and Emile Durkheim – saw the sociological project as a historical one. (It perhaps should be noted that Durkheim proclaimed history to be central to sociology, even though his research was by and large less concerned about history than about the present, modern societies.)

In the twentieth century, historical sociology in America declined in influence. More and more sociologists focused on the present, much like many of the sciences, at least in the sense that many if not most sciences either ignore history or utilize some basic evolutionary model to account for it. In recent decades, some sociologists, including this author, believe that it is important to understand the social world from a historical perspective. This leads one to ask what historical sociology is, and how is it distinct from the field of history?

The field of history is devoted toward an empirical analysis of particular historical events or happenings. The goal is to develop a complete as possible explanation for the occurrence of some unique historical phenomenon or another. The particular and the unique are hallmarks of history. In contrast, historical sociology is oriented toward understanding recurring patterns found in history that could account for one or another historical reality. It is the patternings of the social world found in history that is its focus.

This should not be misinterpreted to mean that historical sociology seeks to discover the social and systematic determining factors that account for the course of history. Historical sociology by and large is not deterministic. Determinism is the position that there is an inevitable course of events that cannot fundamentally be changed. Determinism claims that one or another force is the engine of history, and this force cannot be stopped. As such, from a determinist perspective, history is inevitable. There is a direction or course to history. Thus, a technological determinist might say that technological developments throughout history and into the future are the engine of history. Whether it is the creation of mechanisms to make iron and then steel, or whether it is the Guttenberg Bible, the machine from the 1400s that used movable type and allowed for the mass production of printed books for the first time, technology, these determinists would say, determines the course of history. There are many forms of determinism. One might be a biological determinist, such as E.O. Wilson and his sociobiology which claims that history and social behavior are merely the reflection of the demands of our genes, or one may be an economic determinist such as Karl Marx who claimed to have discovered the logic of history, and this logic was anchored in contradictions that appear in the economic sphere throughout history.

Historical sociology, while influenced by such thinkers, make a fundamentally different claim. The task is not to discover the secret trajectory of history. Rather the task is to understand the systematic social forces that pattern social life in history and to understand how these patternings can maintain social order or foster social change. To identify these patternings historical sociologists either look for similar social formations that occur in different places at different times in history, or they look for similar social formations that occur in different places at the same time in history.

For example, the historical sociologist Michael Mann did a comparative historical study of the rise of fascism in Europe in the 1920s and 1930s (Mann 2004). He wished to understand fascist movements. (Fascist movements are highly destructive radical right wing political movements.) A comparative history compares the social formations that occur in two or more societies. Fascism took over much of Europe during these decades. Mann looked closely at several countries, including Germany (with Hitler and the Nazis) and Italy (with Mussolini), and asked what the movements had in common in these places. He wished to understand how fascism arose and what were the common features of these fascist movements. He identified several common features: transcendence, statism, nationalism, ethnic cleansing, political cleansing, and paramilitarism. A few words can be said on each of these. Transcendence refers to an orientation toward the world that is focused on the beyond. It is an orientation that goes beyond the ordinary, common place. Fascist movements nurture in their membership a sense of being, an orientation, in which they feel like they are part of something extra-ordinary, extra-special. There is a religious, cult-like quality to this. As part of the fascist movements, members feel they are part of a spiritual quest which fills them with a sense of specialness and commitment. They are removed from the ordinary, meaningless day to day existence and are filled with a wonderous sense of purposeful joy (and anger). The rabid devotion of Hitler's followers reflects this sensibility. Statism and nationalist are the next two features. Statism and nationalism, while overlapping, are distinct. Statism is the belief that the state is the embodiment of the people. It is not separate from the people. It is the people, and more precisely the leader of the state – Hitler, Mussolini, etc. – is the embodiment of the state, the party (which conceives of itself as the people), and the people. As such, the state is seen as necessarily all powerful and right in its actions, as it is reflecting the will of the leader, the party, and the people. There is no divide amongst any of these. Mussolini captures these sentiments well in his *Fascist Manifesto* (1919). Nationalism is a belief that one's own nation state, be it Germany, Italy, or the United States, is essentially superior to other nation states. It is an extreme devotion to the nation. A person's national identity becomes central to an individual's sense of self. Fascist movements tend to embrace an extreme version of nationalism, a hyper-nationalism, that goes beyond loyalties and identities toward a nation that many, many people feel in societies that are not fascist. Nationalism in fascism is also often anchored in racist sensibilities. That is, the fascists think their country is superior and they are superior because of the racial genetics of the nation. This is clearly present in Hitler's Germany, and it is present today in America amongst white nationalists.

Mann also found that fascist movements are oriented toward cleansing – both ethnic cleansing and political cleansing. Ethnic cleansing follows upon the ideas of transcendence and nationalism. It is the commitment to purifying one's own country by eliminating ethnic or racial groups presently there. The metaphor of purity and cleanliness and goodness vs danger and dirtiness, and impurity, and evil are central here. The fascist group sees themselves – their racial or genetic composition as pure and good, and they see their society as becoming infested by other racial or ethnic groups deemed impure and evil. These other groups need then to be eliminated. This elimination could be forced expulsion or genocide. Of course, the classic example of this is in Hitler's Germany where the Nazis tried to exterminate the entire Jewish population of Europe. Six million Jews were murdered by the Nazis and their supporters. Half the Jews of Europe were murdered. Hitler also targeted other groups with the same intent. He sought to destroy the Roma people (formerly called gypsies), and others. We see a similar theme present today in America with the white nationalists of the Republican Party who see America as being destroyed by immigration from non-European countries. (The practical realities of Germany in the 1930s and America today are such that while it was possible for the Germans to attempt to ethnically cleanse their country, in America the size of non-white populations – which are estimated to constitute a numerical majority of Americans within the next several decades – makes any sort of similar drive unrealistic.)

Paramilitarism is the last common feature of fascist movement, according to Mann, at least common to those movements in Europe in the 1920s and 1930s. Paramilitarism is the use of non-governmental armies typically by a political party. Paramilitary forces were a major feature of the fascist movements in Germany and in Italy. Mussolini had organized the black shirts as his party's paramilitary wing. He came to power in 1922 after thirty thousand of the black shirts marched on Rome. In Germany, the Nazi party had the brown shirts, formally called the SA (Sturmabteilung) as well as the elite SS (Schutzstaffel), both of which were melded into the Nazi government once Hitler consolidated his power. In some respects we can think of the militias of the radical right wing of the Republican Party, loyal to Trump, as contemporary examples of paramilitary forces.

This description of Mann's study is meant to illustrate the historical perspective in sociology. As we see, fascist movements have a number of features in common. Many, social phenomenon can similarly be studied historically, from family structures to crime, from political revolutions to sexual relations.

We can conclude by noting that the four perspectives discussed above are not mutually exclusive. One can try to combine two or more of the above. For example, one could try to fuse an interpretive with a historical perspective, or a scientific with a critical. But all such efforts lead to the need for more critical reflection as all such fusions produce many conceptual or theoretical problems for the discipline. There is not one and only one right way to do sociology. Each sociologist, being trained in the philosophical foundations, e.g. in epistemology and methodology, is required to determine for him or herself which is the best perspective to take. The task is to decide such matters based not on personal opinion or bias, not on political loyalties, but on informed and reflective engagement with the conceptual issues at hand. The task of choosing fundamentally is an ethical one.

xx -research methods

Chapter Four: Ethics and the Social Sciences

Ethics concerns the set of moral principles that should govern an individual's behavior. It specifically is associated with such principles as they pertain to the proper moral ways of acting in relation to the position or role that one is in. As such, the determination of what is ethical for a medical doctor is not necessarily the same as the determination of what is ethical for a car mechanic. Nevertheless, as we see below a number of elements of ethics are regularly seen as universal and not particular to one or another position or role. As we saw in Chapters One and Two America is currently in a state of crisis. Part of this crisis can be understood in terms of ethics. If one thinks of a teacher or a scientist or a journalist, one of the essential ethical duties is to commit to honesty and objectivity and truth. But as we have seen, the Republican Party under Trump has largely rejected such ethical commitments, though they would deny this. As we also saw, this has created a crisis of trust in America today, where a large percentage of the American public does not trust that scientist, or teachers, or journalists are being honest, objective, and truthful. Democracy cannot be sustained when a significant part of a population mistrusts such groups to the degree that is present today. It is simply not possible.

In recent decades, more people – as least more people in certain corners of the academy -- have come to believe that it has become more important to explicitly and forcefully discuss and focus upon ethics in professional practices, whether these are the professional practices of journalism, or medicine, or the research practices -- or other practices such as teaching -- of social scientists. This heightened awareness of the importance of ethics perhaps is not unrelated to numerous (and typically conservative) political philosophical claims that democracy, at least as it is conceived in practice in the modern world, has within it forces that erode morality and ethics (see Leo Strauss or Allan Bloom) and ultimately threaten its very existence. Modern democracy relativizes all ethical and moral positions. What is deemed right or legal in a democratic society is merely the function of numbers – of the numerical majority. As a result, no one moral or ethical position is deemed superior to any other. All positions are inherently equal. Critics argue that this leads to the collapse of morality and ethics because no standards underlying these can be established, other than the consent of the majority. Our sense of rightness, of ethics and morality, are corroded as a result. Everything becomes relative.

Whatever the foundation of the recent rise of interest in focusing on ethics and social science, it is becoming clear that the social sciences should be addressing these field much more fully and much more explicitly than it has traditionally done. This chapter is written toward that end. Here we focus specifically upon the ethics of social science research, rather than the ethics of teaching or the ethics of any other dimension of professional social science labor.

This chapter is not about democracy or the erosion of ethics in America. Instead, it is an overview of some general ways of understanding ethics in the social science, specifically in understanding ethics in relation to social research. We begin by describing the three basic normative philosophies of ethics – deontology, consequentialism, and virtue ethics. These are three of the more prominent philosophical stances on ethics today. We then briefly discuss some ethical guidelines – the American Sociological Association's Ethical Guidelines and the Nuremburg Code of Ethics. We end the chapter be presenting several thorny examples of ethically problematic behavior in the social sciences as well as in medicine.

The Philosophy of Ethics

Here we describe three forms of what are called the normative views of the philosophy of ethics. Normative views focus on understanding ethics in terms of practical actions, i.e. what is ethical in practice. Philosophers identify three schools of normative ethics: deontology, consequentialism, and virtue ethics. I describe each of these below. As you read these descriptions, ask yourself which of these serves as a foundation for contemporary views of ethics as embodied in such things as the ASA Code of Ethics? Is this code anchored more in deontology, consequentialism, or virtue ethics? Which of the three should contemporary social science ethics be anchored in? We engage these issues at the end of the discussion.

Deontology refers to an ethical perspective that says we should judge an act to be ethical or not in terms of whether the act is based upon a desire to conform to one or another set of abstract ethical principles. The essence of this perspective lies in the a priori ethical rules that should govern behavior. An act is ethical if it conforms to this set of ethical rules, whatever they may be. The classic example of deontology is found in the great German philosopher Immanuel Kant's work. One of Kant's philosophical projects was to determine logically the road map of ethical behavior. For Kant, as for all deontologists, the rightness of an act is determined by comparing the act to a set of ethical principles. If the act conforms to those principles, it is ethical. If it does not, it is not. For Kant it is the motive of an action that is important. Whether the actor is seeking to act ethically or not is the key point. It is not the ultimate consequence of the action that matters.

Consequentialism says that the determinant of whether an act is ethical or not lies in the consequence or outcome of the act. If the outcome of an act produces a greater good, then it is ethical. The focus here is on the ends rather than the means – the latter which is the focus of deontology. The classic figures associated with consequentialism are the utilitarian philosophers, most notably John Stewart Mill and Jeromy Bentham. Utilitarianism is captured in the phrase, that the best, must just society is one in which there is "the greatest good for the greatest number." In its most crass form, one could think of consequentialism by the phrase "the ends justify the means." If one kills one hundred people today in order to save ten thousand lives tomorrow, would it be ethical to do so? This is often the reasoning we hear to legitimate ethically the United States decision to drop two nuclear bombs on Hiroshima and Nagasaki in Japan in World War Two killing hundreds of thousands of innocent civilians – men, women, children. The argument is that by dropping these bombs the United States shortened the war and saved countless lives that would surely have been lost if the United States had to invade the Japanese mainland to end the war. Consequentialists would say yes that it is ethical to kill one hundred today to save one thousand tomorrow. In some ways, this ethical perspective is quite seductive. But in other important ways it is very troubling and can lead to horrendous situations. For example, isn't consequentialism the basis of Hitler and the Nazis' horrendous actions in the 1930s and 1940s. They justified their barbarism by saying that it is justified to kill the infirm, the disabled, and the mentally ill, the genetically inferior – races and others, because such things are caused by genetics and by killing these people (i.e. eugenics) the German people in future generations will be healthier and stronger, i.e. the Germans and Germany will be better off in the long run if they kill these people. In short, a blind embrace of consequentialism can lead to horrendous consequences. Whether it automatically leads to these things, one could debate. But an unreflective embrace of this ethical approach can indeed lead to major problems.

Virtue ethics is our third philosophical perspective. Virtue ethics is in the modern world far less dominant – really far less common -- than the other two, specifically within philosophy, though in recent decades it has gained more followers. It is all but absent in the social sciences. Virtue ethics also has ancient roots. Most notably, one could trace virtue ethics back to the ancient Greek philosophers Plato and most significantly Aristotle. Aristotle systematically describes virtue ethics in his important work the *Nicomachean Ethics* (1999). There has been a bit of a revival of virtue ethics in recent decades, perhaps most notably captured in Alasdair MacIntyre's book *After Virtue* (2016).

Virtue ethics has, at least in theory, traditionally been associated with conservative thought. For example, the history of Christianity, and specifically Roman Catholicism, embraces one or another version of virtue ethics. (Sadly, while religious figures proclaim an embrace of virtue ethics in practical realities one sees that they tend not to live and practice one or another form of virtue ethics but instead proclaim themselves to be doing so while embracing deontology or consequentialism.) Political conservatives also are associated with the championing of virtue ethics, though like Christians, they appear to champion the perspective in words, not in deeds; they tend to live a different form of ethics. (Curiously, the political left has largely remained sadly silent on virtue ethics. It is the claim of this author that we can and should seek to fuse virtue ethics with leftist political practices.)

We can here focus on Aristotle's accounting of virtue ethics. He begins his analysis by asking: What does it mean to live a good life? Or how should we live a good life? He says humans are or should be oriented toward realizing the good in their daily activities. (The good is distinct from the pleasurable.)

Ultimately, humans should strive for happiness or fulfillment (eudaimonia) in their daily activities. This concept goes well beyond our notions of pleasure or happiness. It is more sublime. It is a more elevated understanding of happiness than we would normally give to the term. Moreover, we should, he tells us, strive toward realizing "the fine" (kalos) in our daily lives, which is something akin to acts that deserve admiration, or acts that are done rightly. One strives to act for the sake of the fine in daily life. One strives to realize happiness through the pursuit of the fine. In short, he says that "happiness is activity in accord with virtue" (1999, p. 163).

Importantly, for Aristotle virtue is all about the character of the person and how the person lives and embodies a virtuous character. (Note how this is markedly at odds with the deontological and the consequentialist views of ethics.) It is the form of being that is central to his understanding of virtues and of ethics. How a person is oriented toward his or her world and how he or she acts in it is central. One should strive to be an ethical person in one's daily life. One does this by embodying the virtues and rejecting the vices.

Aristotle's belief in the importance of practice, of living virtuously, is nicely summarized in the following description from the plato.stanford.edu online philosophical encyclopedia:

> Aristotle conceived of ethical theory as a field distinct from the theoretical sciences. Its methodology must match it subject matter – good action – and must respect the fact that in this field many generalization hold only for the most part. We study ethics in order to improve our lives, and therefore its principal concern is the nature of human well-being. Aristotle follows

Socrates and Plato in taking the virtues to be central to a well-lived life. Like Plato, he regards the ethical virtues (justice, courage, temperance and so on) as complex rational, emotional, and social skills. But he rejects Plato's idea that to be completely virtuous one must acquire, through a training in the sciences, mathematics, and philosophy, an understanding of what goodness is. What we need, in order to live well, is a proper appreciation of the way in which such goods as friendship, pleasure, virtue, honor and wealth fit together as a whole. In order to apply that general understanding to particular cases, we must acquire, through proper upbringing and habits, the ability to see, on each occasion, which course of action is best supported by reasons. We must also acquire, though practice, those deliberative, emotional, and social skills that enable us to put our general understanding of well-being into practice in ways that are suitable to each occasion.

In sum, virtue ethics focuses on the character of the person and his or her practical activities. Virtuous behavior is not guided by some abstract principles, but instead is guided by an individual's assessment, learned through training, of the practical realities in front of him and by the goal of acting in a way that conforms with the idea of living a virtuous life.

A central element to his perspective is the idea of balance and moderation. Being a virtuous person means among other things to live a life that is not one of excess. It is tempered, balanced. One should not, for example, wantonly embrace and live to the extreme one or another of the virtues (or vices). Instead, one should moderate these in daily life.

He also says that living virtuously is not something naturally produced. It requires education to become virtuous. It requires education to learn how to be virtuous. In addition, he says that being virtuous does not mean simply living by a set of pre-ordained, logical rules. Being virtuous does entail reason. The virtuous person must assess his or her situation by using reason. But the use of reason (or rationality) in mechanical way goes against his notions of virtue. Being virtuous calls upon the individual to use his or her reason and temper that reason with virtue.

Thus, for someone embracing virtue ethics (as opposed to consequentialism or deontology), he or she would seek to develop and live a particular form of being, he or she would seek to develop a particular character that would be guided in daily life, as a result of education, by the desire to live virtuously.

Of note, his virtues are essential social in character as opposed to being focuses exclusively upon the individual. A virtuous person is oriented toward doing good, toward embodying eudaimonia (happiness/fulfillment), through his or her social interactions. One cannot be virtuous in isolation from the social.

In the *Nicomachean Ethics*, Aristotle identifies, describes, and discusses around twenty distinct virtues (and their converse states, vices). He describes what they are, how they are distinct from one another, how they are distinct from vices, and how they are to be realized in practices. Several of these include: Justice (dikaiosume), temperance (sophrosune), bravery (andreia), prudence (phronesis), continence (enkrates). In addition, he highlights the importance of the virtues of friendship as well as of civic virtues. A few words can be said about a few of these. Temperance refers to a way of being and acting that is oriented toward moderation, particularly as it relates to bodily desires. Prudence can be thought of as the use of practical reason (in contrast to abstract or theoretical reasoning). A prudent person assesses the particular situation in which he or she is in and makes reasoned judgements and actions based fundamentally upon the reality in which the person exists in the present. Again, a prudent person employs practical reasoning. Continence refers to self-control, particularly over an individual's non-rational desires. Incontinence is the vice which is the opposite. It refers to a lack of self-control.

Aristotle devotes the most attention in the *Nichomachean Ethics* to the virtues of friendship and civic commitments. He identities different forms of friendship and different ways of engaging in community life. Virtuous friendship is when people have friends for the goodness of having friends, and not for some other reason, such as utility. Similarly, civic virtue is engaging for the good of the community because this is a value in itself. (MacIntyre (2007) locates such concerns at the center of his contemporary perspective on virtue ethics.)

These are just a few of the many virtues he describes. The question before us then is: how does this relate to ethics in sociology? Since the founding of modern sociology over one hundred and fifty years ago, the discipline has anchored its ethics in either deontology or (to a far less extent) consequentialism. It has largely ignored virtue ethics as a perspective that should embrace and guide sociology and sociologists. We cannot here go into an analysis of why this has occurred. Instead, we can turn our attention to a speculative discussion of what a social science and a sociology based on virtue ethics – what we may call a virtuous sociology --might look like?

It is far easier to understand what a virtuous sociology would not look like than what it would like because it is completely absent in sociology today. Sociology today generally has three components – research, teaching, and community service. Here we focus on research. Conventional sociological research embraces in one form or another a scientistic orientation (see Chapter Three) – either copying the approaches used in the hard sciences –

chemistry, physics, etc. – or in using an interpretive scientistic approach.

Here we can note to necessary themes in any discussion of the development of a virtuous sociology. The first concerns the understandings of subjects and objects in the research project. The second concerns the place of civic commitment or concern. Let us look at each in turn. Conventional sociological research, and the conventional ethical perspectives – either deontology or consequentialism – make certain assumptions about the subject of the researcher and the subject of the object of study, i.e. the people being studied. One of the main assumptions is that the research must negate his or her own subjectivity in the research process. He or she must become objective and unbiased, inhuman. He or she must bracket all that is human in him or her. In a similar way, the researcher must treat the people being studied as objects, not as subjects. As objects, like rocks or chairs, they are to be observed. Causal forces acting upon these objects are to be understood. This is not to suggest that the object of study in sociology is no different than a rock or a chair. Of course, people make decisions, etc., and chairs do not. But their decision making is observed as objects of study and not as purely agentic activities.

Virtuous sociology must reject both of these positions. In a virtuous sociology, the research must embrace not reject his subjectivity, and he must embrace and not reject the true subjectivity of the people being studied. The subjects being studied cannot be turned into objects.

Similarly, in conventional sociology, the researcher, striving to be unbiased and objective, is not seeking to achieve justice in his or her work. He or she is not seeking to realize the virtues of friendship or civic virtues. All of these things must be expunged. But in virtuous sociology, all of these things would be central to the project.

As one perhaps can see, such an approach would require the entire dismantling of conventional, contemporary sociology. One might be tempted to believe that a virtuous sociology would merely turn sociology as we know it today into another humanities discipline, standing aside English, or literature, or the arts. But this too misunderstands the radical nature of any proposed virtuous sociology.

We will have to leave this discussion here and hope that others will recognize the intellectual merits of developing a debate about the need for a new, virtuous sociology.

Ethical Guidelines

All professional associations of scientific researchers that work with humans or animals have their own code of ethics, from medicine to sociology. In addition, some important codes of ethics have developed independently of professional associations. One of the earlier, more important codes of ethics for medical researchers is the Nuremberg Code which was developed by the U.S. and allied victors over Nazi Germany as the result of the horrors of the Nazi researchers' brutal and disgusting and unethical "research" on their prisoners. In this Code we find many of the themes and topics typically found in ethical guidelines of various professions today. For example, informed consent is one of the points of the Code, as is the principle that the researcher should not do any harm to the research subjects.

The American Sociological Association (ASA) has its own code. The **ASA code**, like most ethical codes, consists of a number of the same themes found in the Nuremberg Code, but it tailors its code to the recognition that researching social life is distinct in a number of ways from medical or scientific research on the human body or on some other area of nature. Most notably, perhaps, the ASA code focuses on concerns about inequalities, diversities, and the un-empowered and it focuses in part on being oriented toward making the world a better place.

Since World War Two ethical considerations have been institutionalized within settings that conduct research. That is, all colleges and universities, government agencies, private corporations, etc. that conduct research on humans or animals today have ethical boards that are assigned the task of assessing on ethical grounds whether and if any research at the institution may be conducted by members of the organization. Employees of these institutions, e.g. college professors, must submit their proposed research to these boards prior to conducting any research. These boards are sometimes called Institutional Review Boards (IRB). Sometimes they are called Human Subjects Committees. The members of the boards are member of the relevant institutional community, and sometimes persons not part of the institutional community, such as persons in the external community, a religious leader perhaps, deemed to be one that holds high ethical standards.

Some Thorny Ethical Examples

One of the most important things to realize about ethics in social science research is that ethics and the codes of ethics are not clear and fixed and certain rules to be followed. Being ethical requires more than simply applying mechanically in an unthinking way a set of guidelines or principles. That is, while ethics and the codes of ethics have some if not many clear and unequivocal principles that must be followed – for example, it is not ethical to torture someone during a research study – the essence of ethics and the code of ethics lies in the fuzziness of the lines between what is and what is not ethical. As such, ethics and the code of ethics should not be thought of as a fixed set of does and don'ts mechanically applied to all circumstances. These are not and cannot be rigid rulebooks that allow for blind, mindless application. *The heart of ethics is reflective and informed judgment* - an ethical orientation requires an openness to being intellectually informed. Today, it must be added that ethics also requires people to embrace an open world view, one anchored in a commitment to facts, to objectivity, etc., rather than to a closed, ideological commitment to one or another rigid belief system that is anchored in distortions or fabrications of reality.

What has just been said should most certainly not be interpreted to mean that ethics is just a matter of opinion, i.e. what is ethical for one person might not be ethical for another, and that is fine. This is not the point here. The point is that there are ethical guidelines to be followed, but these guidelines must be understood in a thoughtful and reflective and informed manner. It is this last point – informed manner – that I wish to call attention to here. One might think of layers of perspectives, from the least informed to the most informed. An uneducated person who knows little to nothing of ethical guidelines or the philosophy of ethics will likely have a rather uninformed understanding of ethics, and that person will make decisions regarding ethics based upon this limited understanding. On the other end of the spectrum of layers, one might think of a professional medical doctor or social scientist who has (or at least should have) a significant understanding and appreciation of the ethical guidelines of the relevant field in which he or she works (e.g. medicine, sociology, etc.) and has developed through training a perspective that give him or her a professional judgment that allowed to determine through a more finely intellectual and moral introspection whether an act is or is not ethical. We again are speaking of judgment. Ethics requires knowledge, training, and judgment. And while people can disagree upon the ethical merits of an act, one must also recognize that in the fields of professional labor – medicine, social science, journalism, etc. – the professionals have the added responsibility of self-consciously recognizing their responsibilities in these matters. The responsibility entails in significant measure recognizing the need to learn more about ethics, about the philosophy of ethics, and recognizing the need to discuss matters of ethics with knowledgeable colleagues.

We can turn now to look at a few examples from medicine and the social sciences to explore further the complexities of ethics. The first example is from Alice Goffman's book *On the Run* (2014). Goffman was a student at the University of Pennsylvania studying anthropology. While there she did an ethnography (really a participant observation study) of a group (not a gang) of young black men living in one of the poorer Philadelphia neighborhoods. She became quite close to some of these young men (and teenagers), interacting and engaging with them on a daily basis for many months. She eventually became roommates with one of the subjects. The title of the book *On the Run* nicely captures a main theme: The young men were constantly on the run from the police, for reasons they could not even explain. They knew, or assumed, they were wanted by the police, but often they did not know why. They had so many legal violations, they were overwhelmed. They knew the police would arrest them if they were caught, so they were always "on the run". Goffman chronicles their lives on the street, their daily activities, their hopelessness.

Near the end of her study and near the end of the book, Goffman recounts the murder of one of her subjects, "Chuck," by someone else in the neighborhood. Goffman had become very close personally to Chuck and to the others through the course of her study. She noted how the members of the group she was studying became enraged at his murder and some wished to exact revenge on the perpetrator. Some in the group wanted to kill the person they thought responsible for murdering Chuck. As such, they repeatedly drove around the neighborhood, armed with guns, looking for the person they thought killed their friend. They wanted revenge. If they had found this person, they would surely

have killed him. Here is Goffman's telling of what she did
during one of these incidents:

> Many nights, Mike and Steve [two of the members of
> her group] drove around looking for the shooter, the
> guys who were part of his crew, or women connected
> to them who might be able to provide a good lead. On
> a few of these nights, Mike had nobody to ride along
> with him, so I volunteered. We started out around 3:00
> a.m., with Mike in the passenger seat, his hand on his
> Glock as he directed me around the area. We peered
> into dark houses and looked at license plates and car
> models as Mike spoke on the phone with others who
> had information about the 4th Street Boys [Chuck's
> murderer was thought to be one of these] whereabouts.
> One night Mike thought he saw a 4th Street guy walk
> into a Chinese restaurant. He tucked his gun in his
> jeans, got out of the car, and hid in the adjacent
> alleyway. I waited in the car with the engine running,
> ready to speed off as soon as Mike ran back and got
> inside. But when the man came out with his food,
> Mike seemed to think this wasn't the man he'd thought
> it was. He walked back to the car and we drove on.
> (2014, p. 262)

A few paragraphs later, Goffman reflected upon her
decision to drive Mike around: "I don't believe that I got into
the car with Mike because I wanted to learn firsthand about
violence, or even because I wanted to prove myself loyal or
brave. I got into the car because, like Mike and Reggie, I
wanted Chuck's killer to die" (ibid.). In short, Goffman
volunteered and then served as a driver for one of her
subjects, Mike, as he sought to find and kill the person he
thought was responsible for killing their friend Chuck. Mike
did not kill anyone during Goffman's drives.

Was Goffman's behavior ethical here? Using the ASA Guidelines (2018), we can see that Goffman's actions were clearly unethical. As noted earlier, one of the common ethical considerations found in guidelines in the social sciences and medicine is that the researcher should not do any harm or risk any harm, either to the subjects studied or to others. This is seen is several places in the ASA Guidelines. For example, Ethical Standard Number 12: Research Planning, Implementation, and Dissemination, section 12.1 f says that "In their research, sociologists do not behave in ways that increase risks, or are threatening to the health or life of research participants or others." Clearly and obviously Goffman violated this principle. (It perhaps should be noted that the guidelines being discussed here are those of sociologists, and Goffman is an anthropologist, not a sociologist. As such, she is "governed" by the anthropologists' own set of ethical principles, which include positions quite similar to the above sociologists' principle.)

One could cite a number of other principles found on the ASA Guidelines that were arguably violated by Goffman in her work, though we could debate whether she violated these other principles. These lie in the realm of the fuzzy area between certainty and doubt. For example, in Section 8: Conflict of Interests and Commitment it reads: "If sociologists discover a conflict of interest that impacts their judgment or actions, they must withdraw from the scientific or professional activity or take other reasonable steps to mitigate the effects of the conflict." This principle is related to a phrase – perhaps archaic -- sometimes used in anthropology: "going native." Going native is an ethical problem that potentially confronts anthropologists doing field work, such as ethnographies. At the heart of this type of research is the need for the researcher to live amongst a group of people, to get to know them, to participate in their daily activities – all to understand the perspectives of the people being studied. Yet at the same time, the researcher is supposed to uphold some semblance of detachment and objectivity. It is when the researcher loses this detachment and objectivity during research and in effect becomes a member of the group being studied that we say the person has "gone native." This is a problem, ethical and otherwise. The researcher has abandoned a commitment to engaging in objective scientific inquiry.

The sociological principle described above (Section 8), technically is not written to address issues related to the problems of going native. It is directed more at such things as a researcher doing research that is funded by one or another organization who then manipulates his or her research to appease this organization. Nevertheless, despite the principle being targeted at something else, it is applicable to Goffman's work. It can be interpreted to address this point of going native, and it can be interpreted to mean that the sociologist should also not lose his or her objectivity and become a member of the group being studied. Goffman clearly surrendered her objectivity as she became close friends with the people she studied, to the point where she lost perspective.

Another example of social science, and specifically sociological, research that is today widely deemed to be unethical is the research conducted by the sociologist Laud Humphries in his tearoom study. Laud Humphries wrote his dissertation at Washington University in Saint Louis on tea rooms. The term tearoom refers to public bathrooms in public parks that are used by men to engage in anonymous sex. Humphries published the results of his study in a book titled the *Tea Room Trade* (1970). To begin, we should describe more precisely what the tea rooms are and what he did in his research. As noted, tea rooms are public bathrooms where men go to have sex with other men. Humphries recognized that there was a basic social structure to this activity. That is, it involved three men: Two of the men would have sex with each other in the bathroom stalls and a third man who served as a lookout by the door to warn the others if someone was approaching. This structure was established and known to the participants.

Humphries wished to understand more about who the men were who were engaging in these sexual activities. Were they gay or straight? Married or single? Rich or poor? Black or white? etc. In short, he wished to understand the situation sociologically. He chose to do an observational study. He decided to assume the role of the lookout, without telling any of the participants he was doing research. He did not engage in sex with any of the subjects during the study. As a lookout, he could see into the parking lot where the men would park their cars before coming to the bathrooms. He wrote down the license plate numbers of all of the participants, again without informing any of them he was doing so. Now he had access to some information on the participants, for example through the Department of Motor Vehicles office. He knew not only what cars the men drove, but where they lived, and other such information.

But Humphries did not stop there in his research. He wanted to find out much more about the subjects. The next step was that he pretended to be a researcher in a public health study and went to the homes of the subjects and asked them questions. He disguised himself and knocked on the doors of the homes of the subjects that were involved in the tearoom trade. He did not tell them who he was. He told them instead that he was conducting a public health survey and wished to ask them a number of questions. He asked more detailed sociologically oriented questions, about work, about marriage and home life, about health, etc. Now he had a wealth of information on each of the participants in the tearoom trade. He completed his survey, tallied up the results and ultimately published the results, disguising the identities of the participants, in his book.

Was this an ethical study, and could it be done today? By today's standards, the study was not ethical. It violated a number of basic ethical standards. First, it violated informed consent. None of the participants knew they were in the study. None gave consent. This violated not only the general principle, but also the specifical principle, identified in the American Sociological Association Code of Ethics. Number 11: Informed Consent is quite clear: "Sociologists do not involve a human being as a participant in research without the informed consent of the participant or the participant's legally authorized representative, except as otherwise specified in these Ethical Standards." Further, Section 11c reads: "Sociologists recognize that consent is a process. When sociologists regularly interact with research participants over a period of time (e.g., research panels and ethnographic research), they periodically remind the participants about the nature of the consent, their right to discontinue at any time, and inform the participants if the research procedures change."

However, the issue gets more complicated when we consider Section 11.1 (b): "Sociologists may conduct research without obtaining consent for research carried out in public places where privacy is not expected. They may use publicly-available information about individuals, e.g., naturalistic observations in public places, analysis of public records and archival research." Wasn't the observational research done in *public* restrooms? Any male member of the community could walk into these bathrooms. While there might be some expectation of privacy when one is in a bathroom stall, no expectation of privacy exists in the public bathrooms in general. On the other hand, the part of the study in which Humphries went to the men's homes and asked them questions arguably did violate the principle.

Another ethical principle violated in Humphries' research was deceit. Not only did he not tell the subjects in the bathrooms that they were being studied, when he went to their homes, he lied to them and told them he was conducting a public health study. Section 11.4: Use of

Deception in Research spells out the issues here. Sections a and b are as follows:

> (a) Deception can include misleading participants about the research procedures and/or not providing all relevant information about the research. Sociologists do not use deceptive techniques unless they have determined that the following conditions have been met (1) the research involves no more than minimal risk to research participants; (2) deception is justified by the study's prospective scientific, education or applied value; (3) equally effective alternative procedures that do not use deception are not feasible; and (4) they have obtained the approval of an authoritative body with expertise on the ethics of social science research such as an institutional review boards.
> (b) Sociologists do not deceive research participants about significant aspects of the research that would affect their willingness to participate, such as physical risks, discomfort, or unpleasant emotional experiences.

Section b in particular appears to have been violated here. The researcher should not deceive the subjects if it would affect their willingness to participate, etc. Clearly, Humphries violated this condition.

There is also a matter of harm or potential harm to the subjects. In general, there is a belief today that ethical social scientific research should not harm or potential harm the subjects either physically or psychologically. We see this implied in section 12.1 f of the ASA guide noted earlier during the discussion of Goffman's research. We saw that research should not harm or potentially harm the "health or life" of research subjects or others. It is arguably the case that the subjects in Humphries' study could or would suffer "emotional" harm if they discovered later that they were being observed having sex with men in public bathrooms.

Even though Humphries disguised the identities of all subjects in his writings, it is possible that the subjects still could suffer emotionally or psychological if they become away that their activities were observed and described in writing. Unlike some of the other issues raised in this chapter, this is a debatable issue, one that in keeping with ethical guidelines could and should be discussed and debated with professional colleagues.

A third example of research that raises ethical issues or concerns is the classic research done by the social psychologist Stanley Milgram in the 1950s. In the wake of World War Two and the horrors of the Nazi regime, many scholars in America, including Milgram, sought to understand how and why the average German complied with the commands of the Nazi's to do horrendous things, such as serving as prison guards and murdering millions in the death camps, or conducting or participating in barbarous medical "experiments" on prisoners, etc. One of the sets of research that Milgram conducted toward this end focused upon understanding how or if, and under what conditions, research subjects would comply with the requests of authority figures to inflict harm on others. His research on this subject was made into a documentary film titled Obedience (1963) which has been and continues to be widely shown in college classrooms around the country to this day.

His obedience study involved a fake learning experiment in which he enlisted (male) volunteers from the New Haven, Connecticut area. (The research was conducted through Yale University.) Milgram told the volunteers that they would be participating in a research study on learning and that the volunteers would be randomly divided into two groups. The individuals in one group were to assume the role of "teachers" in the experiment; the individuals in the other group were to be the "learners." The assignment to the positions was manipulated by Milgram and all of the learners were actually actors working with Milgram. In short, it was the teachers who were (unknowingly) the research subjects of the study. The volunteer teachers (subjects) were screened to make sure they were psychologically normal, and they were given directions for the study. They were told they would be participating in a study on learning. They were told that they would be reciting a list of pairs of words, e.g. blue dog, house tree, etc., to learners who sat in a room next to them. (In fact, Milgram changed the locations and physical relations of the learners and teachers to each other and to the research scientist to see if the changes had any effect.) The teachers were told that learners would be strapped to wires and an electrical machine and that the teacher was to administer electric shocks to the learner when the learner did not recall the paired words correctly. The teachers were shown the learner and the wires attached to him. The teacher then was seated in front of a desk with an electric shock machine. On the desk in front of the teacher was an electric machine with thirty or so levers, going from mild shocks to severe or dangerous shocks. This was supposedly the level of shock that was to be administered to the learner if he answered incorrectly. The teacher was instructed to increase the severity of shock each time the learner gave the wrong response, all the way to the severe or dangerous end. (This was all fake. The learners did not receive any shocks, but pretended to be in pain when were told they were getting a shock.) Prior to the beginning of the teaching experiment, the learner informed the scientist and the teacher that he has a heart condition and could not manage severe stress. (Again, this was all acting.)

The research scientist in his white coat sat behind the teacher, in the main segment of the study, while the teacher began the experiment. As the learner answered incorrectly, the teacher increased the severity of the shocks. As this increased, the learner, pretending to be in increasing pain, yelled out repeatedly calling for the research to stop. The teachers largely continued. Some paused and turned to the scientist to complain. But the scientist exhorted them on. "The experiment requires that you continue," he said to the teachers when they hesitated or temporarily refused to inflict any more harm.

Milgram tallied up the results and found that many, many of the teachers willingly complied completely with the demands of the researcher. Depending upon how one calculates the results, between fifty and seventy percent of the teachers were willing to administer the most severe and dangerous shocks to the subjects, to the point where some of the fake learners (actors) pretended to be unresponsive (presumed dead?) but were still subjected to more electric shocks. The point here was to demonstrate how easily ordinary men can engage in sadistic or tortuous behavior (remember the Nazis) upon command.

At the end of the study, the teacher subjects were debriefed by the researchers and told the true nature of the study. The teacher subjects were informed that they were in fact not administering any shocks at all to the learner actors and that the actors were not harmed. Further, the teacher subjects were given a counseling session with a mental health professional to assess their mental status and to address any psychological issues that may have arisen as the result of the study. The learner actors were deemed to not have suffered any significant psychological harm.

Most people today would likely say that the Milgram study violated an important ethical principle -- that of doing no harm. As noted earlier, research that is reasonably expected to lead to physical or psychological harm is ethically prohibited. We saw this in the ASA guidelines where it was stated that research should not produce "unpleasant emotional experience" for the subjects. Arguably, the teacher subjects who thought they were administering severe electric shocks upon command to learner (actors) and who thought at times they may have killed the learners in the process likely suffered from several "unpleasant emotional experience." It was clearly a psychological traumatizing event, which the subjects would reasonably be expected to suffer from in the coming months and years. The psychological counseling and testing the subjects received could not appropriately address the harm that was done. As such, most settings today would not allow the Milgram study to be replicated without significant modification.

Another ethical issue arises with the Milgram study and with other such studies. But this ethical matter is not considered in the ASA guidelines, nor is it considered in most ethical guidelines. The issue is whether it is ethical to use research that was conducted in an unethical manner either in a teaching or a research setting. Let us say that someone discovered some medical "research" in the 1990s that was conducted by Nazi doctors on prisoners in the death camps during World War Two and this research proves that a drug discovered by the Nazis works to cure some illness, say bone cancer, that is a problem for medicine today. In this hypothetical example, the Nazi "medical researchers" tortured the prisoners to death during their experiments, but as a result of these experiments the "researchers" discovered this new cure for cancer. The question is: Would it be ethical for medical doctors today to use this research which was conducted unethically in the 1930s and 1940s? In a far less dramatic instance of the same issue, one might ask if it is ethical for a professor to show the video of Milgram's Obedience study in a college classroom? Afterall, the research is now deemed to be unethical by many people. (As we see below, the answers to these questions depend upon the philosophy of ethics one embraces. We describe these below in detail. Here we can simply note that *consequentialist* ethics would say that it is ethical to use earlier unethical research today if it produces favorable results; *deontology* would say that it is unethical to use this earlier unethical research today.)

One last example: This one too comes from the medical field and from the Nazis. It is about Eduard Pernkopf. Pernkopf was a devout Austrian Nazi. (After 1938, he wore his Nazi uniform instead of his medical clothes to work each day.) He was a medical doctor and a medical illustrator. He drew hundreds of pictures of the internal parts of the human body. He compiled many of these in a textbook titled *Topographic Anatomy of Man* first published in 1937. (The book is informally known as Pernkopf's Atlas.) It was and is considered one of the best medical illustrated books ever produced. It was completed in the late 1930s and early 1940s. Pernkopf dissected hundreds of bodies of people that were killed by the Nazis and used these as his models for all of his illustrations. (It has been reported that over one half of the 800 illustrations in the book came from political prisoners – Jews, gays and lesbians, communists, gypsies, etc. – who were killed by the Nazis.) Today, many would say that even though the book is a classic work of medical illustration, it should not be used today by medical doctors, for reference, for teaching, or for any such reason. Yet some doctors today use it. (A survey of British physicians a few years ago found that 69 percent of the respondents saw no problem in using the book today; 15 percent were "uncomfortable" in using it, and 17 percent were undecided.) It is after all, from a medical illustration standpoint, a work of extremely high quality. The ethical question before us then is: Would it be ethical for doctors to use this book today for reference or for teaching? As we see below, if one embraces a consequentialist view of ethics, then using Pernkopf's book today would be ethical. It also may be ethical using the virtue ethics perspective discussed below, but this would depend upon how an individual develops his or her own formulation of virtue ethics. But the use of the book today would certainly violate the principles of deontology, which in theory is the dominant ethical framework in practice in medicine and in the social sciences today. (Given that, one has to wonder about the British survey results just noted!)

To determine whether or if any of these studies were ethical or not, we can look to the ASA ethical guidelines or to other such guidelines, if applicable. But the issue here is muddier and is not readily addressed and resolved through such guidelines. To address this issue we must turn to the philosophy of ethics. We can use this issue of whether it is ethical to use unethical research as a springboard to discuss some basic features of the philosophy of ethics. As I argue below, I believe the state of American society today and the state of sociology in American society today cries out for, and demands, a more sustained philosophical engagement on ethical issues.

We have framed the above description and discussion of the examples of ethical lapses in sociology by largely applying the dominant, deontological framework of ethics used in sociology today. We can now say a few words about how a virtuous sociology might look at a few of these same examples.

Any assessment of the above cases from a perspective of virtue ethics requires an analysis of the form of being of the researcher in the respective research. Is the researcher seeking to live a virtuous life through his research activities or not? Moreover, the research must treat the research subjects as ethical beings as well. The assessment is not one based upon the consequences of the research or on the methods employed. Arguably, most of the cases describe above – Humphries, Milgram, Goffman, etc. – fail to treat the researcher or research subjects as ethical beings. As such, in and of itself, from the perspective of a virtuous sociology, they would be deemed unethical. One might be inclined to say that Goffman's research in which she abandoned objectively and decided to serve as a driver for someone trying to kill someone else suggests she was being an ethical subject in her study. At least, she was being human. But clearly, from a virtuous sociology perspective, her actions were unethical. Her concept of justice was not solidly founded. Her actions clearly were not prudent or tempered. Indeed, she abandons the very mode of being – one of balance and moderation with reason being infused by practical realities – that is required for virtuous sociology.

Weber, Normative Ethics, and Social Science

One of the classic statements concerning ethics in sociology was that produced by Max Weber in his essays "Science as a Vocation" and "Politics as a Vocation" as well as in a number of other essays. In these essays, he distinguishes between two forms of ethics: the ethics of responsibility and the ethics of absolute ends (also called the ethics of conviction). His analysis of ethics draws upon his analysis of rationality, discussed in earlier chapters. The starting point is to look at the relationship of means to ends. A rational action identifies an ends and logically finds the means to achieve the end. For Weber, a classic example of someone embodying an **ethics of absolute ends** is a religious fanatic. He defines his behavior as ethical if it conforms to his understanding of a timeless truth. The point is to behave in ways that conform to the rigid religious doctrines even if the consequences are horrendous or evil in practical realities. One can think here, perhaps, of the fanatic Islamists, the Taliban, who now govern Afghanistan. They do things that they believe conform to the Islamic faith, to the Koran, etc. even though their actions are by most reasonable assessment horrific. At its heart, the ethics of absolute ends requires the believer to blindly and unquestioningly act in ways that conform to a set of beliefs irrespective to the practical consequences of the acts. The only thing that matters is the ultimate consequence, conforming to religious doctrine.

On the other hand, an ethic of responsibility calls upon an individual actor to actively assess what he or she is doing, how he or she is doing it, and what the practical consequences of his or her actions are. An ethic of responsibility is one that requires the actor to recognize his or her own personal responsibility in making decisions about ends, about means, and about the relationship between the two.

For Weber, these two ethical positions are "fundamentally differing and irreconcilably opposed maxims." Nevertheless, in practice one inevitably finds tensions between the two. In politics, for example, the one tempers or at least according to Weber should temper, the other. A politician needs to be committed to an ideological position, an ethic of ultimate ends, yet he or she must also recognize his or her responsibility for decisions made. A tension exists between the two. In science, the tension materializes in a different form. For Weber, the social researcher should adhere to a value commitment of objectivity, of objectively assessing facts and their relations, of truth.

Another feature of Weber's analysis of ethics concerns values. **Values** are things that are deemed important to someone. We might value social relations, or iPhone, or personal attributes such as honesty, etc. And we prioritize these values or place them in a hierarchy of values. Some things are of more value than other things. Weber wrote a lot about values. Sometimes, if not often, we are driven by value considerations. In terms of ethics and the social sciences, he begins by noting that the very social scientific research project itself is based on a commitment to scientific values and all that comes with it (e.g. objectivity, facts, truth, willingness to change one's position based upon the presentation of new facts, etc.). Importantly, he notes that there is no possible way to claim objectively that one value commitment is somehow superior or better than another. In short, it is all relative. It is only when a people commit to the belief that the value of science should be accorded a higher place than other values, such as political or religious loyalties, etc., that one can engage in meaningful science.

Weber embrace the values of science and anchored his ethical position on that. Weber was deeply committed to a sociology that was anchored in the ethics of responsibility. He claimed that either in the classroom or in social science research, the sociologist should strive to be objective and unbiased in his or her work. (Weber wrote and presented these papers not long before he died in 1920. One must wonder if he would have continued to embrace these same views on ethics if he had lived into the late 1920s and 1930s when Hitler and the Nazis gained power. Would it be ethical to embrace this same ethic while teaching or conducting social science research under the fascist Nazi regime? Or would it be more ethical to proclaim one's opposition to the insanities of the fascist regime in both one's teaching and in research? Would Weber have adhered to his position in the 1930s? Moreover, one might ask, would Weber have adhered to his perspective in 1920 had he known the horrid future of Germany in the coming years? These are all ethical questions of relevance today to consider.)

We can leave Weber to the side for now and ask is how do the three philosophical perspectives on ethics relate to the social sciences, and perhaps to the examples given earlier? What form of normative philosophical ethics serves as the foundation of current ethical codes and guidelines? Most current ethical codes in the social sciences and in medicine are anchored in the deontological perspective. (Thus, the example given above about using unethical Nazi research today would be deemed unethical on deontological grounds.) The ASA code of ethics is also based on deontology. It is clear that consequentialist ethics are largely excluded from current codes. If one reflects upon the reasoning given above to assess the ethics of the case studies – Goffman, Humphries, and Milgram – the reasoning is solidly anchored in deontology. There is one exception, however. That is, the discussion about the ethics of using unethical research in current teaching or research straddles the line between deontology and consequentialist ethics. One might draw upon either one to make claims about this example. On the other hand, at first glance virtue ethics is completely absent in most recent and current ethical codes in medicine and the social sciences. But upon close inspection we can see some subtle indications that the ASA code has within it considerations of virtue ethics as well as deontology, but the former is not well formed, and it is clear there is not a systemic and reflective use of virtue ethics in the creation of recent ASA codes.

Where might virtue ethics appear in the current ASA code? This question itself is a bit awkward and misleading. Afterall, the issue at hand is about proper ways of being, proper ways of practicing. It is not about a set of rules. As such, we might ask, what does the ASA code say about proper ways of being or practicing for sociologists? The ASA Code has two parts. The first part is a summary of six general principles to be followed (e.g. professional competence, integrity, professional and scientific responsibility, etc.). The second part consists of nineteen ethical standards (e.g. competence, confidentiality, discrimination, etc.). It is within the former – the general principles – that we find some shades, however awkward, of virtue ethics, though it bears repeating that the code in general is deeply framed by deontology. Virtue ethics creeps in, for example, in Principle E: Social Responsibility. Part of this reads as follows: "When undertaking research, [sociologists] strive to advance the science of Sociology and to serve the public good." In the next section, Part F: Human Rights, we see similar considerations: "In the course of their research, teaching, practice, and service, sociologists are committed to professional behaviors consistent with promoting the human rights of all people, including other sociologists. In their professional lives, sociologists strive to use their knowledge and skills to advance the cause of human rights worldwide."

Upon reflection, one can see a tension in these and other parts of the code between directives to be scientific, e.g. objective and unbiased, and to embrace a set of values, e.g. human rights, the public good, etc. It is the latter considerations that shade into virtue ethics. You will recall that virtue ethics is all about the proper ways of being. One who follows virtue ethics engages in practices that conform to his or her understanding of the proper, virtuous way of being, rather than in ways that conform to an abstract code of ethics (based on deontology). But the ASA Code does not explicate the calculus of the forms of being that are encouraged here. We are not told which virtues and which organized set of virtues are to be employed in practice. All we are told is the goal or the values to be embraced (human rights, public good, etc.)

An ethical code based purely on deontology (or for that matter consequentialism) would not even include such considerations. These would be ignored. What I am saying here is that the ASA Code needs to be more introspective, and it needs to engage more explicitly and more completely with the matter of virtue ethics. As it is, it acknowledges this need, but falls back unquestioningly on deontology.

I believe this is particularly problematic in the times in which we live, in a society with a faltering or fading democracy, in a society which has corroded its ethical basis. Capitalism and democracy combine, conspire, to elevate deontology and consequentialism and to denigrate virtue ethics. It is time to reverse this. I am not of course championing any sort of religiously based virtue ethics. Indeed, mainstream religions, as I noted earlier, claiming to embrace virtue ethics do not do so in *practice* and this very contradiction reveals one of the many problems with their stances and with our society today. Virtue ethics has been captured by conservatives today and it has been ignored, for the most part, by liberals and leftists. We need to embrace virtue ethics in the social sciences without bringing with it the baggage of conservative ideologies, religious or otherwise. (This in no way suggests that the social sciences are or should be liberal or leftist. It is to suggest that they should not be conservative.) We need a virtue ethics built upon philosophy and we need to integrate this into a code of ethics for the social sciences. What all of this might look like is a mystery at this point. The task now is for people to begin the project of specifying the possibilities.

Chapter Five: Self, Society and the Social

Self

When I think of the individual self today and specifically how the human sciences, the mental health professions, and popular culture understand the individual self, my mind takes me to the famous works of Galileo (1564-1642) and Newton (1642-1726). Among the many wonderous things Galileo did was to demonstrate scientifically that the sun was at the center of the solar system (i.e. the helio-centric view) and that all of the planets, including earth revolved around the sun. This ran counter to the then accepted geocentric theory of the social system – a theory with the full backing of the Catholic Church – which claimed the earth was the center of the universe and that the sun and all the planets revolved around the earth. I mention Galileo here not to highlight the perversions of science that come when powerful political bodies such as the Church demand orthodoxy. Instead, I mention it here to show how an embrace of a science that calls for an objective assessment of empirical facts and their relations has set the table for modern science, including psychological sciences. Newton, the founder of modern physics, is important here for his first law of physics which states that an object at rest will remain at rest unless some force acts upon it, and an object in motion will remain in motion unless some force acts upon it. Thus, an object, such as an asteroid, will remain in the same motion unless forces such as the gravity of nearby stars or planets, or the resistance of one or another atmosphere, causes it to alter its speed and trajectory. In short, the world operates mechanically. Together these forms of thinking – that of

Galileo and Newton – lead us to view all of reality – the reality of the physical world, the social world, the world of self -- as operating under the same fundamental principles, whether these elements of reality are chemicals or humans. Moreover, these forms of thinking see the essence of the world as comprised of distinct elements who passively exist, only to be animated by one or another force imposed upon them. It is a world devoid of agency. It is a mechanical world, not unlike the world envisioned by another of the great early philosophers – Leibnitz (1946-1716) who saw the world as one big mechanical clock.

It is the form of thinking demanded by this that is central here, a form of thinking that has come to dominate the modern world. These factors set the historical table for the emergence of the modern "scientific" understanding of the individual self – as an entity that can be conceptualized as essentially definable as distinct from its relations, lived and dead, close and distant. It sets the table for thinking of the self as having universal and timeless properties which all selves possess. And it sets the table for thinking of the self as fundamentally passive, reactive. The self in this conceptualization acts, like the planets, only when it is acted upon – whether by external forces – be they social or physical or whatever – or internal, e.g. genetics. Sociobiology, for example, captures fully this mechanistic understanding of the individual self.

But I wish to focus here on the other central conceptualization of the self – the self as a distinct, autonomous being with universal properties. It is not a coincidence that this understanding of the self emerged in history at a time not only when new philosophies emerged, but also at a time of industrialization and urbanization when individual selves started to become disembedded from the social context. Prior to the modern era, an eighteen year old would not have to wonder what he or she would be doing when he or she is older. Life was scripted. The person would not have to ask, "Who am I?" "What am I going to do with my life?" The son of a farmer would seamlessly become a farmer; The Catholic daughter of a farmer, would become an adult Catholic wife and mother. The self was deeply embedded, deeply stitched into the social fabric of life. It is only with the modern era that the self emerges as a reflexive entity tasked with deciding what it is, what it should be.

In addition to the disembedding of the self, the modern popular and scientific understandings of the self were and are nurtured by the mode of thinking and being produced by capitalism and by science. Capitalism fragments the world; it treats everything as potentially a commodity, everything is the same; there is an equivalence of all things (rendered in price in the market.

The values of all things can be rendered through the equivalence of the dollar, of a quantity. Apples and labor are equally sold and can be equally valued. The world consists of particular things, all essentially the same – discrete, quantifiable entities. The self, as a part of the world, is thought of the same way. Again, it is rendered into a detached, mechanical object, with timeless features. Science too operates under the same logic. We are suffused with modes of thinking and being that have produced a particular way of understanding the individual self.

Together, the thinking of the intellectuals of the Enlightenment combined with the concrete realities of the modern and early modern society to produce the modern individual self – a self that is autonomous, definable independent of social context and social relations, a self with universal properties. A self that is a universal object and a self that is a distinct subject. In short, individualization has occurred.

Much as individualization was born out of intellectual historical circumstance and concrete, material historical circumstance, so too when we examine individualization today, we see that it has consequences in both the intellectual and concrete senses. In the intellectual arena, individualization provided the fertile soil upon which the modern and contemporary psychological sciences were born. This soil also was the seedbed upon which formulations of the self-employed in other human sciences, from sociology to economics, arose. In psychology, for example, we see the growth of behavioral psychology and learning theories, which treat the individual self as simply a mechanical entity reacting to its environment based upon such things as reinforcements and punishments. But it is of course not only this form psychology that reflects the individualization noted above. Most forms of psychology today treat the individual as a thing not unlike a rock or a chemical, with universal properties that can be understood extracted from lived realties.

The individualization sensibility is also seen throughout the history of American sociology, particularly in the ideas of the social psychology of symbolic interactionism and associated orientations. (Undoubtedly, many symbolic interactionists would contest this description. They would likely say that their theorizing is fundamentally at odds with the individualization described herein. They would say that the living self in social relationships is at the heart of their orientation and that this perspective is fundamentally contradictory to the individualization noted above. This complaint however is only legitimate to a limited extent. When one looks at the perspective of symbolic interactionism closely one finds many of the essential individualization claims present, even if disguised. For example, symbolic interactionism maintains there are universal attributes to the self, e.g. the self has an I and a Me, e.g. the self as subject and as object, and there are universal rules governing its operation. More importantly for our purposes, symbolic interactionism denies or ignores the entirety of the social and of society, claiming that one can understand the individual self without considering such things. As I argue below, this is an ideological fantasy.)

This American penchant to embrace individualization and scientism and its consequences of abstracting the individual self from its full contextual experiencing arguably has deep cultural roots in American intellectual history. It is often claimed that these roots lie in the particular form of Protestantism embraced by the founders of the United States, one that serves as the basis for the putative Protestant work ethic. But it is also anchored in political and economic considerations. In the land of capitalism and democracy, we are told over and over that the self is all there is, that the self is responsible for itself, that the world is comprised, a la Newton and Galileo, of discrete and autonomous entities mechanically reacting to forces bearing down on the self. We are implicitly told, or lead to believe, the self is all there is, that society and the social do not exist, or if they do, they are merely additive things – comprised of nothing more than the tally of the individual selves that make up the group. This is not even to mention the desires and interests of the rich and powerful to maintain a perspective of individualization. If this was to be challenged, then people might start to investigate the social processes involved in maintain the existing systems of inequalities.

Equally if not more consequential are the concrete social practices and policies that arise from an embrace of individualization. This process of individualization has had significant negative effects upon American society's abilities to adequately address a myriad of person and social problems that have expanded over the last fifty years. Most significantly, it has caused people to formulate an understanding that is distorted at best and leads to social policies and practices that are grossly ineffective. I am thinking here specifically about mental illness and criminal justice.

I do not know how anyone today who knows about such things can claim there is not a crisis in criminal justice and in mental health in contemporary America. I am specifically thinking here of the massive increase in the number of mentally ill patients and criminals. The number of people under the control of the criminal justice system – in prison, on probation or parole – is enormous. Over five million people are in the system. Between one and two million are in prison or jails. These numbers rose dramatically from the 1960s through the end of the 1990s and have come down a bit since then, but even today the numbers are significantly higher than they were in 1960. Crime rates have taken a similar trajectory, rising significantly in the closing years of the twentieth century. And while these rates generally have declined in the last twenty years, they are still far, far higher than they were in 1960. We also see an explosion of people identified as having one or another mental illness. Epidemiological data, for example from the National Comorbidity Survey on mental illness shows that almost half of Americans report having had symptoms that would give them diagnoses of one or another mental illness. (Of note, the NCS does not screen for all mental illness, just a select few. As such, one could imagine if people were surveyed for all mental illnesses what percentage of Americans would be deemed ill.) Moreover, the numbers of people being prescribed psychiatric medication has expanded greatly in the last forty years. Relatedly, in the last several decades of the twentieth century, there was an explosion of people in America being diagnoses first with one or another anxiety disorder and then later with depressive disorders.

What is interesting about this for the present discussion is how these problems are understood and responded to. They are almost universally understood as individual problems, problems caused by faulty psychology or faulty biology. If the cause of the problems is individual in nature, then the solutions should be individual, so the logic compels.

We need more mental health professions, more treatments, not less. We need more police and prisons, not less. But if the causes are to be found in the social or in society, then a fundamentally different response would be needed.

These problems are almost never understood as being the products of social conditions, as explainable from a sociological perspective. And this is the point here: Why is it that it is largely forbidden to think about, to present causal explanations for, to present proposals for solutions, the various problems of mental illness and criminal justice from a sociological perspective? Why are the social and society so anathema to these discussions? The answer lies in the powerful forces of individualization, together with the powerful forces whose interests benefit from this form of understanding. Moreover, the very forces that prevent an adequate and sociological understanding of such things are the forces that produce the problems in the first place. It is argued here that this makes the case for the need and value of a sociological understanding.

Society

It is sometimes said that sociology is the systematic study of society and the social. Sometimes it is claimed that sociology is the scientific study of society and the social. Here I wish to show how this second claim must be questioned if the proper object of study is society and the social. That is, the scientific approach that dominates the natural and physical sciences today rely upon the same epistemological and ontological assumptions. This approach draws upon a number of shared claims. Such as the claim that science is the objective study of empirical facts and the causal relations amongst these facts in the quest to determine the laws governing the natural and physical worlds. Similarly, science claims the natural and physical worlds operate mechanically in predictable ways. Almost all sociologists today would reject the claim that sociology should seek to discover the laws – akin to the laws of nature -- governing the social world. But most sociologists would indeed embrace all of the other assumptions of conventional science. As we have seen in other chapters, this approach is called scientism. But is scientism the most appropriate approach to take in understanding society and the social? Is it legitimate or even possible to understand society and the social using a scientistic approach? As I have argued in other chapters, it is not justified to use a traditional scientistic approach in the study of society and the social. (Alternatively, one might seek to modify rather than reject a traditional scientistic approach to study society and the social. This is perhaps possible. But we will need to delay further discussion of such possibilities until after we have identified and describe some of the key reasons that make scientism less than useful in the study of society and the social.)

The essential claim I am making here is that the selection of an epistemological and methodological framework to use is dependent, or perhaps should be dependent, upon the nature of the object that is being studied, and the nature of the objects being studied by sociology, i.e. society and the social, are fundamentally different than the natures of objects studied in the natural and physical worlds. To proceed, then, we must better understand what society is and what the social is.

To begin, a scientistic approach has great difficulties in understanding, let along recognizing, the actual realities of this thing call society. This is so largely because scientism leads to viewing the world as comprised of distinct, autonomous entities, echoing the discussion above about the self. In essence, scientism eschew holism and is lead down the path of individualization. That is, it is lead down the path to believe that the essential composition of the world – including the human world – is comprised of distinct and autonomous entities, interacting with one another. These distinct entities have an essence that is timeless. Their meaning can be determined by abstracting them from lived immediate realities and to assess them out of time and place. The idea of a whole comprised of a combination of these distinct, autonomous entities that has its own, unique properties, has its own reality, independent from the individual parts, is anathema to scientistic forms of thinking, or at the very least scientism leads the scientist to view reality as comprised not of unified and autonomous wholes, but instead as comprised of discrete and autonomous entities. Applied to the social world, we then see a scientistic approach proclaiming that society does not exist, only individuals interacting with one another in stable relations over a period of time exist.

And yet society exists, societies do exist. They are not merely the sum total of all of the individuals within the society. There is a distinct reality to the concept of society. This was one of the main claims of the influential sociologist Emile Durkheim writing more than one hundred years ago. But Durkheim also championed a scientistic form of sociology (as well as championing the flawed logic of functionalism), believing that there was one and only one legitimate way of doing science. One of his theoretical problems lies in this unresolvable tension between an embrace of scientism and its insatiable need to individualize reality and to avoid holism, and his desire to advance a science of sociology which was distinct and independent from psychology, i.e. the study of individuals. His solution to this problem however was flawed. He drew upon the claims that society had a sui generis reality and that there was functionalist imperative embedded in the workings of social life – both claims are flawed.

As a professor of sociology, I often cringe when I hear students say such things as "society does this" or "society makes this happen" or "society wants it that way". My students are not along in using the term society in this way. It is very much the popular way of understanding the term society. I react as I do not because they are using the term society to refer to a unified entity that has causative powers, but because this common usage is too unreflective. It fails to appreciate the complexities of the concept of society, and without understanding these complexities, one is almost doomed to improperly use it, at least improperly use it within serious intellectual and/or academic contexts.

To begin, we should try to define society from a sociological perspective. Here we run into a conceptual issue that is systematically ignored in sociology, to the peril of sociology. That is, there are two fundamentally different ways of defining society. One of these ways sees society as merely the aggregate of one or more qualities embodied within individuals within the group in question. In this formulation society itself does not have properties and does not "act" in ways that are independent of the membership of the group. When, for example, using this perspective one says, "America has decided to go to war." The claim is that individuals, perhaps many – even a majority – who are members of the society have decided to go to war and they have directed the military to act thusly. This formulation is anchored in scientistic forms of understanding realities. In effect, when this perspective is used to understand the workings of society, it inevitably leads to the isolation of parts of society and then sees the parts as the "real" forces that propel the aggregate, i.e. society, into action. In essence, this perspective negates the existence of the concept of society that has its own powers and its own realities independent of the individuals who comprise it. In short, this perspective inevitably leads to the rejection of the concept of the social, as I describe below.

On the other hand, a very different perspective, taken for example by Durkheim, gives an autonomy and uniqueness to society. Society here is seen as something distinct from the elemental parts, i.e. individuals, that make it up. Here society is seen as a thing-like entity -- acting, causing things to happen, operating under its own rules or laws, independent of the individuals within society. But this is also flawed perspective. It uses the metaphor of a thing to describe society and then treats the reality of society as if in reality it was a thing when it is not. It confuses the trope of metaphor with the reality being represented. Anytime one treats the tropic construction, for example the metaphor, as if it was the real thing without thoroughly appreciating the difference between tropic representations of reality and reality itself, and then confusing the distinct logics and mechanisms of tropes with the logics and mechanisms of social realities, then one inevitably distorts reality.

In short, the two forms of understanding of society – the one that sees it is little more than the composite of individuals and the other which sees it having a reality distinct from the parts – each lead to unsettling problems. One negates the existence of sociology; the other necessarily engages in fanciful and distorted understandings of reality.

What then should sociologists do with the concept of society? We assert here that society does has a reality in itself, as is claimed by the second argument. But we should not, and cannot, think of it as a thing-like entity, without fully appreciating a number of factors. First, we recognize that society must be thought of as a trope and we should not blind ourselves to this reality. The questions then for sociology are which trope should we employ in our understanding. The influential social and literary theorist Kenneth Burke claims there are four master tropes, i.e. four most important tropes: metaphor, metonym, synecdoche, and irony. The unreflective, tropic sociological understanding of society draws upon metaphor, and sometimes an unreflective fusion of either metaphor and metonym, or metaphor and synecdoche. At the very least, a sociological understanding of society requires a reflective understanding of the particular tropic formulation one is using, as the particular formulation will lead one to certain understandings and away from others. I agree with Burke when he champions the trope of irony, and specifically the concept of "dialectical-irony", demonstrating his indebtedness to Marx, as the master trope to draw upon mostly in understanding the contemporary world. In addition, any analysis of society should understand how and why the members of the society understand the concept, i.e. which tropic formulations are being used, and only then can a full analysis begin. We will have to leave such discussions of tropes for another time. Here suffice to say, these are necessary and central concepts to employ in understanding sociologically the concept of society.

The most significant difficulty of employing a tropic understanding of society is that one runs the risk of sliding into endless, circular discussions of language and symbolic formations while ignoring the material reality underlying these formulations. Indeed, this is one of the essential dilemmas of contemporary sociology, a dilemma ignored or insufficiently attended to by most sociologists today. Society is, as is all social reality, at the nexus between the material and ideal, and it is realized in and through lived social practices.

A second theme we must appreciate in trying to develop a sociological understanding of society is the notion of group identity. We, us, them, them. Society is defined to a significant degree by such terms. This implies a self-conscious awareness of group affiliation. While these are important factors to consider, they are in themselves to limiting. That is, you may self-consciously believe you are not a member of a society when in reality you are a member of that society. It is the form of being rather than the self-conscious awareness of group identity that is of importance here. This is reflected somewhat in Weber's influential book *The Protestant Ethic and the Spirit of Capitalism*. One of the points Weber was making was that the religion of the

Puritans in the 1600s led them to have a particular orientation toward the work (the protestant work ethic, asceticism, etc.) that led to the emergence of modern, rational capitalism, and ultimately transformed the entire modern world. Of significance, the factors that united the members into one society were not the self-conscious awarenesses of members believing themselves to be such members. Instead, it was the shared ways of thinking and being which constituted them as members of a society.

From another perspective, one can identity three parts of society, any society: economics, politics, and history. Society at its heart is the realization of the lived intersection of these three domains. To study society then means to study these three domains and most importantly to recognize that in reality these domains are fused. One must recognize that it is an intellectual fabrication to analysis any of these three in isolation from one another. And yet, here again we run into the same form of opposition, the same dilemma, that we encountered above: To understand society we must understand that these three elements are fused in reality, but to understand society we must parcel out the three elements and study each separately, as if each was autonomous. The task for the sociologist is to recognize that he or she must constantly seek to appreciate the intrinsic interconnectedness of the domains of the political, the economic, and the historical.

I believe it is one of the biggest limitations of American sociology today, that scholars have tended to shy away from the concept of society because of their commitment to scientism and the implied rejections of wholes and because of the inabilities to effectively conceptualize society as a whole. Yet it is society that should be at the heart of the sociological project. The founders of sociology, particularly the European founders – notably, Durkheim, Weber, and Marx – in their very different ways recognized the central importance of the concept of society in the sociological project. But in America and in American sociology in particular, there is a tendency to stray away from the concept of society. This has had significant harmful effects upon the sociological project in America.

The Social

In contrast to the concept of society, the concept of the social is far more amendable to the sensibilities of contemporary American sociologists who gravitate toward scientistic forms of understandings. We may think of the social as comprised of two domains. The first is the organized, patterned and patternings of social relations that produce routinized social interactions often taking the form of formal and informal social institutions. Here we have anything from families to bureaucracies, from corporations to the military, etc. At its heart, we are speaking of patternings of social relations that are structured. The second is the reality of the breakdown of such patterns and patternings. From deviance to revolutions, stable patternings are often confronted with social realities that confront them.

The social has constituted much of the research focus on American sociology since its founding. Scholars have applied scientistic understandings of social formations, from bureaucracies to friendships, from health care to mental illness. In this mode, scholars tend to employ a curious fusion of nomothetic and idiographic sensibilities. Nomothetic forms of understanding seek to determine the laws governing natural phenomena. The physical science and the natural sciences tend to draw upon nomothetic orientations. Idiographic knowledge in contrast looks to determine the uniqueness of a given situation. The discipline of history is an example of one that uses this form of understanding. Scientistic sociology has for centuries now abandoned any attempts to establish laws governing the social world, as is often part of nomothetic understandings, but it does nevertheless seek to establish the causal facts that produce one or another social reality, with the assumption that if the identical social setting were to occur again, complete with an entire set of the same facts, then one would expect the outcomes in the two situations to be the same. This sounds precariously close to embracing a claim that there are indeed laws governing the social world akin to laws governing the natural world. This is an issue that most contemporary sociologists would just as well not engage. Nevertheless, that is the implication.

There is a seductive quality about the social that attracts American sociologists, particularly the many predisposed, knowingly or not, to scientistic forms of understanding. We can identity and measure much more easily manifestations of the social than we can society. This allows sociologists to convince themselves they can proclaim truths about the structures of the social. Even if one wished not to measure the observed social phenomena in order to understand the observed social interactions, such as the techniques employed by various micro-sociological approaches including symbolic interactionism and the like, one is still led to a perspective ensconced in a scientistic perspective, even if one wishes to deny this reality. The claims of discovering patternings and structures of social interaction are not the essence of the perspective. Instead, it is the belief that one can capture with certainty the empirical observations of social interactions and extract from these observations certainties of these patternings and structurings.

This ineluctably leads to conceptual problems that are parallel to those noted above in the discussion of society: How do we fit the round peg of society into the square hole of the social? The social can be fragmented, segmented in analyses; society cannot. The issue then is how can or do we fuse the two – the social and society – into one in an analysis of the human condition? It would appear that taking the assumptions of one or another of these two domains necessarily negates the other. Indeed, I believe this is correct, and I believe we must begin with the assumptions of society and use this as the foundation point for an analysis. The social should be understood within the framework – ontological, epistemological, methodological – of the society. For example, we cannot sociologically understand the family if we abstract it from its political, economic, and historical context, and more fully from the context of the society in which it operates. Abstracting it from such things necessarily distorts our understandings. The same for any other institutional or social arrangement. The same also for any violations of the order.

Chapter Six: From Production to Consumption

Sociologists have long recognized that an understanding of the social world requires an understanding of how the economy affects this world. But which aspect of the economy is important here? The economy has three parts: the organization of production, the organization of consumption, and the organization of the distribution of goods and services. From the founding of modern sociology in the early eighteen hundreds through the middle of the nineteen hundreds sociologists tended to focus on understanding the organization of production rather than understanding the other parts as the key economic factor influencing the rest of society. This is perhaps not too surprising given that modern, industrial capitalism was expanding greatly during this period and the productive, rather than the consumption, aspect of the economy was far larger and more influential. In the early nineteen hundreds, for example, factories and cities were expanding greatly, but shopping malls and movie theaters were not, or at least they were not at the same pace. But since the nineteen fifties, the American capitalist economy (and society) has significantly changed. Now the largest sector of the economy lies in consumption rather than production. Manufacturing in America plays a relatively smaller role in today's economy, particular when compared to one hundred years ago, and production more generally has been supplanted by consumption. If everyone stopped shopping tomorrow our economy would fall apart. (And the American economy is not the only economy so impacted. The entire world economy is based in part upon the assumption that Americans will consume and consume. If this stopped, much of the world economy would grind to a halt.) We have a consumption based economy, and as a result sociologists have turned their attention more to the understanding of the organization of consumption rather than of production – or at least in addition to production -- in recent years. But prior to discussing consumption further we should first describe some of the earlier influential ideas related to production in the history of sociology.

Perhaps the most famous social thinker who saw the organization of production as the key part of the economy and as the key to understanding how all of society works was Karl Marx. Marx was a German Jewish nineteenth century intellectual and revolutionary and was the founder of the idea of modern communism (though he undoubtedly would have been aghast at the ways his ideas were put into practice in various communist countries, such as the Soviet Union or North Korea). He was not a sociologist. He was a social theorist, a philosopher, and a political revolutionary. Marx developed a theory of history in which he argued that history should be thought of as a series of modes of productions – one mode replacing another until we reach the modern world in which the capitalist mode of production arises. The term **mode of production** refers to the type of economy a society has, and specifically it refers to the way a society organizes its production. One can imagine many different ways a society can do so. Think for example of Native Americans prior to the arrival of the Europeans. They had an economy. In fact, there were many different Native American groups, and each had their own particular form of economic organization. All societies need to have economies. They need to have some system by which the needs and wants in a society are produced, distributed, and consumed. Most Native American groups hunted for food and clothing and picked berries and the like for food, though some planted crops. Each group needed to decide how to get what it needs to survive, and it needed to coordinate its members to achieve this. The Native Americans did not have factories or any such thing, but they did have economies. One might call the Native American economies forms of primitive communism. All societies have economies. A different type of economy is slavery. Slavery is a mode of production in which one group of people, the slaves, are treated as property. They are owned by another group, the slave owners. The slaves worked for their owners to produce other things owned by the owners. In the American South prior to the civil war, the slave economy was an agricultural one, with the slaves doing the work in the fields and the plantation owners reaping the benefits. Feudalism in the Middle Ages in Europe was a different mode of production. This mode of production was also largely agricultural, with the nobility owning the land and the landless peasants living and working on this land. The peasants produced crops using horses and farm and hand tools and the like. Capitalism is a different mode of production. It requires things like capital and factories and machines to produce things. The point is that there have been many different types of societies based on the different types of modes of production.

According to Marx, each mode of production has a particular means of production. The **means of production** consists of those things that are needed to produce whatever is being produced. Specifically, it includes the things and the organization of social relations that are needed for production. In feudalism, the means of production consisted of things like land, and horses, and farm and hand tools to do the farming, but it also included the social organization of relations of the peasant farmers as well as the organization of their relationship to their feudal landlords. In capitalism, the means of production consists of things like factories and machines, but it also includes the organization of the factory workers and their relationship to the owners of the factories.

Marx shows that each mode of production in history has been riddled with conflicts and these conflicts grew and grew until they finally caused the ultimate collapse of the mode of production and of the entire social order, and this order is replaced by another social order and another mode of production which eventually suffers the same fate. At the heart of the conflict throughout history, he says, lies a conflict between the social class, or economic group, that owns the means of production and the workers that need to work for this class if they are to survive. In feudalism, it was the conflict between the aristocracy or nobility and the peasants. In capitalism the social class that owns the means of production, that is, the rich people, is called the **bourgeoisie**. The industrial working class is called the **proletariat**. The bourgeoisie own the means of the production, and the proletariat do not own much else besides their own labor, their ability to work. They sell their labor to the bourgeoisie in order to survive.

At the heart of Marx's analysis lies the concept of private property, and specifically private control over the means of production. Marx saw the creation of private property as the key historical fact that has led to the seemingly endless series of modes of production in history. That is, when one group owns the means of production and another does not there inevitably will be conflict. Marx believes that the workers in any mode of production eventually rebel, and the entire mode of production comes crashing down, only to be replaced by a new mode of production. This will go on and on according to Marx as long as the concept of private property is embraced. To end this, one needs to eliminate private property (over the means of production). Only with the elimination of the private control over the means of production, he says, will the essential conflicts in society that have propelled history forward be ended.

Importantly, for Marx, the organization or mode of production, i.e. how a society arranges its production, determines everything else (or at least all else that is consequential) in a society. It is foundational for the rest of society. Everything else in society, from family organization to cultural tastes, from political organization to war, all can be explained in terms of the mode of production. In short, the organization of production is the key to understanding anything in society.

Other scholars during the eighteen and early nineteen hundreds also saw production as the key to understanding modern society, though most understood economics quite differently than Marx. Max Weber, the influential early twentieth century German sociologist, was one of these. Weber, who certainly was not a Marxist, believed the organization of the economy and specifically the organization of production were necessary to understand if one wished to explain social phenomena sociologically. This is seen clearly in his great book *The Protestant Ethic and the Spirit of Capitalism* (1905) which was an explanation of the rise of modern, rational capitalism, and specifically the rise of the productive system of capitalism. Weber wished to know why it was that the West, that is, America and Europe – and particular Northern Europe – became so prosperous and so dominant in the world in the modern era and why other great civilizations such as China and India did not. What was it about Europe and America that led to these placed becoming the dominant economic forces in the modern world? He concluded that one central reason for the development of the modern Western world and its dominance in the world lay in the development of modern, rational capitalism. Moreover, he reasoned that it was a particular ethos or psychological orientation toward the world that people in Northern Europe and America had that allowed for capitalism to growth over the last several centuries.

Weber specifically saw a particular cultural orientation, inspired by Calvinism, a branch of Protestantism, as a main source of the growth of this new economic system. The

Protestant Reformation of the fifteen hundreds was centrally important to the history of the Western world, according to Weber. The Protestants of the times were devote Christians, and were originally Roman Catholic, who believed the Roman Catholic Church had become corrupted. The Protestants broke off from the Catholic Church and create their own Christian churches. Whether it was the followers of Martin Luther in Germany or of John Calvin or of many, many others, a new form of Christianity had arisen, particularly in Northern Europe. This new type of Christianity was called Protestantism, and it included most of the Christian religions that are not Roman Catholic. For example, Baptists, Methodist, Quakers, Lutherans, Episcopalians, and so many others are Protestant groups. Weber believed that modern rational capitalism could trace its roots to the rise of Protestantism, and specifically to the Calvinist branch of Protestantism. The religion of Calvinism instilled a particular value orientation, a Protestant ethic, a particular way of being in the world, that led its followers to desire to work hard and to produce effectively. The Calvinists, also known as Puritans, were serious and sober in their daily lives. They were compelled to work hard and to live seriously as a result of the ways they interpreted their version of Christianity and the Bible. At the heart of the birth and growth of modern, rational capitalism, according to Weber, was this serious and sober mindset, born out of Calvinism, that led to serious, disciplined, and productive leaders of industry. The Calvinists believed that God had a plan for each individuals life, and the task of the individual was to discover his or her calling, that is to discover the vocation or job that they think God wished for them to do. If the Calvinist selected a vocation and did the work very well, then they could convince themselves they were in God's good graces. As such, they worked hard and they worked well. In addition, Weber believed this value orientation led the Calvinism to reject rampant consumerism. They believed

God called upon them to live ascetic lives, lives that shunned pleasures such as ice cream or iPhone or popular music or other sensual delights. In itself, such an anti-consumerism orientation could be seen to work against the spread of modern capitalism. But according to Weber, it did not. The Calvinists, because of their religious commitments, were prohibited from engaging in wanton pleasures. As a result, they worked hard, made a lot of money, but could not frivolously spend it. Instead, they invested their monies in their businesses, and capitalism grew. (In effect, the Calvinist embodied the ways of being of a good businessman, one that we can see today in a corporate office or on Wall Street, though today the religious foundations of this ethos have long since been abandoned.) As such, this Calvinist orientation applied to the productive realm, rather than the consumption realm, and it holds the key to understanding the history of modern capitalism, according to Weber.

The point here in this discussion of Marx and of Weber is that the earlier sociologists and early social thinkers focused on the production side of the economy rather than the consumption side to explain social happenings. Production was seen as the defining element of an economy. Along these lines, some scholars distinguish between three conceptual types of economies, largely based upon the different forces that determine production. That is, societies create mechanisms that determine what is produced within the particular societies. One can identify three distinct types of economies here. The first is a **market driven economy**. Capitalism is the classic example of a market driven economy. In capitalism, it is the market itself that is supposed to determine what is and what is not produced. That is, supply and demand determine production. Thus, if everyone wishes to drink coffee (demand), then some people will grow and sell coffee (supply). As such, the market itself determines and regulates production, at least in theory. It is the desires, want and needs of individuals that are said to determine what is produced in a market driven economy. A very different type of economy is a command economy. A **command economy** is one in which production is determined not by the market, not by supply and demand, but by some central authority. This central authority might be a dictator, a king, a bureaucracy, or some group of people. The former Soviet Union and other "communist" societies such as Cuba had command economies, as does the communist state of North Korea today. Thus, a centralized authority, rather than the market, determines whether the society should produce coffee or not, or whether it should grow wheat or rice, or whether it should produce big automobiles or small ones. If the members of the ruling body determine that one or another thing should be produced, then that is what is produced. If the ruling group believes the society would be better off if more wheat was produced and fewer washing machines were manufactured, then they would order this to occur. That is what would occur even if the public wanted more washing machines and less wheat. (To be fair to Marx, who the North Korean and the Soviet Union leaders claimed as their godfather, in his vision, the decision to produce one or another thing would not be determined by the market, nor would it be determined by some central authority – as it was in the "communist" Soviet Union and other communist societies in the twentieth century. Instead, it would be determined by "the people". But what this exactly means is an open question – a question which countless scholars have debated over many years. Arguably Marx's vision was really a form of a culture based economy, which is described below, and not a command economy. Nevertheless, in practice communist societies were based upon command economies.) The third type of economy is one based upon cultural principles.

A **culture based economy** is one that determines production based upon the values, beliefs, morality, aesthetics, and ideals of a population. If a society values one thing or another, then it will produce these things. If a society values certain activities and certain ways of acting, then this will determine what things are produced. If a society values one thing or type of thing more than another, then those are the things which will be produced. Traditional, pre-industrial, religious societies are examples of such forms of economies, at least loosely speaking. If a society is deeply religious, and if that religion champions a life of simplicity, then one might imagine a society that is not very dynamic, and one that is not consumer oriented. What may be produced may be subsistence agriculture and cultural productions honoring the religious deities. But a culture based economy need not be driven by religion. One could imagine, for example, that a particular society values nature and the environment, and organizes an economy around the protection of nature and the environment rather than around other values, such as material gain or iPhone. Thus, a culture based society might say that the society should produce only those things which do not unalterably harm the environment. Such a society perhaps would not have global warming or plastics or nuclear energy or perhaps airplanes and smartphones. One could imagine a society that heavily taxes carbon based products and heavily taxes non-renewable energies used. Or even more, one could imagine a society that bans such things as carbon based products, plastics and non-renewables based upon a cultural ethos. Another example: One can imagine a society that accords traditions in which old people and children are cherished in and of themselves and are seen as people of primary importance – of more importance for example than the total amounts of economic productivity in a society, or as more important, more cherished that workers. In a market based society, the value of an individual is based upon the value of productivity of the individual. In this alternative society, the value of an individual would be based upon something else. In such a society, economic decisions would be based upon whether these values are realized in practice or not. Poverty amongst the elderly and children would not exist. There are many forms of culture-based economies, both in theory and in reality. One might look at the Amish society in Pennsylvania as one that has a culture based economy. Of course, the Amish actively participate in the capitalist market based economy of America today, but they do so in highly restricted ways, ways determined by their values. In history, one tends to find such things as tradition or religion as the guiding principles in such societies, but one could readily imagine other such cultural principles as foundational. Traditional hunting and gathering societies, for example many Native American societies prior to the arrival of the Europeans, rely upon culture based economies. The Native Americans living on the plains of Kansas in 1200 AD likely relied upon the hunting of buffalo and the like. The hunters would kill the buffalo and bring it back to the village. How would they distribute the buffalo meat? Would they sell it to their fellow tribesmen? No. They likely had a cultural tradition which has rules for who should get the first and best pieced of buffalo meat – perhaps the elders or the children? – and who should get the rest. Such decisions are anchored in culture, in traditions.

These three types of economies are conceptual models, and one cannot find in reality any of the three in operation in pure form. Instead, one finds in reality elements of more than one of these three at the same time. Thus, in contemporary American society, largely anchored in a market based economy, one finds countless examples of values influencing if not determining what is and what is not produced. For example, can one sell one's heart or kidney online, on eBay or some other such site? Can one sell oneself into slavery? Why are their minimum wage laws? Why are there some environmental laws and regulations restricting the economy? All of these things are distorts of a pure market based economic model. All of these are in place at least in part because of a cultural value commitment to such things as the value and dignity of human life, of the environment, etc.

We thus far mostly have been discussing the organization of production. But is production the most important dimension of the economy to understand if one wishes to understand the workings of a society? Since the nineteen forties and growing into the present, more and more sociologists have come to recognize the central importance of the organization of consumption rather than that of production for an understanding of the workings of society. Consumption rather than production lies not only at the heart of understanding the workings of contemporary capitalism in the United States, but since World War Two it has become the dominant sector of the economy, constituting over seventy percent of economic activity. In short, sociologists are beginning to recognize this important shift from production to consumption, and in an effort at understanding consumption sociologists have developed a number of concepts and themes, though a persuasive theory that unifies these concepts into a systematic accounting of the social world is arguably still waiting to appear. We look at some of these concepts here.

We begin with **consumerism**. Consumerism is based upon consumption. Consumption is the buying and using of goods and services. We buy and eat food and buy and enjoy music or sporting events. We consume. Consumerism is an orientation toward social life that elevates consumption to a place of significance in individuals' hierarchy of preferences. It elevates consumption over other competing value orientations. That is, one who has a consumerist orientation accords a high value to the buying and consuming of goods and services and generally accords a higher value to these things than to other aspects of human life, such as morality, or beauty, or social relations, or the environment. But consumerism is less about an individual's orientation toward the world than it is about a shared orientation amongst a people in a society. Thus, it is better applied to a description of a society than it is of an individual. If most people in a society share a consumerist orientation, then we might speak of the society being defined by consumerism. America can be described as a consumerist society. In effect, it is almost second nature for Americans today to think that they should consume, and should consume more and more. They should consume the latest innovations, and they should embrace the endless changes in products to be consumed. The mad rush of costumers at the mall on the day after Thanksgiving, on "black Friday," almost appears to have religious or sacred overtones (see Chapter Eight). People line up at stores, such as the Apple store, to buy the latest products as soon as they appear. Such things attest to the importance accorded consumption now. Consumerism in effect has become an ethos toward life in America. It is the proper way of being oriented toward social life in America today.

A second set of central concepts in our consuming world is **commodities** and **commodification**. A commodity is nothing more than something, anything, that can be bought and sold. An iPhone is a commodity, so too is an automobile. One might also sell their expertise, as a medical doctor does. As such, the medical doctor's work is commodified. The prostitute sells her (or him) self for money. He or she has commodified his sexuality or body. Commodities lie at the heart of capitalist society. Capitalism is built on the production, distribution, and consumption of commodities. Everything has a price, so the saying goes. Commodification is the process of turning some thing that was not once a commodity into something that is a commodity. Water, for example, has become commodified. One could imagine that for thousands of years people got their drinking water from the local river, or from the local well, for free. For much of history people did not pay for water. Now, one pays for water. I am thinking here of tap water in your home. One pays the water department for this water. (This is not even to mention the buying of bottled water.) It is not only things that have been and can be commodified. Abstract things such as knowledge as well as relationships can and have been commodified. The medical doctor's knowledge is abstract, and the doctor sells this knowledge to his or her patients. The prostitute sells her (or his) sexual relationship to the customer. But commodification as a process is far more extensive than medical doctors and prostitutes. One can look around the world and see everywhere relations and knowledge that has or is being commodified, from the ways in which children are born in hospitals to the paying for childcare. Did people pay to have their children born a thousand years ago? Most people did not. Do people pay to have their children born today? Yes. The hospital sends them the bill. And what about childcare? Today, it is common for people to pay others, for example at daycare, to watch over their children. This did not really happen in years or centuries past, at least not to any appreciable extent. We can go on with other examples. Think about the fact that we can now own slogans. Corporations own their sales slogans, not to mention their logos. It is illegal to use them without permission. Words have become commodified. Music too has become thoroughly commodified. A thousand years ago, if someone was playing a guitar and singing songs in a bar in Europe, would they have to pay someone else royalties for playing a song that this other person wrote? No. But today, popular musicians are very protective over their music and charge people for playing their music. Music has been copyrighted, a legal guarantor of ownership. Music has been commodified. In sum, ideas have become commodified. Think of patents as well as copyrights here. (As an aside, Benjamin Franklin invented a number of things in his creative and productive life. One of these was the Franklin wood stove. A friend of Franklin once urged him to get a legal patent for his invention, noting that Franklin could make a lot of money on the invention, but Franklin rejected the idea. He believed that such discoveries should not be privately owned. He never took out any patents on his inventions, at least not on the wood stove.)

The concept of commodification is often associated with a Marxist or critical perspective (though it need not be). It is often seen by scholars taking such perspectives quite negatively. Marx and Marxists see commodification as one of the central dynamics of the modern world, and they see commodification as an essential force in capitalism. Capitalism demands that more and more things become commodified. Capitalism has an insatiable appetite to expand, and one way of expanding is to turn more and more things into commodities. But according to Marxists, at what costs? Marx himself focused on the alienating nature of labor in the productive process of capitalism. The worker was him or herself turned into an animal or perhaps more fittingly a machine, a thing, as he or she is forced to do repetitive, mindless tasks on the factory floor (on in a McDonald's restaurant). The workers' labor, and thus the worker him or herself, become commodified. He or she becomes a thing no different from the things he or she produces, and the worker sells himself and his labor to the owners of the factory. Moreover, Marx argues that commodification leads to people, to workers, treating other people as things, as commodities to be used. Humanity, he suggests, is negated by the workings of capitalism.

Another concept from the Marxist tradition on commodities needs to be mentioned here. This is the concept of the **commodity fetish** (or commodity fetishism). Marx wished to understand how an economic system like capitalism could manage to survive given what he saw as its exploitive and oppressive nature. How could a system such as capitalism – however productive and wealth producing it is -- that turns people into things be able to continue? How could a system which is built upon exploiting workers, paying them little, forcing them to work in inhumane conditions, and turning them into machines, continue? One way capitalism manages to continue, Marx argued, was that capitalism itself produced a way of thinking and being that prevented people from seeing the true, exploitive, and oppressive workings of the system. People become blinded to the *real* workings of capitalism by the normal workings of capitalism, thus allowing the system to continue. One way this occurs is through commodity fetishisms. The term fetish itself in a traditional sense is one that is derived from psychology. In psychology a fetish is a non-sexual object that gives sexual pleasure to someone. Thus, someone might have a foot fetish, in which this person becomes sexually aroused by feet. The types of fetishes are endless – shoes, clothing, food, etc. The concept of commodity fetish draws upon this original psychological meaning, but it is not exactly the same. By commodity fetish, Marxists refer to the superficial and unconscious pleasure produced by the purchase and consumption of commodities, and this purchase and consumption, like a drug, causes the consumer to emotionally lose themselves in the blissful act of consumption. This process in turn prevents the consumer from seeing the larger picture of how the whole system of capitalism works and how it harms people, social relations, and nature. It blinds people by distracting them with the superficial (and sensual) pleasures of consuming, of consuming tunes on iTunes, or of consuming a coffee drink at Starbucks, or of consuming the wonders of Disney or Las Vegas, or of playing an online game, or whatever. That is, it prevents people from seeing or even being concerned about, according to Marx, the true or actual exploitive and oppressive nature of capitalism, including the harmful things it is doing to the individuals themselves. And this in turn allows the system to continue, because people are so busy happily consuming that they do not care to reflect upon these realities.

When this concept of commodity fetish is paired with the earlier concept of the commodification of work and of life more generally, we have a powerful force, according to Marx, by which the normal workings of capitalism prevent most people from accurately seeing what is happening. Together, these things produce a very mechanical and non-critical form of thinking and being which allow the system of capitalism to continue uninterrupted.

Another set of ideas related to consumption comes from the theorizing of Jean Baudrillard. Baudrillard was a French philosopher and social theorist. In his youth he embraced Marxism, but he quickly rejected that theory and came to embrace a theory that is associated with postmodernism. At the heart of his theorizing is what we may call sign consumption. This is not a term he used, but it captures well what he is focused upon. Baudrillard argues that the ways that signs – a stop sign, language, images, movies, advertising, etc. – makes meaning has dramatically changed in history. Each sign is comprised of the representation of the sign and its meaning or referent. If I say, "the dog is walking down the street," the words are the representation for the reality of a real dog really walking down the street. In this example, a direct connection exists between the representation and the meaning. The meaning of the sign – the words – is based upon its relationship to the reality. Baudrillard says this was the dominant ways that signs made meaning prior to the 1400s in Europe. But from the 1400s through the 1900s, this changes. Technology emerged allowing for the mass production of books with the inventions associated with the Guttenberg Bible. Prior to the 1400s, how were books make? They had to be made by hand. They were handwritten. But with the invention of the printing press, everything changes. But it was not merely this one invention that changed the landscape of signs. The mass production of goods in the 1800 and 1900s – textile factories, automobile factories, soup factories, etc. – all became dominate. And with this dominance came a different way in which the representation and meaning of a sign was made. No longer were these two thinks directly linked. Think for example of what the original Coke-a-Cola can means? In the era of mass production the meanings of the sign system change. The meaning of signs no longer was derived from the relationship of the sign to the thing represented. This relationship becomes weakened in the modern era.

Baudrillard then takes the next step, which is by far his most provocative. He argues that in the last several decades the ways that signs make meaning has been fundamentally altered. The loosing of the relationship that occurred with mass production has now become complete. The meaning of a sign no longer is based in any relationship to its referent. The sign systems take on meanings themselves and have no relationship to actual realities. We live in a world of hyperreality – a world in which nothing meaningfully exists except signs and their relationships. It is a world of free-floating signifiers, of symbols whose meanings are no longer based on the relationship between the signs and their referents. Our world is a world of simulacra – copies without originals – detached from the real world.

Most main-stream scholars would reject Baudrillard's claims here, claiming that at best they are hyperbole. Nevertheless, when one considers contemporary realities in America today where millions believe things that are not true, as discussed in other chapters in this book, one might ask whether Baudrillard was actually on to something. After all, are the Worldwide Wresting Entertainment (WWE) matches real or fake? The point is that today it does not matter. Is Disneyland actually more real than places outside of Disneyland? Baudrillard would say it is. This is America today.

Sociologists have developed numerous other concepts to make sense of consumerism that are not directly or indirectly drawn from Marxist theory or from postmodern theory. One such idea is **conspicuous consumption**, a concept first coined by the sociologist Thorstein Veblen (1857-1929). Conspicuous consumption occurs when someone buys something, typically something that they cannot readily afford, as a means of trying to convince others that the person is of a higher social status, that is, has higher prestige, than he or she actually has. When one engages in conspicuous consumption, one is using consumption as a social vehicle to send a message to others that one is more successful than one actually is. Thus, if a poorer person buys a fancy car, such as a BMW, even though they cannot realistically afford to purchase and maintain this car, to show off to others that the person is actually wealthier and more successful than he or she actually is, then this person is engaging in conspicuous consumption. This occurs in a wide array of commodities, not just automobiles. People often buy things, from handbags and other fashion accessories to smart phones because the brand name of the product is thought to bring with it a certain level of prestige. It is meant to convince others – or perhaps to convince the individual him or herself -- of the higher status of the individual while at the same time that it is meant to make the person engaged in conspicuous consumption feel better about themselves. In some situations, it could be argued that people engage in conspicuous consumption because they otherwise do not have a positive sense of self-worth or self-esteem. Conspicuous consumption can be seen as a tool an individual may turn to as a way of warding off negative self-evaluations. In effect, people are not simply buying commodities for practical needs, but for other things, like status and prestige and self-esteem.

Another concept related to consumerism in advanced capitalist societies is the **commodification of feelings** (or emotions). This is a concept that has been developed by among others the American sociologist Arlie Hochschild. Whether it is at McDonald's restaurant, or on an airplane, or at Disneyland, or at your doctor's office, the management of feelings or emotions has become an important part of many, many organizational activities. This is particularly true of corporations in the private, for profit sector of capitalism. The goal is to make money. Part of the typical strategy is to make the costumer happy and content. It is to manipulate the customer as far as possible into being happy and content. Toward that end, workers are trained to sell themselves as pleasant and comforting. Emotions then simply become another piece of the puzzle of the process of production, distribution, and consumption of capitalism. Disneyland (and Disneyworld, and all things Disney) is well known for focusing on the commodification of feeling -- after all, it is the "happiest place on earth." All the features of the park are designed to elicit sets of feelings in the customer, as they walk around and consume their experiences of the wonders of Disney. Of note, it is not simply the manipulation of people to get them to feel happy and content that is at issue with the commodification of feeling. This commodification often entails the manipulation of a broad array of feelings, from fear to sadness to glee. Amusement parks and movies, for example, are often if not typically designed to manipulate a whole assortment of feelings, and toward what end? Toward the end of profit. Emotions in this sense have simply become another element of our lives which can be boxed and sold like a candy bar.

As the forces of capitalism, particularly commodification, expand into more and more areas of human life, domains of life once not part of the market to any significant degree – for example, domains such as feelings and relationships – become absorbed by market dynamics, as we have just seen. But capitalism produces other effects upon the forces and organization of consumption. One of these is a trend to create prosumers and prosumption. **Prosumption** is the fusion of production and consumption. It is a situation in which consumers are required to be simultaneously consumers and producers. It is when consumers are put to work to produce that which they consume. When a fast food restaurant requires its customers to fill their own drinks rather than to have their drinks filled by workers at the restaurant, we have prosumption. Similarly, when restaurants expect customers to bus their own tables, we have prosumption. In effect, the line between consumption and production is being increasingly blurred as corporations seek to transfer labor, and the costs of labor, onto the customer. It is not simply in a fast food restaurant where one finds presumption. One can find it increasingly in a wide array of settings. One finds it for example when engaging in consumption on the internet, through Amazon or other retailers.

Consumption has become a central feature of contemporary society, and this has produced many new phenomena. One of these is the **cathedrals of consumption**. Cathedrals of consumption refer to retail sites, such as massive shopping malls, such as the Mall of America in Minnesota or the King of Prussia Mall in Pennsylvania, where people go to consume, that have taken on an aura of religiosity and grandeur. They are sites within which social practices and rituals – rituals that bear resemblance to sacred religious rituals -- occur. These cathedrals are generally not seen by the general public as religious in quality, but they operate in religious ways (see Chapter Eight). The sociology Emile Durkheim writes that religion is essential a social phenomenon, rather than an individual phenomena, and it entails "beliefs and practices relative to sacred things, things set apart and forbidden." By the sacred, Durkheim is referring to things, ideas, events that are extraordinary, that fill the participant with a sense of wonder and awe. He argues that humans have a need to conceptually partition the world into two distinct domains: the world of the sacred and the world of the profane or ordinary. The profane for Durkheim is the part of daily life that is not special. Much of our lives are spent in the realm of the profane. But the sacred is distinctly different. It is a time or place or event that has extra-worldly significance. Think about religious sacraments such as a marriage ceremony or Confirmation in the Roman Catholic tradition, or sacred religious sites such as Mecca in Islam. The sacred, for Durkheim, could be religious, for example when one participates in a sacred religious ritual. But it could also be non-religious, or secular, at least non-religious in the traditional meaning of the word. For Durkheim, celebrating the Fourth of July or Thanksgiving or some other national holiday could be considered a form of secular religious practice and could be considered a sacred activity. He argues that these sacred happenings are social. People come together and experience what he calls a collective effervescence, in which people get so consumed in the sacred experience they feel as if they are touching the sacred in their lives at that moment. It is a transcendent experience. Cathedrals of consumption embody most of these elements. The concept refers to the almost mystical quality of the experience of shopping at these reverential palaces. In short, they have assumed a religious or at least a quasi-religious quality to them in the world today, however secular they may formally be. And yet, at the same time there is no deep meaning attached to these cathedrals. Indeed, there is an utter emptiness to the experience of shopping. One does not touch the sacred, the transcendent, the spiritual, while shopping at the Apple store in the mall. It is the sacredness of this void, this emptiness, that characterizes the cathedrals of consumption. It is this dialectical process – of simultaneously attending and participating in practices at cathedrals in a sacred way all the while knowing there is nothing sacred about the practices – that captures the concept of cathedrals of consumption.

A different approach toward understanding consumption has been taken by some sociologists studying the environment. Some environmental sociologists look at capitalism and express concerns that the system of capitalism creates a treadmill of production and a **treadmill of consumption**. Both of these – the treadmills of production and consumption -- refer to the idea that capitalism creates a self-reproducing system that operates on its own dynamics, and that it operates in ways that are independent of the wills of the people working with the system. It is the imperatives of capitalism that pushes things forward. The logic and practice of capitalism dictates that we endlessly consume, and consumer more and more. We are on a treadmill – of production and consumption. To understand this, we must recognize that capitalism is built on the assumption and on the need of a never-ending expansion of the economy. More and more things must be produced in capitalism, if capitalism is going to survive. It must endlessly grow. As such, if capitalism is to survive, more and more things must be consumed. Capitalism is based upon appropriating and using things of nature, of the forests, of oil, of minerals, of whatever, toward the end of producing profits. The nature of capitalism is that nature is a resource to be used or exploited for short term private ends. Among other things, nature (and the environment) is merely seen as a bottomless pit in which the endless production of waste is thrown. Thus, we have our oceans filled ever more with plastics, plastics that will not melt back into nature but will accumulate endlessly. (Plastics do not biodegrade in any sort of appreciable manner.) At the same time, we have oceans with fewer and fewer fish, as they are being caught and eaten at an unsustainable rate. Nature is not accorded any special significance. The treadmill thus leads to the destruction of nature and ultimately to the destruction of the social.

At the heart of many of the critical perspectives taken on consumerism discussed above lies the implicit understandings of needs and wants. What is a need? What is a want? Where do needs and wants come from? Is consumption in capitalism organized to fulfill needs or wants, both, or neither? Does one need a smart phone? Does one need to go to Disneyland, or to have cable television? Such questions call upon us to clarify however briefly the concepts of needs and wants. In its most basic sense, a need is something that is necessary for survival. A plant needs the sunlight to survive. It needs water. A dog needs airs to breathe. A human needs warm clothes to wear if he or she lives in Alaska. A want is something different. One may want needs. Indeed, people want warm clothes if they live in Alaska because they need these to survive. A plant may "want" sunshine because it needs it to survive. While the needs of plants and animals may be parallel to the basic needs of humans (i.e. food, water, shelter, air, etc.), the concept of wants is fundamentally different in humans than it is in animals. To say a dog wants something is generally to say it needs that something. As such, we must think of human wants in a fundamentally different way than the wants of animals. I may want a new car, but do I need one? I may want a particular brand of car, say an Audi, but couldn't I get by quite nicely with a Honda Civic? A new smartphone, but do I need one? A new pair of shoes, but do I need them? In effect, human wants should be understood to be humanly produced, and specifically *socially* produced. What is wanted by people in a society is determined by the historical, social, cultural, and economic context. If I am a conservative Calvinist Protestant living in the 1600s in Germany and subscribe to the ethic of asceticism – of a life of rejecting sensual pleasures of all sorts – then I am not likely to be driven to want to consume frivolous things for pleasure (though I may be driven to produce such things for others to consume). In America today, we are schooled to want, to want more and more.

The claim that wants are produced by social forces rather than by nature is a claim raised by Marx, and by many other scholars. Marx or later Marxists took this further and saw capitalism as producing wants in ways that were destructive to people, to social relations, to the environment. All the while, Marx said that capitalism also systematically fails to provide for needs. But what about human needs? What are they? Is it possible to identify or rank human needs? The psychologist Abraham Maslow many years ago did just that in his hierarchy of needs. He created a pyramid to illustrate this hierarchy, with the most basic human needs at the bottom, and the most human of needs at the top. From the bottom to the top the needs are: physiological, safety, love/belonging, esteem, and self-actualizations. Maslow argued that the base needs, i.e. physiological (biological), needed to be fulfilled before the more human needs at the top could be fulfilled. From a sociological perspective, one might ask two questions here. First, is the hierarchy that he proposes an accurate accounting of basic, universal, and timeless, human needs, or is it a description that reflects the biases of the humanistic era of the twentieth century? That is, how are we to know or to claim that self-actualization is a universal and timeless need, and how are we to say that this is need is the supremely, human need, i.e. at the top of the pyramid? Second, how do social forces, and the production of wants, intersect with these needs. For example, does contemporary post-industrial society allow for the fulfillment of the highest needs in a society that produces wants as it does? Does post-industrial, rational capitalism allow for the realization of the needs of love, esteem, and self-actualization, or does it impede these realizations? We will leave any discussion of answers to such questions for another time.

We end our discussion of consumption by briefly mentioning the theory of **risk society** proposed by Ulrich Beck, a contemporary German sociologist. Beck argues that the central force or dynamic in society today is fundamentally different from the main force or dynamic that operated one hundred years ago. He says that during the nineteenth and twentieth centuries, during the era of industrial capitalism, that economic conflict and specifically class conflict, as Marx argued, was the central dynamic determining the main social events and activities of the period. Class and class conflict were the forces driving society. These were the overarching forces dictating what occurred in these societies. But we now live in a post-industrial capitalist society and the central dynamic is no longer class conflict rooted in economic conflict. Instead, Beck argues that the main driving force in today's society is the production and management of risk. One can readily see this when one looks at how private corporations operate. One of the central activities of these corporations is the management of risk and the relation of risk to reward. Corporations try to maximize rewards, most notably in the form of profits, while minimizing risks. These risks come in many, many forms. There is a risk to profit, to a company's reputation. There is a risk of labor conflict. There is a risk of government intervention in the workings of the corporation. There is a risk to the environment or health as the result of the practices of the corporation. A general tendency is for private corporations to structure their interactions in ways that minimize risk to the corporation often by having the other party involved in a transaction assume the risk. (For example, a corporation would like to say, "caveat emptor", buyer beware, which means that the corporation's responsibility ends when it honestly sells a consumer something, assuming the corporation was honest about what it sells. The risk is thus assumed by the consumer.) This process, Beck suggests, permeates all of society. It goes far beyond the private economic domain. The management of risks can be found as a driving force in all sorts of institutions, from governments to schools, from private corporations to religious organization. Beck argues that the risk, the management of risk, etc. is the central driving force in society. We are risking the environment as we pollute and as such are risking human health and risking the future of humanity. We are risking our bodies and health as people in society get heavier and heavier, as we wantonly consume more and more potato chips. A sports team takes a risk in trading away one player for another. For Beck, if you wish to understand society today, you should understand how risk operates.

Risk is centrally related to consumption, as was suggested above. Mass consumption comes with risk. The question is: How does society manage this attendant risk? The sociologist oriented toward such a question could look at the organization and workings of the institutions in society, from government to private corporations, from religious organizations to voluntary associations, such as environmental groups, to better understand how risk operates today.

This chapter has described a number of concepts related to consumption that have arisen in sociology in recent decades. Thus far, aside from a unified Marxist theoretical framework, scholars today have not yet effectively combined these various concepts into a unified perspective or theory of consumerism. Sociology today, arguably, is waiting for such a theory to arise.

Chapter Seven: Marketization

Marketization is the process of turning an exchange process of goods and services into one based upon the principles of capitalist economics. It is a process in which goods and services that were once exchanged in ways not based on market principles that are now exchanged based upon these principles. When we speak of the capitalist marketplace, we are referring to a setting in which people are allowed to buy and sell goods and services in the open and competitive market. The price of these goods and services are determined by the fundamental relationship between supply and demand. If the demand for something, let us say coffee is great, and the supply is very limited, then the price of the coffee will rise. The marketplace is based also upon the assumption that individuals and groups (e.g. corporations) are free to produce and to consume whatever they wish, within the confines of law and reason, and producers are free to sell their products for any amount they wish. Marketization is fundamentally based on the sanctity of private property. The idea is to allow for and encourage private ownership of goods and services and to have these exchanged in a free market. Perhaps most centrally marketization concerns the allocation of value. All economies are, at the core, mechanisms to allocate value. Economies dictate what is and what is not more valuable to a people. Markets are based upon the assumption that the most efficient and effective way of allocating value is through the market.

If one looks at the broad sweep of history – in the West and now around the world – one sees the enormous expansion of marketization through time. This is most easily seen in the spread, conquest really, of modern capitalism.

The economic system of capitalism is based upon the principles of the free market, noted above. Modern capitalism has largely overtaken the world economy in the contemporary world. Even China, nominally a communist society, i.e. an anti-capitalist society, is a capitalist country. (It has a form of state capitalism where the state highly controls and regulates the free market, and where state actors, such as the People's Liberation Army, actually owns significant free market firms. While China is economically a capitalist country, politically it self-consciously professes to be communist, i.e. to be following in the lines of Karl Marx, though arguably Marx would disagree with this self-assessment.) One need only contrast the economic systems in place ten thousand years ago with those of today to see the expansion of marketization.

All societies have had economies, systems of production, distribution and consumption of goods and services. Economies are a vital part of any society. Hunting and gathering societies, which were common thousands of years ago, were based upon people hunting animals for food and goods, such as clothing, and picking fruits and berries and vegetables from wild grown plants. The market was not the force that dictated economic actions in these economies. For example, one could imagine Native Americans living in what is now Kansas ten thousand years ago. They perhaps had a hunting and gathering society. (In pre-Columbian America, Native America societies were quite diverse. While some had hunting and gathering societies, others had horticultural and agricultural societies.) Perhaps this tribe hunted buffalo for food. The men would kill the buffalo and bring it back to the village. Would they sell the parts of the buffalo to others in the village? Would they rely upon market principles? Likely not. They would likely distribute the buffalo mean based upon traditional or religious values. Perhaps the elderly or the children would be given the best choices of meat, etc. The point is that marketization was not a force here. But it is, of course, now.

Marketization is closely related to the concept of privatization. Privatization refers to the process of turning market or market entities that are controlled or owned by the state sector, i.e. by the government, into entities that are privately owned, i.e. owned by individuals or group of private individuals. Privatization concerns ownership; marketization concerns the organized structure of the processes of exchange. Of course, these two things are compatible, but do not necessarily go together automatically. The charter school movement, which we discuss below, is an example, of marketization but not of privatization. Charter schools are privately owned and managed, but charter schools are still funded by the state. But they operate in an environment which is created to mimic the capitalist marketplace.

Marketization can occur in two distinct ways. It can occur in a sort of natural way. That is, marketization can arise and become established without any group or groups specifically intending to create markets. Markets here emerge and become solidified as the result of unreflective habits of people. This natural emergence of markets describes much of the history of the world. One can imagine how the markets for eastern spices or silk arose and became established thousands of years ago in Europe. But there is a second way that marketization can occur. This is in a self-conscious and designed manner. It is the self-conscious imposition of the market on one or another dimension of social life. While the first form of marketization has been around for thousands of years, the second is rather more recent. One might argue that marketization in this second sense began with the self-conscious efforts to create a formal capitalist system in the 1600 and 1700s in the wake of mercantilism. While this is true, marketization as a widely use principle did not appear in full flower until the late 1900s in the United States, accompanying the accenting power of the New Republicans, as discussed in an earlier chapter. Today, it is a common understanding amongst not only Republicans but mainstream Democrats today, that the solution to one or another social issue or problem is to marketize the issue.

A few examples might illustrate this process. Space has become marketized in the United States. NASA – the National Aeronautics and Space Administration agency -- was created as a branch of the United States government in the late 1950s, during the Cold War. NASA was a governmental agency. Everyone working for NASA worked for the government. All of the materials, from the launch pads to the spaceships were owned by the government. NASA was given the task of space exploration and of conducting research in and on space. It was also used in the service of the military. NASA sent hundreds of missions to space and sent humans to the moon on several occasions. The first major turn toward marketization was in 2011 or so when NASA created the Commercial Crew Program, which allowed for private companies to send people to the International Space Station, a task that was until then completely done by NASA itself. SPACE X, the private space company founded by Elon Musk, became part of this and contracted with NASA to send numerous satellites into space along with shuttles to and from the space station. This was the beginning of the marketization of space. This marketization has continued apace since then. We see this for example it three separate private space companies run or owned by some of the richest people on earth – Jeff Bezos (the founder of Amazon.com), Elon Musk, and Richard Branson, the British billionaire and founder of Virgin Air. These three men led their own space companies into a competition for which company would be the first to send lay people – rather than formally trained astronauts – into space. For a hefty sum, lay people could purchase a ticket on one of these rockets and go into outer-space, however briefly. This competition was more of a commercial stunt, advertising for the supposed business of "space tourism" but it highlights the point of marketization here. Space and the space program have become marketized. The belief propelling this is that if one creates an open, competitive marketplace of space and space exploration, that there will be much greater outcomes, than if the country continued to rely upon the monopoly of NASA. Space and space exploration, the argument goes, would be more effectively and efficiently engaged if it is done through private companies competing with one another.

Another example of marketization in recent decades is the charter school movement. Charter schools are privately owned and privately run schools that contract with local school districts to provide K-12 education. They are funded through the contracts with the cities, but do not have to submit to most city policies governing their operations. The idea of charter schools was to provide individual, privately owned and run schools greater autonomy such that they would be allowed to be more innovative. They would also be forced to compete with other charter schools for students and funding and would compete with public schools for the same. This competition, the argument goes, would create a more efficient and effective field of operation for schools. It would improve the quality of education and reduce the cost – which is the essence behind marketization.

While some trace the origin of the charter school movement to arguments put forth at the University of California, Berkeley and other universities in the early 1970s, in fact the charter school movement largely was born and largely expanded on the backs of concerted and sustained support by private and wealthy right wing think tanks who ultimately and successfully lobbied more and more cities across the country to adopt the charter school movement. (Some have argued that these right wing think tanks greatly disliked the fact that teachers in many school districts were unionized, and as they were unionized it was hard for cities to reduce their pay and benefits and thus hard for city school districts to cut costs. Moreover, teachers unions had a significant say in curricula being taught. Not being able to effectively address these concerns within the public education system itself, conservatives took it upon themselves to champion charter schools, places that can and have addressed the conservatives' concerns, at least to a degree.)

Charter schools have expanded significantly in the past thirty years or so. They have expanded in part because of the seductive nature of the ideology of the market, i.e. that competition in a free market produces more efficient and effective products. This is seductive to the general public today and to politicians. And it is again all the while urged on by conservative and wealthy think tanks and other such groups.

Many other examples of marketization could be cited here. Let me mention just one last one. Under President Obama, the Affordable Care Act (Obamacare) was passed in 2010. This was the Democratic attempt to provide health insurance to all or at least most Americans. (The United States is the only industrial or post-industrial country in the world that does not have a nationalized health care system, i.e. that does not guarantee medical insurance to all its citizens.) Because of the trenchant opposition to creating a standard nationalized health care system, Obama sought to compromise in developing the ACA. What occurred was an instance of marketization. The ACA sought to expand and to require all Americans to have health insurance (the latter was a provision that was struck down by the Supreme Court). But the Democrats knew they could not create a state run health care system (e.g. Medicare for all). As such, they sought to develop a program that took elements from the private markets with elements from government controlled programs and built the ACA. In effect, the ACA seeks to draw upon things like private ownership of medical companies and competition, i.e. things fundamental to marketization, with things like state control and funding of the overall program.

Commodification and Value

To understand marketization and to evaluate this process we need to understand the concepts of commodification and value. A commodity is nothing more than anything that can be bought and sold in the marketplace. **Commodification** is the process of turning things that were once not commodities into commodities. A key element of modern capitalism, as Marx and many others have noted, is that it turns more and more things into commodities. Commodification is central to capitalism, and it is a feature of marketization as well. Think about water. How did people get drinking water ten thousand years ago? Likely, they went to the local river or lake to get the water. They did not have to pay anyone to do so. Water, like air, was simply a part of nature to be used. In contrast, today people pay for water. I am not thinking here of the bottled water that people buy in supermarkets. I am thinking here of tap water. A homeowner has to pay a water bill each month to get water. Another example of commodification: childbirth. Imagine how people had children ten thousand years ago and contrast that with today. In the past, a person likely gave birth with the assistance of relatives, friends, tribe members, etc. There was a good chance that each tribe or village had a midwife who helped to deliver the baby. One might argue that because the midwife was undoubtedly compensated in one way or another for her help, that childbirth at that time was already commodified. But this is not quite accurate. The entire process was embedded in culture and tradition, not in an abstract model of exchange. In contrast, childbirth today, if it occurs as the large majority of births are, in hospitals is commodified. One has to pay the hospital substantial sums of money to deliver the baby. It is not only things, like water, or services like childbirth, that have been commodified. Social relations have also been commodified. For example, think of childcare. Today it is common to pay people to watch over your young children. In the past, this was not the case.

Commodification is related to the important concept of value. Value is a central concept in economics as well as in sociology. Capitalism says that the value of something should be determined by an open market whereby the supply and demand for something dictates its value and its value is reflected in its price. In capitalism, value is all about quantification. The value of something is noted by a number, a price. Marketization is also driven by the need to quantify value.

But it is here that we see some potential limits or problems with marketization as well as with capitalism. By claiming that value can and should be reflected quantitatively, one is making the claim that all things are, or can be, or should be able to be rendered equivalent. A bushel of apples might be equivalent to a shirt in this sense, i.e. they might be the same price. This seems reasonable. But the notion of value is far more complicated. For example, there are values associated with the objective world, such as apples or shirts. But values are also associated with the subjective worlds and with the world of social relations and the process of quantification and of assessing equivalence between, for example, a social relation and a bushel of apples is problematic. People and social relations are essentially different forms of values than values of the objective world. At best, it is a fiction, however useful for a time, to claim there is one and only one form of value. In short, the values of the objective world – the world that exists independent of human consciousness – are essentially different from the values of the subjective world, and the values of the subjective world are fundamentally different from the values of the social (relational) world. Quantitatively treating them all the same is to claim the form of value of the objective world is and should be the form of value for the other two worlds (cf. Habermas 1984).

But the problem becomes bigger when we examine such things more closely. I am specifically thinking of the valuations of the objective world. Marketization is based upon the premise of quantitative equivalence, e.g. a pound of coffee is worth two gallons of milk because both costs the same in the market. And yet there are complications in the valuation of the objective world that go beyond this. The main issue is one of morality. The marketization basis of value is based upon the assumption that morality does not come into play, and should not come into play directly, in an exchange of objective goods through quantitative equivalence. A buyer or seller relies upon the law to govern his or her acts, and not upon his or her morality, at least not explicitly and not directly. Morality only plays a role indirectly or informally. If a person owns all the drinking water supply in an area, can he or she decide not to sell this product to people, even though they would die without it? Likewise, can someone sell their kidneys or their liver on eBay? Now they cannot, but why not? It offends the moral sensibilities of many people to do so. This moral offense is imposed upon the market from outside.

We have been discussing commodification and value, but the discussion leads us to consider another fundamentally important concept related to marketization: private property. What is private property? This is a fundamental question, one that is central to understanding marketization, as well as to understand contemporary American society. To begin, we should note that we are here focused on productive private property, i.e. private property related to the production of goods and services, as opposed to one's own private property, e.g. one's iPhone or car, etc. The real question that should be addressed here is, what is the nature of private property? Does private property exist in nature or is it a social creation? How should we think about such things? In the Enlightenment tradition, at least in some major sectors, we see the opinion that private property, as opposed to communal property, is based upon labor. That is, if I labor, or work, to make something, then by right it is my property. If I pick some apples from a tree, I labored to pick those apples, and therefore I own the apples. Similarly, if I plant an acre of corn and raise the corn, then the corn is mine because I labored to do so. This is a basic labor theory of value. The great Enlightenment philosopher John Locke makes this argument. He presents a labor theory of value. As he notes in his Two Treatise of Government, within the section "of property: "Though the earth, and all inferior creatures, be common to all men, yet every man has a property in his own person: this no body has any right to but himself. The labor of his body, and the work of his hands, we may say, are properly his. Whatsoever then he removes out of the state that nature has provided, and left it in, he has mixed his labor with, and joined to it something that is his own, and thereby makes it his property. It begins by him removing from the common state nature has placed it in, it has by this labor something annexed to it, unquestionable property of the laborer, no man but he can have a right to what that is once joined to, at least where there is enough, and as good, left in common to for others" (2015 [1609] p. 111).

Locke goes on to note that fair communal agreement will establish laws of ownership, but the point here is the origins of private property. For Locke, private property is not part of nature, per se. It is a social convention, anchored in labor, anchored in the idea that one has a right to the fruits of one's labor.

Locke is generally seen as a seminal figure in the development of modern, democratic capitalist theory. But one can look at a position that takes an opposite view towards democratic capitalism and see that others too embraced Locke's labor theory of value. I am thinking here of Karl Marx, the nineteenth century father of communism. Marx largely agrees with the labor theory of value. He largely agrees that the labor one puts into the production of something makes that something personal property. But importantly, Marx sees capitalism as corrupting this process, whereas Locke, within limits, sees capitalism as reaffirming this process. For Marx, part of the problem of capitalism is that one's labor is no longer owned by him or herself. In capitalism, labor becomes just another thing bought and sold in the marketplace. I sell my labor to the factory owner for eight or ten hours a day and the owner pays me for it. As such, the actual things I produce in the factory owned by someone else do not belong to me. They belong to the factory owner. For Marx, this has many significant and negative implications, which we cannot describe here. The point is, that both Marx and Locke saw the essence of private property being rooted in labor.

It is telling that Jefferson's first draft of the Declaration of Independence said that humans have inalienable rights to "life, liberty and property." These are lines originally written by Locke, but as we saw above, the concept of property must be understood by way of the labor theory of value. In the final version, he omitted property and substituted the pursuit of happiness: "Life, liberty, and the pursuit of happiness." We need not get into a discussion of why Jefferson changed the line. Suffice to say, that Locke in his important Essay Concerning Human Understanding actually does write about "the pursuit of happiness" as being foundational.

More telling is how Locke's ideas about property have been changed, molded, and shaped by the needs of others through history, and this molding has come to change his original understandings. Now, private property has assumed a transcendent status: The right to private property is not based upon labor, but simply exists. It is a transcendent right, with no history, like the right to life or liberty. This molding had a strong early impetus in *the Federalist Papers*, written by Madison, Hamilton, and Jay to support the newly developed constitution in the 1780s. Madison, in particular, repeatedly supports the idea of private property being a part of nature, as something that just exists, rather than as the product of labor. In any event, today the ruling classes in America see private property as inviolate and chose to ignore Locke (and Marx's understanding).

It is not merely Locke or perhaps Jefferson who had more complicated understandings of the nature of private property. I think here of Benjamin Franklin and his refusal to take out patents on his inventions. For example, Franklin created a new style of wood stove, called the Franklin stove. He friends repeatedly urged him to get a patent, telling him that he could make a lot of money out of it. Franklin regularly refused, claiming that such things as innovations and discoveries are not and should not be the personal property of any one individual. Instead, they should be common property. Curiously, we see here that one of the more well-known founding fathers – Franklin – is taking a position that is in many ways more radical than Locke's labor theory of value. Franklin is saying that at least some forms of labor – labor that produces innovations, discoveries, etc. – essentially should not be taken as private, but as social.

What we have then is a more complicated picture of the notion of private property than in popularly discussed in America today. And this is important for the purposes of a discussion of marketization because marketization, as it is self-consciously embraced and practiced today, is fundamentally based upon a reject of the labor theory of value and is based upon the rejection of things such as Franklin's beliefs about patents. For marketization to work, at least in theory, we must begin with the notion of private property being a part of nature.

Criticisms of Marketization

Marketization is a powerful force in contemporary American society. It is a common frame of understanding upon major elements of powerful institutions in this society. From politicians, to corporations, to the courts, believers in marketization are centrally important figures in shaping American policies and practices. Supporters of marketization say this process will produce the most efficient products. It will create mechanisms in which innovations will continually improve products, whether in space or in the classroom. It will reduce costs and increase benefits, just as the rest of the capitalist market does. Yet when one looks at the recent examples of marketization, one has to question whether this has occurred. Are schools more cost effective now, with the great expansion of marketization? Space exploration? Health care?

The claims that marketization makes schools more effective and efficient, that it increases the learning of students, etc., is not supported by the evidence. Similarly, the claims that marketization has made the health care system more effective and efficient is also not supported by the evidence. The evidence suggests that students in charter schools do not outperform students in public schools, all things considered. The health care example is more complicated. As noted earlier, the Affordable Care Act (Obamacare) was designed to expand coverage of health insurance to most if not all Americas, but it was designed to do so not be nationalizing the health care system. It was not designed as a form of "socialized" medicine, as conservative critics sometimes wrongfully note. Instead, it sought to meld elements of marketization with state funding and oversite. The entire plan is based upon private health care companies competing for customers (patients) in an open market. The ACA has expanded health care coverage (though major provides of the act were rejected by the Supreme Court). As such, one could argue that it "worked." On the other hand, health care costs continue to rise and rise in America. As such, the idea that it would reduce costs and enhance benefits might be questioned. The reasons why the ACA did not reduce costs is not clear. But at best, one can say that the marketization strategy employed in the ACA has not worked in this regard.

Space X presents a different set of issues when assessing marketization. Specifically, it concerns the public funding of science. How and why does a government decide to fund one or another scientific endeavor? The traditional view in America, one that has been sustained and supported through marketization, is that there is a difference in science between basic research and applied research. Basic research is research that is designed to discover the fundamental ways the world works. It is not interested in discovering how these discoveries may be useful or profitable in practice. Instead, it seeks to research those basic areas of scientific disciplines that might not ordinarily be investigated by private corporations. On the other hand, applied research is research oriented toward discovering how one or another scientific discovery can be put to practice use, for example in the construction of a new product, etc.

The conventional and long-standing view in America is that the government should provide funding for basic research, but it should in general not provide funding for applied research. The idea is that private corporations will not be likely to fund basic research because it will likely not yield results that are practically useful to the company in the marketplace. On the other hand, private corporations likely will finance applied research as this is directly related to the goal of producing innovations in the marketplace that will enhance profits.

The rationale for the marketization of space is based, at least in part, on the above formulation. The government decision to fundamentally alter the space program and to encourage marketization was based in part on the idea that much of NASA's work to date has been oriented toward basic research, but now that it has developed technologies and knowledge to the extent it has, it is now possible to allow and encourage applied research. As such, NASA now has outsourced such things as travel to the international space station and the putting private satellites into space. Federal funding of primary research (mostly through university funding) in health, in chemistry, in physics, etc., has clearly demonstrated a great effectiveness, and leaving the applied research largely to the private sector has also demonstrated effectiveness. But the translation of this to space is more complicated. While basic research in space is rather straightforward, applied research in space is not. Presumably, the applied research being conducted by SpaceX or its competitors in the tourist commercialization of space travel will improve the efficiency of getting people to space. But to what end? It is one thing to conduct and apply applied research in the health care field, e.g. to find a cure for one or another ailment, but it is quite another to do so in space. The argument in support of the marketization of space is that we may not know the practical benefits of doing so yet, but history shows, so the argument goes, that it will likely produce benefits. But is this assumption legitimate?

There are numerous problems and potential problems with marketizing space and space travel. Many of these were implied in earlier discussions. For example, the idea that all value is or can be rendered quantitatively equivalent has its limits. The value of human body parts, of social relations, of nature, etc. all are essentially determined through social processes. The market might be best to allocate value of some objective things in the world, like the price of a tomato. But it may not be best to allocate things like, who owns space, who owns the moon, etc. Such things cry out for a different form of social management than marketization.

Marketization and the Professions

The sociology of the professions emerged as a subspecialty within American sociology in the early to mid-1900s. This was the field that focused its attention on the putatively unique features of such occupations as medicine, accounting, law, psychology, etc. It was claimed that these professions as a group of occupations shared a number of characteristics that other professions, such as being a businessman or working at McDonald's did not. The professions were considered distinctive and as such operated in a different manner than occupations operating with the economic arena. For example, working in a factory, a factory worker is doing things fundamentally in his own interests. In contrast, the medical doctor is not supposed to do things to their patients because it serves the medical doctors' interest. The doctor does not prescribe a medication or order a procedure because the doctor will financially benefit from doing so. Instead, the doctor is supposed to do what is in the best interest of the patient, with the doctor's own self-interest viewed as secondary.

The sociology of the professions is based upon the assumption that the professions do not operate in the same way as non-professional, economic groups. While this assumption has been challenged by some, it is embraced by this author. Moreover, as we see below, there is now, partly through the pressures of marketization, a move to treat the professions as no different than any other occupation. Many, many decades ago, the conservative economist Milton Friedman wrote an essay making this very argument. His article was specifically about the field of medicine, and he argued that health care would be better off, the American public's health would be better, if the profession of medicine abandoned its anti-market, monopolizing practices and instead created open markets where doctors could compete with one another. Friedman was arguing for the marketization of medicine. At the heart of his argument was the claim that medicine's monopoly should be eliminated.

Before examining the current forces of marketization on the professions, we should first describe some of the central features of **the professions** (e.g. medicine, law, etc.). Monopoly is one of the central features of the professions. The cornerstone of a monopoly in general is when one group has complete control over the production and distribution of goods or services. If there was only one automobile company in the world, it would have a monopoly. Monopolies are the opposite of capitalism. Capitalism is based upon the idea of competition in the free and fair and open marketplace. The argument is that this competition will drive down costs and improve products. But in a monopoly there is no competition, and as such the dynamics of costs and product improvement are different.

Most professions have a monopoly over their particular jurisdictions. By jurisdiction I am referring to a specific area of specialized knowledge and skill that one or another group claims. For medicine, it is health. The profession of medicine is given complete, legal jurisdictional control over the jurisdiction of medicine. Only medical doctors are authorized to practice medicine. Only medical doctors can perform surgery, or admit a psychiatric patient to a mental asylum or an inpatient facility against the will of the patient. These are just a few of the many, many prerogatives given medicine.

Medicine is a monopoly. Only those authorized by medical associations are allowed, legally and ethically, to practice medicine. Medical doctors are the gatekeepers to their own profession. They decide who is allowed to become a doctor and who is not. They decide such things through controlling medical schools, e.g. who is allowed to become a doctor, and controlling things such as licensure. One needs to be licensed to practice medicine, and the medical doctors have control over this process. As such, the medical profession controls the number of medical doctors in society. The market does not dictate how many medical doctors there are, the profession does. (One might thing that doctors compete against each other for patients in practice, and as such do not have a genuine monopoly over their work. It is true that doctors can and do compete for patients. But the practice is regulated and ultimately controlled by the medical profession, in terms of the numbers of doctors and in terms of what these doctors may do.)

Another set of features of the professions are professional training and licensure. Whether it is law or medicine, professionals are required to complete specialized graduate training in their specialty, and this training is heavily regulated by the professional associations. To practice medicine or law one not only has to graduate from an accredited academic program, but one also needs to get a license to practice. The license largely consists of an exam which one needs to pass. Again, the professions themselves dictate what the exam and what the licensing entails.

Another feature of the professions is that their work is anchored in abstract knowledge, as opposed to concrete knowledge. Auto mechanics is not a profession, in the sense described herein, in part because it deals with concrete knowledge, i.e. knowing how the parts of a car work. Professions, on the other hand, are required to understand conceptually the field of study and to understand theoretically this field.

One last feature of the professions can be noted here: Professions are said to be other-directed rather than self-directed. Some roles are said to be more other-directed; other roles are said to be more self-directed. A self-directed role is one in which the person acts primarily to further the person's own self-interest. The classic example of a self-directed role is a businessman selling things in the marketplace. His primary interest is in making money. An other-directed role is one in which the person acts primarily to serve the needs and interest of another and not him or herself. The role of mother or father, for example, are said to be other-directed. The mother is to put the needs and interest of her child ahead of her own.

Medicine and the other professions are said to be other-directed. The medical doctor is supposed to place the interests of the patients, as suggested earlier, ahead of her own. This is conceptually the most controversial of the elements of the professions. Numerous critics of this claim that doctors are other-directed argue that the claim is an ideological one rather than a scientific one. That is, critics claim that this is an idealized view of medicine rather than a realistic one. It is a view that doctors would like others to believe is true, when it is not true, or not consistently true, according to critics. We can leave this debate to the side for now.

When we look at the professions historically and when we relate their development to the concept of marketization, some important insights arise. Specifically, the modern professions arose in the 1800s at a time that modern capitalism was becoming established and embedded in the United States. Commodification and marketization were becoming anchored. Value was increasingly being allocated through the market. The professions, such as medicine, consolidated as a monopolized force at the time because the professions largely were responsible for managing value considerations not readily managed by the market. That is, the market could rather easily assign value to such things as coffee and steel, but in its earlier phases it could not as easily assign values to such intangible and human factors such as health. How much is a human kidney worth? How much is a life worth? Such things cry out for an organized social response, a response that the market was (and perhaps still is?) incapable of giving. As such, we may think of the professions from the mid-1800s through the late 1900s, as a safety valve, as an intermediate between the realm of the market and the realm of the human. The professions existed effectively as monopolies – in distinction from markets – throughout this time to manage, contain, and distribute values that are not readily amenable to marketization.

But in recent decades, with the ever expanding marketization, this role of the professions is being questioned. We can see the pressures on the professions, and in medicine in particular, in many ways, from the advertising of prescription medication on television to the medical professions acceptance of the D.O. degree (doctor of osteopathy) by the mainstream medical community, from allowing non-medical practitioners, such as nurses, the right to prescribe at least some medications to the increasing acceptance of non-medical professions, such as Ph.D.'s in the medical research community. The question of relevance here is what are the limits to marketization in terms of the professions? Is Friedman right to argue, as noted earlier, that medicine would be more effective and less costly if it abandoned its monopoly? I will leave it to the reader to assess such questions. Suffice to note, that some human considerations should give one pause before one embraces the full marketization of the professions. Are there or should there be limits to marketization? Should one be allowed to sell one's kidney's on eBay? Should we abolish medical control over prescriptions and allow anyone to buy fentanyl, a highly dangerous opioid over the counter like one buys aspirin without a prescription? Should we allow anyone who wishes to call themselves a surgeon to perform surgery, as is implied in Freidman's open market model? Presumably, most would recognize a need to regulate somehow such professional practices. Presumably, most would recognize that there are limits to the effectiveness of marketization.

And yet, this process of marketization continues unabated, as if it had a life of its own.

Chapter Eight: Sacralization

This chapter takes on the rather important concept of religion in America, today and in history. We do so through the lens of the sociology of religion. In the opening chapters of this book, we explored the rather cult-like devotion that a large minority of Americans have for Donald Trump, embracing and propagating his delusional lies and tearing America apart. The very idea of a "cult" is a concept very much within the field of the sociology of religion. We discuss this further. But in a more general sense, we explore in this chapter the rather curious relationship between several sociological concepts: McDonaldization, rationalization, and secularization. And we put forth the concept of sacralization to make sociological sense of what is happening in America today.

Rationalization is one of the most central concepts in the great German sociologist Max Weber's theorizing. We briefly discussed this concept in earlier chapters. Here we tackle it in much greater detail. Weber wrote about rationalization within his attempts to understand the course of history and specifically how modern society – and for Weber, modern, Western society emerged. But he was not only interested in understanding how modernity developed in the Western world. He was also very interesting in understanding the future. What would be the consequences for a world dominated by rationality? He expressed concerns about this future, based upon his theorizing. This chapter addresses these issues.

To begin, we need to understand what rationalization means. For Weber, rationalization is the historical process by which formal rationality is taking over (from substantive rationality). It is a process spanning hundreds of years. To understand this, we need to understand the meaning of the term rationality, and the meanings of formal and substantive rationality. Rationality is nothing more than logical behavior. One identifies an end (or goal), and one identifies the means to reach the end. Logically doing so, makes the act rational. Thus, if someone wishes to pass a class in college (perhaps an end or a goal), there are certain things the student likely will need to do (means) to achieve this end, such as coming to class, doing the assigned readings, taking the exams, etc. Thus, a rational action here would be to logically do what is needed to reach the ends.

Formal rationality is the lining up of means and ends in a logical way in a social context without considering values. Substantive rationality is the lining up of means and ends in a logical way in a social context while considering values. These definitions need to be unpacked. The first thing to note about both forms of rationality is that they are referring to the organization of a social setting and its relationship to individual social action. The terms are not in themselves simply referring to abstracted individual behaviors. As such, when we speak of rationality, we are describing social contexts and how they bear down upon individuals. Some settings or contexts are formally rational; others are substantively rational. Examples settings that are formally rational include: the Army, bureaucracies in general, corporations, football teams, etc. Examples of setting that are substantively rational include: the family, friendship groups, religious cults, some other forms of religious organization, etc.

The difference between formal and substantive rationality concerns the presence or absence of value considerations. In substantive rationality, values shape or influence the means, the ends (goals), or the relationship between the two. In formal rationality, values do not influence any of these. Thus, we have the Amish community in Pennsylvania today largely organized along substantive rationality and the McDonald's restaurant chain organized along formal rationality.

A term associated today with rationalization is **McDonaldization**. The term was popularized by George Ritzer in a number of books with this title. McDonaldization is similar to, if not the same, as rationalization, i.e. as formal rationality taking over. McDonaldization is the (historical) process in which the organizational form of McDonald's restaurants is increasingly being the form used by more and more organizations today. Thus, we have McUniversities, McDentists, etc. Ritzer identifies four basic elements of McDonaldization: efficiency, calculability, predictability, and control (by non-human technologies).

Weber and Ritzer each express concerns about this process of rationalization or McDonaldization. Though they recognize the positive consequences of rationalization, for example, bureaucracies in many ways make things easier and better, and of course science is anchored in formal rationality, and this too is a good thing, they were also greatly concerned about the social consequences of rationalization and McDonaldization. One concern about rationalization was the irrationality of rationality. If formal rationality takes over, it could lead to a situation in which people acting rational, without considering values, could produce irrational situations. One thinks here of the German Nazis. The Nazis in World War Two developed a highly rational, highly organized mass killing machine. Six million Jews and millions of others – communists, gay people, etc. -- were exterminated through this methodical, rational system. But of course, it was insane. It was completely irrational. Similarly, the nuclear arms race between the United States and the Soviet Union in the 1950s was also utterly rational and irrational at the same time (as is the current existence of nuclear weapons). It was rational in that it was the product of science, a thoroughly rational enterprise; it was irrational because it could (and may) lead to disaster.

Other problems with rationalization have been noted. Dehumanization is one of these. When one extracts values from the equation, rationality does not consider humans. Humans are treated as things rather than as people. One thinks of the effects of bureaucracies on individuals. At McDonald's too individuals – customers and workers – lose their humanity as they mechanically comply with the rules. (Formal rationality is the rationality of a machine.) Another problem, noted by Weber, was the disenchantment of the modern world brought about by rationalization. Disenchantment is the opposite of enchantment. Prior to the modern world, the world was enchanted. It was filled with wonder and awe. It was filled with things that could not be explained through reason and logic. Fireflies, electric eels, lightening, earthquakes, mental illness, and on and on, could not be explained by rationality in the pre-modern world. Yet humans have a need to make sense. In an enchanted world, humans turned toward religion, to gods or spirits, to explain such things. But Weber notes that we now live in a disenchanted world, in a world in which all things can be explained or at least we believe that if we do not know the explanation of one thing or another, we know that someone – some scientist or expert – can give us a rational explanation for this or that.

There is one other effect that rationalization has upon the social world, according to Weber. Weber argues that we are now living in "an iron cage" of rationality. That is, formal rationality is impose upon us and saturates our being, but we cannot see it and we are trapped, metaphorically by it. To exist normally in the modern world, one must bow down to and accept the legitimacy of formal rationality. To fail to do so, marks one as a deviant.

All of this drains the world of meaning. For Weber, this was a characteristic of the modern world. Rationalization drains the world of, of purpose. We are just producing and consuming machines left with little to no purpose. For

Weber, this was associated with secularization. It was widely accepted amongst European academics in the 1800s and 1900s, that secularization accompanied modernity. Technically, secularization has two meanings. One meaning is the increasing separation of the church and state. The second meaning – the one we will be using here – means the historic decline of religion. A secularized society is one in which fewer and fewer people believe in god or participate in religious practices.

Two important and interrelated questions emerge from all of the above. The first question is what does a secularized future world hold for us? In a world of meaninglessness, etc., what happens to things such as social order? What are the social implications of secularization? The second question is whether the claims about secularization are right? Should we think that secularization is simply a fact of the modern world, or alternatively should we consider it a hypothesis that may or may not be correct? The remainder of the chapter is devoted to addressing these two questions. But first, we need to describe some things about the sociology of religion. It is only by doing so can we effectively answer the two above questions.

The Sociology of Religion

To understand American society today and specifically religion in America today, from a sociological perspective, we need to present some central sociological ideas on this topic. We begin with a classic sociological definition of religion put forth by Emile Durkheim over one hundred years ago. Durkheim defines religion as follows: "A religion is a unified system of beliefs and practices relative to sacred things, that is to say, things set apart and forbidden – beliefs and practices which unite into one single moral community called a Church, all those who adhere to them" (1915, p. 62).

There are several key parts to this definition. To begin, we should note the importance of the concept of the sacred. Not that Durkheim is stating that a religion – from a sociological perspective – does not need to have a god or gods but it does need to have the concept of the sacred. The sacred refers to things, placed, times, or events which are transcendent, extra–ordinary. The sacred is a thing that goes beyond the common, daily occurrences of life and gets on in touch with the eternal. God is a sacred thing. So too are religious holidays and rituals. Durkheim distinguishes between the sacred and the "profane" (i.e. the mundane or ordinary). Much of most peoples' lives are spent in the profane realm. For Durkheim, all religions clearly demarcate the line separating the sacred from the profane. This could be the city boundaries around the sacred city of Mecca in Islam or the designation of midnight on Christmas Eve designating the date of Christmas. For Durkheim, the concept of the sacred is central to all religions. Another part of the definition is that religion involves beliefs and practices. For Durkheim, religion consists of social practices. People come together and worship. They come together during sacred rituals, etc. A third element of the definition is the focus on the idea of a moral community. (Whether it is technically called a Church is not important.) Morality, for Durkheim, is central to religion. But Durkheim describes morality in a broader way than we might normally think of morality. For him, morality is about shared evaluations and judgments about right and wrong, proper and improper, good and bads. Lastly, for Durkheim it is about moral community. All religions, he says, are essentially social. You cannot have a religion of one – as he sociologically defines religion. This social dimension is central to his understanding.

When people come together to worship or to engage in one or another sacred ritual, e.g. marriage, funerals, etc., Durkheim says, they may think they are worshiping some god or some sacred entity above or beyond the people, but in reality they are worshipping their membership in the collective. They are worshipping themselves as a community. They are worshipping their collective as something sacred. For Durkheim, religion, as a moral force, binds the community together.

Durkheim was of course not the only sociologist to put forth a sociological understanding of religion. Countless other scholars have. Two of the other classic understandings are those developed by Karl Marx and Max Weber. Marx's view of religion can be summarized in his well-known line: "Religion is the opium of the people." Opium is from the poppy plant and is the source of the highly addictive and dangerous drug opium. (Opium has been synthesized into increasingly more powerful and more dangerous drugs – from methadone to heroin and more recently fentanyl.) When high on opium, one feels happy and content, blissful. For Marx, religion is a form of ideology or belief systems used to maintain systems of inequality. Belief systems – religious or otherwise – that support the existing system of inequalities will organically emerge and will be supported by the rich and powerful, as they are the ones who benefit from existing systems of inequality. Marx believed that belief systems such as religions convinced the poor and working classes to be content with their lot in life and not to rebel against the rich. This is a far different understanding of religion than that of Durkheim, who argued that religion ultimately serves as a form of social solidarity. It binds people together.

Max Weber also wrote a great deal about religions. But he viewed religion very differently from either Durkheim or Marx. One of Weber's primary interests, as noted earlier, was to understand how and why the Western world – Europe and America – became so economically wealthy in the modern world and how they came to dominant the rest of the world. What was it about Western Europe and America that caused these areas to develop so much economically from the 1600s through the present? And what was it about other civilizations, from India to China, which prevented these places from doing the same, at least until very recently. Weber provides a thorough sociological inquiry into these questions and argues that there are numerous factors to account for these things. Rational bookkeeping, the forms of language, cultural commitments to family groups, and a host of other factors, he says, help account for the rise of the West and the lack of economic growth in other areas. But the key factor – the factor that Weber is most well-known for describing – is religion. In his book *The Protestant Ethic and the Spirit of Capitalism*, Weber argues that it was the religious ethic of Protestantism in the 1600 and 1700s in northern Europe and in America that provided the foundation for economic growth.

Weber believed that the **Protestant Reformation** was the key to understanding why Western Europe and America became so prosperous and so dominant in the modern world. To understand this, we must first understand the Protestant Reformation. The Protestant Reformation began in the 1500s and continued through the 1600s. Prior to the 1500s, in Europe, there were no Protestants. Almost all Europeans were Roman Catholic (though a small and important Jewish population existed as well). But beginning in the 1500s, particularly in the north and Western European countries, religious people – both in the Catholic orders – and religious secular people began to protest against the Catholic Church. The protesters believed the Catholic Church had become corrupted and had lost its way. Protesters such as the German Catholic monk Martin Luther (1483-1546) and The Frenchman who migrated to Switzerland John Calvin (1509-1564) complained vociferously that the Catholic Church had gone astray. These were just two of the most famous figures associated with the Reformation. Luther, for example, complained about the medieval Catholic Church practice of selling indulgences as one of the many corrupt practices of the Church. Indulgences are notes of forgiveness of sins that are written by the Church and could be purchases. Thus, if you are rich, you may commit a sin and buy an indulgence and have your sins forgiven.

Weber looked at the economic activities of Europe and America in the 1600s, and he noted that economic development and expansion was growing faster in some parts and was not growing fast in other parts. The parts that were getting wealthy were the Protestant areas, i.e. the north and west of Europe and the Massachusetts Bay Colony. He looked closer and found that capitalism was taking root in areas dominated by one particular Protestant group, the Calvinists. The Calvinists were followers of John Calvin. Once the Protestants broke away from the Catholic Church, they had to reconstruct their faith. They no longer had the Pope to tell them what the Bible meant, what Jesus meant, etc. Calvin reconstructed Christianity in a particularly austere and extreme manner. Calvinists believed in predestination, the idea that God knows what will happen to you after you die even before you are born. Your fate is scripted. Some people were chosen by God to go to heaven; most were chosen to go to hell. But God does not tell you which group you are in. Calvinists also believed that God wished for people to live ascetic lives, i.e. to avoid sensual pleasures. A 17th century Calvinist likely would not drink alcohol, would not dance, would not eat ice cream, etc. Another part of the system was the idea of the calling. Calvinists believed that God had a particular vocation for each individual. He might wish for you to be a carpenter or a schoolteacher or whatever. Your task was to find your calling. How do you know if you have found the calling that God has assigned to you? If you pick a vocation and you are good at it. If you are productive and efficient, then you can think that this is your calling. If you find a job that you are not good at, then you can think that it is not your calling. Still another part of the belief system was that followers should seek signs of election. That is, they should look for signs in this world that may convince them and others that they are part of the group that God has selected to go to heaven. The primary sign of election is through the calling. That is, if you become a carpenter and do well, then you can convince yourself that you have found your calling and that you are one of the elect.

How does this "**Protestant Ethic**" translate into the emergence and ultimate conquest of capitalism in the modern world? The answer is that the Calvinist were so fearful of their God and so fearful of eternal damnation, which they took extremely seriously, that they were racked with burning anxiety, an anxiety that need psychologically to be managed. It was managed by the Calvinists working hard in the vocation and working well. They were economically quite productive and made a great deal of profit. But they could not simply spend the profits on pleasurable things for personal gratification. That would violate their faith. They lived ascetic lives. So they reinvested their money and grew their businesses. Because of this work ethic and overall religious sensibility they outcompeted non-Calvinists. As a result, if you were a non-Calvinist, for example either another Protestant or a Catholic, then to compete with the Calvinists in the economy you would have to conform to this way of being, i.e. being serious, sober, hardworking, etc. This got the ball rolling for modern capitalism.

Of note, Weber, like most of his contemporaries believed that the modern world, the world of modern capitalism, produces secularization, as was noted earlier. It is one of the great ironies of history that capitalism was born out of religion, but it then turns to destroy religion.

The Future of Religion?

While Marx and Weber arguably believed that secularization was a part of the modern world, Durkheim had a more nuanced (some might say contradictory) view. While Durkheim believed traditional religions were declining in modernity, he also believed the essence of religion was such that it was always going to be around, perhaps in different guises. That is, at the heart of religion lies its function to provide moral solidarity for a group. Any society has to have some sense of shared morality if it is to survive. For Durkheim, religion traditionally served this role. It morally bound people together. Yet how are we to reconcile this with the decline of religion in the modern world, at least in Europe? Durkheim suggests the following at the end of his book *The Elementary Forms of the Religious Life* (1965 [1915]):

> Thus there is something eternal in religion which is destined to survive all the particular symbols in which religious thought has successively enveloped itself. There can be no society which does not feel the need of upholding and reaffirming at regular intervals the collective sentiments and the collective ideas which makes its unity and its personality. Now this moral remaking cannot be achieved except by the means of reunions, assemblies and meetings where the individuals, being closely united to one another, reaffirm in common their common sentiments; hence come ceremonies which do not differ from regular religious ceremonies, either in their object, the results which they produce, or the processes employed to attain these results. What essential difference is there between an assembly of Christians celebrating the principal dates of the life of Christ, or of Jews remembering the exodus from Egypt or the promulgation of the decalogue, and a reunion of citizens commemorating the promulgation of a new

moral or legal system or some great event in the national life? (1965, p. 475)

Durkheim is saying here that in the modern world religion may take on a different form than it took in earlier times. It might not appear as religion, but it is – based upon his definition – still a religion. We will recall that religions provide moral solidarity for a group. This solidarity is affirmed and reaffirmed through public ceremonies in which believers come together and engage in sacred rituals that reaffirm the collective. For Durkheim, religion is really all about worshipping the collective. People may be consciously worshipping a god or some sacred thing, but sociological they are worshipping the sacred collective us, and the individuals membership in it. Thus, Thanksgiving and the Fourth of July are not formally religious holidays in the United States, but in the Durkheimian sense, they are essentially religious. In short, religion is not going to disappear as is suggested by the secularization hypothesis; it will instead simply change form.

Civil religion

We are speaking here of the concept of **civil religion**. The concept was first used by Jean-Jacques Rousseau in the eighteenth century, but it did not really enter sociology as a fully formed concept until Robert Bellah wrote several essays and books explaining the term several decades ago. Bellah was a prominent cultural sociologist at Berkeley and he wrote within the traditions of Tocqueville and Durkheim, focusing on the elements of culture that bind a people together. He was particularly interested in understanding the moral and political culture of America. Several decades ago Bellah along with several of his colleagues wrote an influential book, *Habits of the Heart*, where he examined several different moral and political cultural orientations in

America. In some ways the book was an optimistic telling of how Americans disagree. In other ways, it was rather prescient of the problems afflicting this country today. But here we will focus on civil religion.

According to Bellah, in line with the above Durkheim quote, Americans share a deep moral connectedness that can be called religious, even though the beliefs and practices associated with this are not explicitly religious. Most Americans are part of this civil religion even if they do not know it. They share a set of beliefs and practices relative to sacred things that bring them together into a community called the United States. For Bellah, the concept of civil religion included elements from three distinct but overlapping traditions. One of these elements is the Judeo-Christian tradition. Bellah says that the central beliefs of this tradition are part of the civil religion. That is, the most basic and most widely shared elements of this tradition are part of it. Thus, we have "In God We Trust" on the penny (and not "In Jesus We Trust"), and people get sworn into office and in court by placing their hand on the bible. There used to be much discussion of the separation of church and state in America (though these discussions have largely become muted in recent decades), but Bellah notes that religion does regularly enter the public square. But it does so in a broad, sweeping, and inclusive way, reflecting the great diversity of Judeo-Christian traditions in America. A second element of civil religion concerns the basic elements of the Enlightenment, for example liberty and equality. These concepts and others associated with the Enlightenment saturate the American moral and political culture, the civil religion. Bellah suggests that these concepts are elevated to a place of sacred status. The third element is patriotism.

Like all religions, civil religion has various things that are sacred. There are sacred practices and rituals where members of the religion come together and worship the collective, i.e. the United States, and their membership in this society. We have noted earlier the Fourth of July and Thanksgiving as high holidays in America's civil religion. But it goes well beyond this. The flag is sacred. And there are sacred practices. Before a sporting event, the national anthem is sung in a solemn way. Many places in Washington, D.C. are deemed sacred, e.g. the White House, the Washington Monument, etc.

Altogether, this civil religion binds Americans together, or so says Bellah, even if they do not know they are members of this religion. But is this claim about the existence of a civil religion actually true? Scholars who make such claims often note America's "exceptionalism." Many scholars over the years have argued that one reason that American has managed to maintain a democracy and has managed to become more prosperous compared to other countries lies in the unique qualities of America, from history through the present. One element of this supposed uniqueness is the significant religiosity of Americans compared to other industrial or post-industrial countries. Research and survey data over decades and decades now clearly show that Americans are in fact more religious than people in most of Europe. Whether the question is whether people believe in god or whether it is whether people attend religious services regularly, the data is clear. This all suggests that one element of the civil religion hypothesis is confirmed – the Judeo-Christian tradition remains vibrant in America.

But is this really true? When one looks more closely at the research and survey data, there are reasons to question the above claims about American religiosity. Specifically, when one disaggregates the data and looks more closely at individual states or regions of the country, one finds, in keeping with one of the claims of this book, that there are two Americas. Religiosity is very strong in red America, specifically in the South up through Oklahoma. But religiosity appears to be more in line with other industrial or post-industrial countries, such as in Europe, when one looks at blue states in America. That is, residents of the blue states are not very religious. Their religious beliefs and practices are much, much less religious than those living in red states. While the belief in god and church attendance in these areas are a bit higher on average than those found in Europe, they are more comparable to each other than are the data on religiosity in blue state versus red state America. In short, a religious divide exists in America; there has historically been a religious divide in America.

When we return to consider the secularization hypothesis noted earlier, we can see that in blue America the hypothesis has generally been confirmed. On the other hand, it has been disconfirmed in red America. This presents the interesting question why religiosity has continued so strongly in some parts of America?

Sacralization

How are we sociological to account for such things as civil religion and the reality that much of America continues to be religious? Specifically, what are we to think of the secularization hypothesis? This evidence suggests that the secularization hypothesis may be wrong or at the least must be modified to effectively explain religion in America today. I would like here to propose the idea of sacralization as a way of making at least some sense of all of this. In some ways sacralization is the opposite of secularization. While secularization is the claim that religion declines with the development of the rational modern world, sacralization is the claim that there is a universal and timeless need to believe and to enact the sacredness of membership in a community, much as Durkheim argues. Weber's argument too is quite compatible with this claim. His theory of rationalization and secularization suggests on first glance that religion will die in modernity. Yet he also posits that the conquest of formal rationality, i.e. rationalization, over substantive rationality, produces an emptiness, a loss of meaning. It produces a world filled with people living in a sea of meaninglessness; a world in which people are by nature compelled to seek out some source of meaning. In a rather prescient line, Weber warned before 1920, that this may lead a population to gravitate toward a charismatic leader, one who will fill the void of the rationalized world. Hitler a few years later did just that.

But Weber does not theorize there will be a systematic push for the re-emergence of one or another religious sensibility. He leaves it to the side. But the consequences of formal rationality taking over may compel a population to embrace a form of substantive rationality, one anchored in one or another set of values, as a way of addressing the emptiness of a world of formal rationality. This suggests the possibility of sacralization.

Sacralization perhaps could most easily be understand in contrast to McDonaldization. Like McDonaldization it has several features. And like McDonaldization, one should not think of this description as an account of the real world. Rather, in Max Weber's terms, we should think of these things as ideal types or as pure types – as abstraction. There are five features of sacralization: 1) closure; 2) oneness and transcendence; 3) purity; 4) social; and 5) ritual. It is important to recognize that these features are not specifically features of consciousness, nor are they features of the concrete world external to the individuals. They are features of human experience and of social reality, and most importantly, they are features of the intersection of these things. We can now briefly look at these things one at a time.

To understand closure, we can contrast the fundamental workings of science with that of religion. Science, as an embodiment of formal rationality, is open in its orientation to the world. The essence of science is the claim that empirical investigations can produce tentative understandings about the natural workings of the world, but these understandings must be subject to further investigation and it must be recognized that these understandings can and will change as the result of future empirical investigations that challenge the claims of earlier research. In short, science is endlessly open to change. In contrast, religion is closed. Religious beliefs are not subject to change based upon changing empirical evidence. They are timeless. The interpretations of this timeless reality may change. One may engage in theological disputes with others, but the putative reality at the core of the beliefs does not change. Sacralization embraces this closed nature of the world.

Oneness and transcendence are the second feature. Durkheim notes that one of the essential features of religions is the public sacred rituals. He notes that the followers come together – in the modern world we can think of religious sacraments such as weddings, funerals, births, first communion, etc. – and experience an altered state of religious ecstasy. He notes that the members share a "collective effervescence" in these rituals, at least in the pre-modern societies he describes. The individual members lose themselves in the moment; they lose themselves in the blissful joy of sharing their religious devotion of other like-minded people. They become one not only with fellow believers. But they become one with the timeless truth of the university. They touch god, or at least they touch the sacred. They are spiritually removed from the mundane during these events and transcend the meaningless of the secular world. We can see how such an experience, institutionalized somehow, can serve to counter the effects of rationalization, at least in the short term. Sacralization does just that.

A third feature of sacralization is purity. Purity is associated with the first two features, but it is distinct. When we think of purity, we can contrast the world of a shopping mall or of Disneyland with that of a downtown in an American city. The downtown likely will be gritty, dirty.

Litter will be spread about on the streets. The wretched smells of garbage and urine might be sensed. Homeless people might be seen. This is not the world of purity. In contrast, in the shopping mall or in Disneyland, one does not see or smell or experience any of these elements. These are worlds of purity. In short, purity is very much like the sacred, as Durkheim conceives it. And much like Durkheim argues that the world is parceled out into two distinct domains – the world of the sacred and the world of the profane (mundane/ordinary) – so to sacralization does the same. It embraces the sacred through purity. Experiences, times, events, are rendered pure, in contrast to the rest of the world which is impure.

Sacralization is also essential social. This too is in conformity to Durkheim's understanding of religions as being essential social. Sacralization brings people together and fosters a collective sense of oneness, and oneness as purity. It is characterized by individuals being self-consciously identified as members of a collective us, of course a very special collective us. (One might think of the concept of tribalism here. A number of scholars have argued that it is a universal feature of the human condition, that humans need to divide themselves into us versus them, our tribe vs the others. Sacralization does not make such a claim, though it does implicitly make the claim that it inevitably produces conflicts or tensions between groups, particularly as it appears in a world that has become rationalized. But the nature of this conflict is essentially different than the nature put forth by the tribalism argument.)

Sacralization is essentially social in two ways. First, it is social in that the experience and practice of the fervent of the commitment to the sacred, to purity, to transcendence, in daily life as one experience the profane, or mundane world. The ordinary is saturated in its daily occurrence by the specialness felt and experienced by the sacred. Secondly, as Durkheim notes it involves rituals. And like Durkheim, it does not matter whether these rituals are officially and self-consciously understood as being directly related to, or expressions of, the sacred. Their existence is enough, along with the other features, to affirm sacralization.

Religion and America Today

Given all of the above, how are we to make sense of the religious landscape of America today, and how is this landscape implicated in the crisis, described in chapters one and two, that is America today? Some if not many who are reading this might wish to dismiss or deny the claims made herein that America is in a state of crisis. These people might say that America has always been conflicted on important issues, or they might say that there are not two defined sides in opposition but there are many different views on various matters, and this has always been the case in this country. To those who make such claims, I urge you to look at what is happening in the country today. There is a deep and significant divide. We can now return to our topics covered in this chapter – rationalization, secularization, civil religion, sacralization, etc. and ask how these may help us to better understand.

As noted earlier, in terms of traditional religious sentiment America is and has been quite divided with red states being quite religious and blue states being significantly less so. The rationalization thesis appears to be vindicated in the latter, but not so in the former. The concept of civil religion is more complicated here. While many of the public and social practices in the country today seem to suggest the legitimacy of this concept, when one looks more closely one finds again a divide. Superficially, one can see Americans from Alabama and from Boston waving flags and participating joyfully in the sacred secular holidays such as Thanksgiving and the Fourth of July. Americans from

Mississippi and California readily volunteer to join the armed forces to defend the country. An abundance of such evidence exists suggesting that in fact most Americans do share a commitment to some civil religion. And yet, the symbolic meanings and social practices which ostensibly reflect a shared religious sensibility may not in fact be doing so. When the radical right wing Republican insurrectionists attacked the Capitol on January 6, 2021 and sought to overthrow the legitimate election of Joe Biden and replace him with Donald Trump, many were waving the American flags. Many were proclaiming they were acting to defend rather than to defeat democracy. The point here is that the symbolic and social practices arguably have two very different meanings for the two Americas.

And what about rationalization and sacralization? Is the great divide produced in part by rationalization, and how does sacralization come into play here? To answer these questions we should address another thorny product of rationalization. I am thinking here of tolerance. Rationalization is the foundation for modern democracy. What could be a more rational form of political organization than democracy, where we assume every individual is inherently equal to every other individual? But democracy produces a difficulty when it comes to morality. Democratic decisions are not based on the moral rightness of a position but on whether the position has the support of more than half the population. In effect, democracy fuels a decline in morality. This issue has been noted by such disparate writers as Tocqueville and the late twentieth century conservative moral philosopher Leo Strauss. Tocqueville, for example, expressed concerns in the early 1800s that democratic systems might lead people to believe if their candidates won elections that their moral positions were right, and further that the people whose candidates lost the election might also believe this. This runs counter to the essence of democracy. Democracy does not mean that the majority is morally right.

Strauss also expresses concerns about morality. He believed that democracy by its very workings weakened and ultimately destroys morality, or at least moral consensus, because there is a plurality of moral beliefs in democracies and no one belief is deemed right. All of this spawns moral relativism.

When we combine such ideas with the emptiness brought about by rationalization, we can see an elevated crisis. Moreover, such ideas must be understood within the context of looking at the actual, social, and political and cultural realities to understand their effects. We described some of these in the first few chapters, e.g. the American political system is skewed to favor red states, etc. Combining all of this we can see how sacralization is supported in the contemporary American context as a response to such things. But in the American context sacralization is realized in two contradictory ways. On the one hand, we see it with the assertion of conventional Christian beliefs and practices. I am thinking here of the inordinate power conservative religious groups such as the Baptists and Mormons have on the political landscape in America today. But as was suggested earlier, sacralization also appears within secular institutions, such as shopping malls and Disneyland. And it is this fusion of the secular sacralization and the religious sacralization, combined with the political and institutional realignment that is fostering an increasing divide in the United States.

Romanticism, Rationality, and Fascism

Sociologists writing in the early 1900s sometimes focus on the theme of social change. These sociologists tended to look at the broad stokes of history to make big claims, typically about cultural forces that drive societies for hundreds if not thousands of years. This form of sociology which was largely speculative – focusing on the sweeps of history – is no longer in vogue. Very few practice this approach today, perhaps because it does not readily lend itself to scientific investigation. We end this chapter by invoking a form of social change sociology, and by tying it into the themes already presented in this chapter – religion, secularization, sacralization.

I wish to discuss here the historical forces of romanticism, rationality, and fascism, and wish to explore their relationships. Rationality is a primary theme of this book. Following the arguments of Max Weber, I believe that rationalization is a predominant feature of the modern world. This process has only been amplified in recent decades. Romanticism, the second force of note, is the term used to refer to the cultural style that emerged in Germany, France, and other parts of Europe in the late 1700s and flourished in the 1800s. It is found in the writings of the German author Goethe as well as the German classical music composer Richard Wager. **Romanticism** is a cultural style that at its heart is a rejection of the perceived dehumanizing qualities of the modern, industrializing rational world. Romanticism embraces the emotional side, the ineffable side, of human experience. It embraces the undefinable beauty of the non-rational aspect of human experience. Romanticism stokes a passion and a longing for the pursuit of genuinely human, in its fullest sense, existence. It calls for a response in the viewer, listener, or reader that is one of warm and wonderful mystery, of what it truly means to be a human being in its fullest form. Many have argued that romanticism was a reaction against the Enlightenment (The Age of Reason), with its almost obsessive elevation of rationality above all else. Some also have argued that the tradition of romanticism served at least in part as the seedbed for the rise of fascism in the early 1900s. We will revisit this idea below.

Fascism is a radical right-wing political ideology and political system that in many ways stands in direct opposition to democracy. From the 1920s through the early 1940s, this system took control over much of central Europe. The fascist movements of Mussolini in Italy and then Hitler's Nazis are the two most well-known examples. World War Two was defined in large measure by the opposition of three ideologies – fascism of Central Europe, democratic capitalism of Western Europe and America, and communism of the Soviet Union and its satellite states. World War Two was a war between, on the one hand, the allies, which were comprised of the democratic capitalist countries, led by the United States, and the communists of the Soviet Union, against the axis powers, which were comprised largely of the fascist governments in Germany, Italy, and others. The Western powers combined with the Soviets defeated Germany and their allies, and with this came an end to the fascist experiment in Europe. Most in the popular imagination ever since believed fascism was an ideology and political system that has been buried in history, never to reassert itself. But what is fascism?

As was just suggested, the reader is encouraged to think about Hitler's Germany and Mussolini's Italy when thinking about what **fascism** is. Numerous scholars have provided academic definitions of fascist movements and fascist societies. Here we can describe several of these. First, we described the political sociologists research on fascism as well as his definition in Chapter Three. Briefly to recap, he says fascists movements in Europe in the 1920s and 1930s has several common traits, all of which are captured in his summary definition: "Fascism is the pursuit of a transcendent and cleansing nation-statism through paramilitarism." Fascism has been described by the historian Robert Paxton in a more detailed way. He writes: "Fascism may be defined as a form of political behavior marked by obsessive preoccupation with community decline, humiliation or victimhood and by compensatory cults of unity, energy, and purity, in which a mass-based party of committed nationalist militants, working in uneasy but effective collaboration with traditional elites, abandons democratic liberties and pursues with redemptive violence and without ethical or legal restraints goals of internal cleansing and external expansion" (2005, p. 218).

A third definition, in addition to those presented by Mann and Paxton, is offered by Umberto Eco, the Italian author and rhetorical philosopher. Eco provides a list of fourteen or so features of fascist societies. We will not describe each of these here. Suffice to highlight just a few. One of the features of fascism is the rejection of modernism. Modernism refers to a cultural style of art, literature, etc. that was quite popular in Europe and America in the early 1900s. In art, it often times embraced abstract paintings, in contrast to representational paintings. Hitler and the German fascist hated modern art and modernism in general. This is famously seen in the Nazi's infamous art exhibit titled "Degenerate Art." The Nazi's gathered up a fine collection of modern art and they presented it in an exhibit titled degenerate art in the late 1930s. The exhibit was meant to show how bad and evil modern art. Below the paintings on display were descriptions of how the art was bad. Some of the art was done by Jews, but much was done by non-Jews. The Nazis saw modern art as degenerate, a term commonly used by scientific racist of the day. It refers to evolutionary throwbacks to early stages of evolution, e.g. ape-like forms of being. For the Nazis modern art captured much of what was wrong with the world.

Another feature identified by Eco was machismoism. Machismo refers to cultures which accord masculine, and really hypermasculine characteristics (in men), an elevated value. (The term traditionally was applied to Latin cultures.) Machismoism says that men should be manly, hyper-manly, and manliness should be prized about all things non-manly.

This is clearly a common feature of fascism, one not discussed by Paxton or Mann. Still another feature cited by Eco is the cult of action for action's sake. That is, for the fascist it is better to do now and think later, than think now and do later. Being fully human, being a full nationalist, means asserting oneself in the world through one's action. We can mention one last item on Eco's list of characteristics of fascism: Fascists speak "newspeak." The term newspeak refers to George Orwell's famous dystopian novel *1984*. In that book, one way the oppressive authoritarian government maintained control over the population was by constantly filling the public with false and changing information, such that they could not believe anything to be true, and they could only rely upon the government to tell them what to believe is true. (Newspeak is not unlike the concept of "fake news" propagated by Trump and his followers. (See Chapter Thirteen).)

By its very nature, fascism, at least as it was realized in the early and mid-1900s, is a self-imploding system. It calls out for endless militarism, conflict, and war. Struggle lies at the heart of this system. Eventually, this ends. In the 1940s, it ended with the destruction of fascism as a movement and as a political system. In the many decades since then, many – at least in popular consciousness – came to believe that fascism was a threat in the past but is not one now. It has been seen as a dead ideology with no prospect of reasserting its ugly head. And yet in the last five to ten years, in America and elsewhere, we have seen the rise, if not the dramatic rise, in authoritarianism – from Russia to the United States, from Hungary to Brazil. This authoritarianism has clear connections to fascism. Whether democracy – a system essentially opposed to fascism – can withstand this rise and can endure is now an open question.

We can conclude by saying a few more words about the relationship between romanticism, rationality, and fascism. It is sometimes said that romanticism and fascist are both anchored in a rejection of rationality. Some have argued that fascism in Europe in the early 1900s was fueled in part by romanticism, by the embrace of the irrational and transcendent. The emptiness of the modern, rational world is filled by the wonderous embrace of fascism, or so its followers felt. And yet today on the cultural landscape – in art, literature, etc. – we do not find romanticism. This leads to the question of whether fascism requires as a seedbed the sensibilities of romanticism or not? Arguably, it does not. It does, however, require some of the essential features of romanticism, including the embrace of passion and emotion and the rejection of rationality.

We can end, by returning to Durkheim's ideas about religion. If all societies in fact do need some sort of religion, as he defines it, if they wish to remain cohesive, Americans should now ask: What is this religion, this moral unity, that binds the society together. As I have suggested in other chapters, this goes to the center of the crisis that is America today: There is no moral unity that binds America together. America, as a unified society, does not exist.

Chapter Nine: Rationality, Science, and Technology

Rationality and the related concepts of science and technology are major themes of this book. One only needs to glance about the world today, or for that matter the world of the last two hundred years, to see that these ideas have become central to the organization of the social world. Some of the founding figures of contemporary sociology, such as Marx and Weber, recognize the importance of these things. Some such as Weber expressed concerns about the possible social consequences of the spread of rationality, science, and technology. It was not that Weber or other early sociologists were luddites, opposed fundamentally to the spread of technology. It was not that Weber saw rationality and the associated concepts as being unequivocally harmful to individual, social relations and social order. Weber indeed like most early twentieth century people welcomed the seemingly endless new technologies arising in the world. But Weber also expressed great concerns about the possible negative effects that rationality, science, and technologies were having and would be having on the social world. We discuss all of this in this chapter. One of the concerns that Weber and others had about rationality and the associated ideas was that the embrace of such things might lead to the hollowing out of individual experience and the hollowing out of social relations. People might become more and more machine-like in their thinking —less reflective -- and in their social behaviors as a result of blindly accepting rationality. This could create a void, an emptiness in individuals that longed to be filled. It was the blind and passive acceptable of rationality, science and technology that concerned Weber.

Yet today in America we seem to be experiencing the opposite. Instead of blindly accepting and following rationality, science, and technology, millions and millions of people are in fact rejecting such things. I am thinking mostly of the millions of New Republican Party followers of Trump who simply deny rationality and science (and reality) time and again. Rationality would dictate that people accept the fact that Biden handily won the 2020 presidential election. Yet millions today reject this fact. Rationality and science would dictate that people embrace the COVID-19 vaccines as safe and effective and recognize the rational way to address and to contain the COVID-19 epidemic is for everyone to get vaccinated – using vaccines produced systematically through legitimate scientific means. Yet a third of America is today not vaccinated (and this failure has contributed to needless deaths and to the prolongation of the epidemic). Rationality would tell us to accept the scientific consensus amongst climate scientist that climate change and global warming are real, and they present a significant threat to social life. Yet millions – many of the same who believe the above false claims – believe that climate change and global warming are a hoax, are not real.

This presents an interesting sociological question. Why is it that these realities seemingly contradict the claims and warnings issued by Weber and others? Weber assumed that people in the modern world would unquestioningly embrace and accept rationality, science, and technology, and that embrace would create problems (which are discussed below in more detail). Weber expressed concerns about the negative and harmful consequences when people embrace unquestioningly rationality, science, and technology. But as we have just seen in America today there are numerous examples of Americans doing the opposite, i.e. rejecting rationality. How are we to make sense of this? We might simply believe that Weber and countless other sociologists since then who have warned about rationality, etc., are simply wrong. But I do not believe this to be the case. In this chapter, I describe the basic concepts related to rationality and I describe some sociological approaches to the sociology of science and technology. Along the way, the seeming contradiction noted above is explained.

To begin to understand the sociological complexities related to rationality, we can turn to the 2019 Women's World Cup of soccer. One of the things talked about the most during the 2019 Women's World Cup of soccer, aside from the dominance of the American team, was the controversies surrounding VAR – Video Assisted Referee, which is simply another term for instant replay. As in American sports, VAR is the use of video replay to check to see that a ruling on the field by an official was correct. Instant replay and VAR were instituted largely because people felt that technology could help provide objective, fact-based judgments. It was assumed that technology would remove the errors of human judgment and as such would lead to better, more accurate calls on the field. All of this was meant in part to reduce or eliminate arguments amongst the spectators about the correctness of the calls. Afterall, one cannot argue against the rational, objective, fact-based decisions made by the video. Cameras don't lie, the saying goes. Yet something curious happened at the World Cup. Rather than reducing the arguments and disagreements amongst spectators (and players) regarding the rightness of a penalty call, the VAR seems to have increased the arguments and disagreements. The amount of time spent debating the VAR decisions was significant. The goals of the implementation of the VAR did not appear to be realized. The implementation of technology to solve a problem actually fostered the very problem it was designed to solve.

We can turn to another example of technology and sports to see a related dilemma. I am thinking here of the prospect of having computers replace umpires in baseball to call balls and strikes. Today, when one watches a baseball game on television, a computer program creates an image of the strike zone and shows whether a ball goes through it or not, i.e. whether it was a ball or a strike. As such, one might wonder, why we need umpires if the computer can do it more accurately? The problem with such a proposal for many baseball fans is that part of the fun of watching a baseball game, or for that matter any sporting activity, is complaining about the actions of the officials. If this is taken away, arguably the soul of the game is taken away.

These are two distinct examples – the soccer one was about the failures of technology to solve the problem of the correctness of calls, the baseball one was about the failures of technology to take into consideration the intangible qualities of the game. Yet curiously, the soccer VAR example might lead one to conclude that technology cannot solve the problems of getting the call right, while the baseball example suggests the opposite. The point here is that there is in our society much hope that the implementation of technology, built upon science and rationality, can be a good thing and can solve problems, but when looked at more carefully one finds at best that there are complications which should give us pause.

Without question rationality, science, and technology have come to be dominant forces in our world today. How are we to understand these forces sociologically? As we see below, some sociologists express concerns about the spread of these things – concerns about social relations, social stability, and about what these things are doing to the individual self. The conquest of rationality, science, and technology might not be all good, or at least this conquest might have consequences that are both good and bad.

It perhaps should go without saying that science and technology have an enormous impact upon our lives. Scholars, and artists – from movie makers to music makers, cultural critics, academics, and others -- have long commented upon this. But what sort of impact has it had, and what impact does it have? On this, there is great disagreement. Crudely, one can identify two basic and opposing camps based upon how people answer this question. On the one side are those that think technology is an oppressive force. Those thinking this see technology as robbing people of their autonomy, morality, or political voice. These people see technology as a force that is harming individuals and society, perhaps by turning people into soulless machines doing the bidding of forces beyond them, whether these are political forces or technology itself. Such critics sometimes see social relations breaking down or becoming corrupted as the result. For example, the dominance of technology and rationality, some have said, have turned social relationships into mechanical exchanges instead of human encounters. In the other camp are those who look about a world filled with technology and see the wonders of it all. Whether iPhone and the internet or airplanes, pharmaceuticals or air conditioners, technologies have greatly enhanced our lives, as individuals and as a society. These are two very different views. Which is right? In this chapter, we examine the many ways that rationality, science, and technology impact our lives, and we are introduced to the various ways that sociologists have understood such things. We find that the impacts of technology are both positive and negative, and that the impacts are more complicated than is sometimes thought.

Rationality and Its Discontents

We briefly discussed the concept of rationality in Chapter Two. Here we dive deeper into these ideas. To begin, we should define what it is we are looking at here: rationality, science, and technology. **Rationality** is the lining up of means and ends (goals) in a logical way. If one identifies a goal and employs logical means to reach this goal, then that is a form of rationality. For a student to graduate from college (a goal), for example, there are certain logical things she needs to do (means), such as attend classes, take notes, do the assignments, take and pass the exams, etc. For a football coach to win (a goal), he needs to get his team to practice and to learn how to effectively play (the means). The noted German sociologist Max Weber distinguished between two types of rational actions: instrumental (or means-ends) rational action and value rational action. **Instrumental rational action** is lining up means and ends in a logical way without considering values. The examples just given – the student and the football coach – reflect instrumental rational action. **Value rational action** is lining up means and ends in a logical way while considering values. Values are things, ideas, beliefs, etc. that one assesses to be important. One might value a guitar, or a personal relationship, or god, or your religion, or honesty, or your sister, or whatever. The values can influence the ends, the means, or the relationship between the means and ends. When a teenage girl asks her sister to borrow a sweater, the sister very well might decide to loan her the sweater. Does she charge the sister a fee for the loan? Presumably not. Had she charged the sister stating she could borrow it if she gave her five dollars, then this would be an instance of instrumental rational action. (Economic exchanges in a capitalist market are largely instrumentally rational.) But she likely did not. She acted in a way that was driven by value considerations. That is, she values her family and her sister, in and of themselves, and this influenced her actions. This valuing does not make her action irrational, but it is instead using a different type of rationality than instrumental. Similarly, religious communities such as the Amish, in Pennsylvania, arguably act very rationally on a day to day basis, but their rationality is infused with their religious values. They drive horses and buggies rather than ride cars. They do not use modern technologies, such as iPhone. It is not instrumentally rational to refuse to use automobiles or smartphones, but it is value rational to do so. The Amish have a form of Christianity that leads them to believe that modern technologies threaten their pure, religious experience, and as such goes against the will of god. It would be more "efficient" for them to use telephones and drive automobiles, but their values prevent them from doing so.

Weber noted that instrumental rationality has increasingly become prominent in the modern era. In pre-modern societies, value rationality is more prominent. Instrumental rationality is closely aligned with science and technology. Science is based upon instrumental rationality. It is the pursuit through logical means of understanding the workings of the world. The sciences of the natural world, from biology to physics, are about using logical means, i.e. through research, to understand the laws of nature. (The sciences of the human world, such as the social sciences, have a more complicated project because there are not laws governing the social world as there are laws of nature.) When one thinks of a scientific experiment, one can see instrumental rationality in action. The scientist is not supposed to allow his or her values to influence the research. He or she should be purely objective and unbiased in his or her work. Technology can be thought of as a tool. It is the application of science in the real world. Technology generally seeks to control or manipulate this world in some way or another.

Weber introduces us to another set of concepts that further help us to understand rationality in the modern world: formal rationality, substantive rationality, and rationalization. A technical definition of formal rationality is as follows: **Formal rationality** is the lining up of means and ends in a logical way in a social context without considering values. A technical definition of **substantive rationality** is as follows: Substantive rationality is the lining up of means and ends in a logical way in a social context while considering values. Upon reflection, one might note that the definition of formal rationality sounds quite similar to instrumental rational action, and the definition of substantive rationality sounds quite similar to value rational action. Indeed, they are similar, but these sets of concepts are also very different. Formal and substantive rationality refer to the organization of a social context while instrumental and value rational action refers to individual social behaviors. Thus, one could have a social setting or context organized in a formal or substantively rational way. A McDonald's restaurant is organized in formally rational way; the Amish community is organized in a substantively rational way. Most settings today are organized along formally rational way, for example, bureaucracies, the military, sports teams, businesses. In contrast, in all earlier times in history, many, many sites were organized along the lines of substantive rationality – family, religion, aristocracies, etc.

Briefly, we can consider the relations between the types of social action – instrumental and value rational – and the types of social settings – formal or substantive. Formally rational settings demand or at least encourage individuals operating within them to think and to act in instrumentally rational ways, while substantively rational setting demand or at least encourage individuals operating within them to think and to act in value rational ways. But this does not mean that an individual will always act or think in an instrumentally rational way in a formally rational setting. It does mean that the setting bears down upon the individual and imposes a form of rationality upon the individual. Think about a worker at McDonald's who is a vegetarian – I know it is a stretch of the imagination to think so. McDonald's formal rationality dictates to the vegetarian worker that he or she flip the hamburgers – dead animals -- even if the individual on value or moral grounds does not wish to do so. The point here is that there can be a tension between the two which cries out for resolution.

Rationalization is the historical process by which formal rationality is taking over (from substantive rationality). This is one of Weber's central concepts. (Do not get this sociological concept of rationalization confused with the psychological concept of rationalization. The two concepts have nothing to do with one another.) Rationalization is a historical force in which people are encouraged or required to think and act in a formally rational way. While Weber very much embraced the modern world and all the wonderous things rationality has brought about, from new inventions to the growth of bureaucracies, he also was quite concerned about the potential harmful effects that would come with the spread of formal rationality. That is, he was concerned about rationalization. In his famous book *The Protestant Ethic and the Spirit of Capitalism* in which he argues that the emergence and spread of modern capitalism has its roots in a particular form of Protestantism in the 1600s, he uses the phrase "the iron cage" of rationality to describe the modern world. We are, he says, trapped in an **iron cage of rationality**. It is a cage that we cannot see, but we are trapped in it nonetheless. It is imposed upon us. We are forced by our social environment to think and to engage in the world using instrumental, rather than value, rationality. In effect, we are becoming more like machines and less like humans and are blinded by instrumental rationality from seeing this. This is associated with another concept used by Weber: **disenchantment**. The modern world has become disenchanted. Disenchantment is the opposite of enchantment. The pre-modern world was one that was enchanted. It was filled with wonder and awe. It was filled with things that could not rationally be explained. Imagine yourself to be a Native American living in what is now San Francisco in the year 1200 AD. You look up at the sky and see a rainbow, a beautiful rainbow. How might you explain it? You would not say it occurs because of refractions of light through the clouds – a scientific and instrumentally rational explanation. Instead, you likely would assign some spiritual or religious meaning to it. Similarly, how might you explain an earthquake? Would you say it was caused by shifts in plate tectonics, or would you again say it was the gods or some such thing. Endless examples could be offered, from mental illness to fireflies. The point is that in a rationalized, modern world, the explanations are scientific and boring. One does not invoke mystical or religious or value-laden accounts in the modern world to explain things – to explain anything. Weber argues that disenchantment leads to a loss of meaning. When everything can be explained, what is the point to anything? It creates a hole in our existence. It empties our lives of the richness of mystery. Rationality drains meaning from our worlds and casts us adrift. It leads to secularization, the decline of religion. Meaning is drained out of our lives. Our lives become flat and listless, meaningless. This is an emptiness, as we see below, that cries out to be filled. Formal rationality also produces a dehumanization, where individuals come to treat other individuals as things to be used instrumentally rather than as humans with values. Think of a large bureaucracy with employees simply following orders. The employs interact with others and with others outside of their organization in mechanical ways. The employees are just doing their jobs, in mechanical ways.

But Weber and others following in his footsteps also see rationalization having effects not only on individuals but on social organization and policy. For example, numerous scholars have written about the **irrationality of rationality** that is said to come with rationalization. The irrationality of rationality refers to an irrational outcome that comes about when social actors are put in situations in which they are required to act instrumentally rational. Under some situations, when individuals act in instrumentally rational ways – particularly within formal rational settings, this could lead to irrational outcomes, both for the individual and for society. This is counter-intuitive. It runs against the commonsense notion that when individuals acts rationally then this automatically leads to rational outcomes – either for the individual or the society. But there are many, many examples of the irrationality of rationality. Examples that illustrate the irrationality of rationality abound. One such example is the German Nazis. On the one hand, Hitler's Nazi regime appears as a fundamentally irrational enterprise, with its quest for self-destruction and the inhumane destruction of six million Jews. All told, the wars created by Hitler led to the deaths of fifty million people and the utter destruction of Germany. (Russia alone lost twenty million people.) This hardly seems a rational enterprise. And yet, an expression about the German character captures some of this insanity. It is said that in Germany the trains run on time. This expression is meant as both an insult and a compliment to the German character. It is a compliment in that in Germany things run as they are supposed to. They are efficient. If a train from Munich to Berlin says it is departing at 10:34, then it likely will depart at that time. The claim is that the German character is one of punctuality and efficiency. But the trains also ran on time to Auschwitz, to Bergen-Belsen and all the rest of the Nazi death camps. Hitler created a methodical, rational killing machine. And yet the enterprise was utterly irrational.

Another example: MAD. MAD stands for Mutually Assured Destruction. MAD was the official United States policy regarding nuclear weapons during the cold war (1945-1990) with the Soviet Union. The MAD doctrine was that the United States should build more nuclear weapons than the Soviets such that the Soviets will know that if they attached the United States first with nuclear weapons that the United States would respond immediately in kind, and both countries would be annihilated. The policy is quite rational, but it is also completely irrational. One last example: capitalism. Capitalism is fundamentally a formally rational system. But it is the major reason for global warming and climate change – processes that are destroying the environment. (Supporters of capitalism like to point out such things as electric cars to argue that capitalism has within itself the possibility of adapting and of addressing climate change. But the logic of capitalism – the demand to rely upon instrumental rational action – suggests that it in fact is incapable of addressing the problems at hand.)

The idea that instrumentally rational action can lead to irrational outcomes is famously captured in **the prisoner's dilemma**, an example developed in game theory. The dilemma shows that when an individual acts rationally in his or her own self-interest, it does not always lead to the optimal outcome for the individual. The dilemma is as follows: Imagine two people, Tom and Harry, who robbed a bank together and were arrested. Tom and Harry are held in separate cells and cannot talk to each other. They are each interviewed separately by the prosecutor, who does not have enough evidence to convict either of the main crime, but he does have enough evidence to convict both of lesser charges. The prosecutor seeks in the interviews to get them each to confess and/or to implicate the other in the crime. Th prosecutor offers each prisoner a bargain.

Tom and Harry are given a choice. They can implicate each other, or they can remain silent.

> -If Tom and Harry each implicate the other, each of them serves two years in prison.
> -If Tom implicates Harry, but Harry remains silent, then Tom will be set free and Harry will serve three years in prison (and vice versa)
> -If Tom and Harry both remain silent, both of them will serve only one year in prison (on the lesser charge)

The question is: What is the most rational, self-interested thing for each of the two men to do, and using rationality, will each likely do the most rational thing? What will each likely do? The most rational, self-interested thing to do is for Tom and Harry each to implicate the other. By doing so, each would get no jail time. But if both do so, then each gets the worse outcome. The best outcome is not the most rational self-interested one: That is, if both Tom and Harry remained silent, each gets only one year in prison.

Many variations of this dilemma have been offered over the years, but the point is always the same. The point of the prisoners' dilemma, again, is that sometimes acting in a self-interested rational way does not lead to the best outcome. This calls into question a number of things about rationality. It questions whether we should assume rationality leads to the best outcome. It questions whether individuals do act rationally, if rationality is defined in terms out best outcomes? It also suggests that a social or economic system, such as capitalism, which assumes that we should encourage (enlightened) rational, self-interested action, as this will lead to the best outcome – which is a basic assumption of capitalism – should be questioned at least to some extent.

Another concept related to a discussion of the consequences of rationalization needs to be mentioned here. This is the idea that rationality must be understood in relation to the social context in which it is employed. What is and is not rational is determined in part by the context. If a chef on the Titanic was cooking dinner right before the Titanic hit the iceberg and then the chef continued to cook the dinner after the crash, would his actions be deemed rational? Assuming his actions while cooking were instrumentally rational, one might say that his cooking was rational even though in the broader context it is irrational for the cook not to try to get off the boat after it hit the iceberg. Similarly, economic actors in contemporary capitalism generally act in instrumentally rational ways, but as noted above, capitalism is destroying the planet. If one looked simply at the individual actor's actions, one would say the actions are rational, but if one looks at the larger picture, i.e. at the global environment, one would say that the actions are not rational.

A final idea related to rationality is reason. We should distinguish between these terms. Rationality is abstract. It was discussed above. Acting rationally means acting mechanically by relating logically the means to a given end. Reason is different. Reason is using logic to relate means and ends, but it does so while considering common sense, practical and human factors. Is it rational for a police officer to give a speeding ticket to someone who is driving 56 miles an hour in a 55 mile and hour zone? Technically, if a police officer did so, then she would be acting rationally, by our definition. But is it reasonable? No. If violates common sense. Reason requires the tempering of rationality about judgments about such things as decency and common sense. Reasonable behavior is not rigidly fixed to a set of abstract principles, but instead is based upon a human assessment of the present realities. It is an argument of this book that one of the sociological problems of the present age is the surrender of reason to rationality.

We can return now to the riddle posed at the outset: Some if not many people in the United States today reject rationality, e.g. the science of global warming, of vaccinations, etc. and as such claims about instrumental rationality taking over may not be correct. How are we to reconcile this rejection of rationality with the claims made by Weber and others that rationality is taking over? It would appear from these recent examples that this is not the case. And yet, some sociologists (for example the members of the Frankfurt School; see below) argue that the irrational rejection of science – of global warming, vaccinations, etc. – actually reflects rather than contradictions the main claims regarding the irrationality of rationality. The key here is to remember that with rationalization comes disenchantment, a loss of meaning, the iron cage. As meaning is drained, people are compelled to look for it wherever they can. We are after all a meaning making species, a species driven to provide meaning in our lives. As meaning is drained by rationalization, people are compelled to find meaning elsewhere. One such place is putting one's faith in the hands of some mythic or charismatic leader, who professes that his people are great and that he is the embodiment of this greatness. In effect, rationalization creates a society of lost sheep looking for a leader who will restore order and a sense of purpose in the peoples' lives. Surrendering one's autonomy to the leader and feeling the warmth and fulfillment of this surrender is a powerful force in a world dominated by formal rationality.

Technology and History

What role has technology played in history? Has it played a central role in moving history forward, or is its importance only secondary to the forces of such things as economics or culture? These questions revolve around the topic of technological determinism. **Technological determinism** is the claim that technology is the engine of history, and that other forces that might propel history forward, such as economic arrangements (for example, Marx claimed that economic factors and class conflict were the engine of history) or culture (such as the introduction of new ideas in a society, such as the Protestant Reformation in the 1500s in Europe leading to changes in social and political life) are merely secondary to technological changes. Technological determinism says that one can explain the march of history by looking at changes in technology. Changes in technology produce all of the other changes in society and history, according to technological determinism. Technology produces changes in the cultural, the political, and the social orders. Technology is fundamental. For example, a technological determinist might say that the invention of moveable type and the modern printing press (a technological innovation) in the 1400s facilitated the Protestant Reformation in the 1500 and 1600s, a period in which Christians throughout Europe, and most notably northern Europe, theologically rebelled against the Roman Catholic Church, then the only Christian Church in Western Europe. Martin Luther, one of the main leaders of the Protestant Reformation, and the founder of the Protestant denomination Lutheranism, relied upon the new technology of the modern printing to print out his statements of protest against the Catholic Church on a mass scale to the general public. Luther went on to translate the Bible into German and to print it – to mass produce it, so that the general public could read it directly rather than having to have it read and interpreted to them by Catholic priests. Luther gave direct access to the general public the actual words in the Bible. (Can you imagine how few books and Bibles existed prior to the moveable press? Each book had to be handwritten.) The people now could assess for themselves, rather than having to rely upon priests, what the Bible means. It fostered an independence in thought. The new technology arguably contributed not only to the Protestant Reformation, but to many subsequent historical events which in themselves were arguably influenced by the Reformation. Things such as the great democratic revolutions of the late 1700s – the French and American revolutions – could be seen as having been influenced by the Reformation.

A technological determinist might say that the introduction of a new technology, be it the printing press or the internet, is the fundamental driving force in society. The anthropologist Leslie White, for example, embraces technological determinism. Other scholars recognize the central importance of technology in shaping human history, but they see it as one of many factors that drive history forward. Other factors such as culture, material conditions, population changes, social arrangements, and others also play crucial roles. Gerhard Lenski takes this view, though he argues that of all the factors it is clearly technology which is the most important. He develops a theory that gives technology a prominent, but not a determinative, role in historical development of societies. Lenski developed an ecological-environmental theory in which he argues that there is a pattern to the evolution of societies. This model is elaborated by Lenski and his colleague Patrick Nolan (2014). They identify several types of societies in history and show how technology was key to the historical shift from one to another of these. Lenski and Nolan show how the introduction of new technologies was instrumental to major social, cultural, and political changes. They identify several distinct types of societies in history: hunting and gathering; simple horticultural; advanced horticultural; simple agrarian; advanced agrarian; and industrial.

Hunting and gathering societies were the first to appear. They lasted from approximately 40,000 B.C. to 8,000 B.C. Hunting and gathering societies relied upon killing wild animals and picking fruits, grains, and vegetables from native, uncultivated plants to survive. A key technological development characterizing this period was the innovations in tools and weapons, specifically the development of spears and later bows and arrows, but also the use of hand tools such as the ax. **Simple horticultural societies** came next. They began between around 8,000 B.C. in the Middle East and remained a dominant form of social organization until 4,000 B.C. In simple horticultural societies, people began to plant and raise crops. Slash and burn farming was also introduced as a new technology of farming. This was the practice of burning the crops after the harvest to fertilize the soil for the following year. The next period was **advanced horticultural societies**, which lasted from 4,000 B.C. to 3,000 B.C. This period was characterized by the introduction of copper used in the making of tools and weapons. It was during this period that herding of animals, and the domestication of animals arose, though there is much debate about the precise location and dates of the emergence of the first herding societies. Next to arise was the **simple agrarian society** which began in 3,000 B.C. and lasted until 1,000 B.C. The plow was a key technological development during this period, and Mesopotamia and Egypt were two areas in which early simple agrarian societies. **Advanced agrarian societies** followed. These are characterized by large scale systematic farming using tools and farm animals. Iron was discovered between 1,000 and 2,000 B.C., but it was not until the stage of the advanced agrarian societies that iron was widely used in tools. Advanced agrarian societies began around 1,000 B.C. and lasted up until the early modern era in Europe, in the 1500 and 1600s. This was followed by the emergence of **industrial societies**, which began in the 1700s and lasted until the 1950s. Industrial societies are characterized by widespread use of machines and the mass production of goods in factories. In addition, science as a foundation of technology became central during this period. Lenski and Nolan end their historical description with the industrial, but many other scholars have argued that we are now in a **post-industrial society**, starting perhaps in the 1960s. The principle technological development was the emergence of digital technologies, which now drive much of the internet era.

It is important to note that the timelines just described should be understood as a rough guideline of the emergence and spread of different types of societies. It is not meant to be a rigid sequence of stages whereby one type of society emerged, then disappeared only to be replaced by another type of society. History is far more complicated than this. For example, we find in history different types of societies co-existing. Moreover, some societies have jumped from one type of society to another. One can think of European colonization in the industrial era. Europeans conquered many peoples in the world whose societies were in one of the "earlier" forms of development, such as simple agrarian, or horticultural. Nevertheless, the point should not be lost here: The argument is that technological innovations are said to be a driving force in history.

Sociology of Science

One of the many areas of specialization within sociology is the sociology of science. This subspecialty calls for the social scientific study of the activities of scientists as they do their research, in for example the laboratories; as they proclaim their findings; and as they produce or refute accepted truths. Several main, competing perspectives exist within the sociology of science. To understand the differences in perspectives it is first necessary to recognize that they embrace opposing views on the nature of science, and specifically they differ on the philosophical concept of what is real and how claims about reality are made, and how they are supported and accepted. For example, some perspectives claim that there is an objective reality that exists independent of our judgments about this reality. If a tree falls in the forest and no one is there to hear it, it still makes a sound, or so this perspective would claim. Others argue that whether there is or there is not such an objective reality, the only way of making claims about any reality is through a social process. People have to come to some sort of agreement about what claims are deemed true and what claims are seen as false. As such, one should study the social processes involved through which the claims about reality are made. Using conventional scientific principles and methods, we may, for example, develop and understanding of the workings of the world that is factually wrong but is nevertheless embraced and believed to be true. The famous historical case of Galileo and his rejection of the geo-centric theory of the solar system (also called the Ptolemaic model) illustrates this. The scientists in the Middle Ages built and used a geo-centric, scientific model of the solar system which had the earth, rather than the sun, at its center. Because this was factually wrong, but nevertheless was believed to be true by the scientists of the day, the scientists had to create ever increasingly complex models (however wrong) to account for their observations of the real movement of the planets in the sky. (For example, some theories claimed that the planets did not move around in a simple circular orbit, but instead they looped around and around in circles within the overall circular orbit. Ever increasing complicated numerical calculations were needed to fit the theory with the observation of the planets in the sky. The point is that the perspectives in the sociology of science differ from one another in the approach they take to such questions. If the sociologist assumes there is an objective reality that is independent of the observer, he or she will approach the social scientific study of science in a very different way than if the sociologist assumes otherwise. For example, if the sociologist of science assumes there is an objective reality that is independent of any claims about it, then he or she will likely examine how and why the scientists go about their work in ways that help or hinder their discoveries of real truths. On the other hand, if the sociologist of science assumes there is no such objective reality, or at least no such objective reality that can be known independent of the social processes which produces claimed truths, then he will focus on the social processes through which the scientists engage to produce agreements or disagreements of claimed truths or falsities.

The oldest approach in the sociology of science is what we here can call the traditional approach. This was the classic perspective embraced by scholars such as the

American sociologist Robert Merton in the mid-1900s. Merton sought to develop an approach that was based upon an assumption that there is an objective reality, and that science is defined in part by methods that lead to knowledge that is ever increasingly accurate.

Merton, following in the footsteps of Talcott Parsons and Emile Durkheim, embraced a structural functionalist perspective in understanding the social world. As such, he begins by asking what are the social conditions necessary for science to work effectively? He then identified four normative values that need to be present in a scientific (research) setting for science to work effectively. These are: universalism, communalism, disinterestedness, and organized skepticism.

Universalism is the normative value that calls upon the scientist to embrace the idea that scientists in their practices should embrace and employ practices that could be replicated anywhere at anytime. That is, the procedures and methods, and findings, of science should be able to be conducted at anytime and anywhere. The research should in effect be reproducible. Moreover, adhering to the universally accepted rules of science produces results are true irrespective of when and where they are produced.

Disinterestedness refers to the value of objectivity and freedom from bias. The scientist should not distort his or her understandings by any sort of moral or political or other preconceptions. He or she should also not manipulate the research to achieve one or another end, such as personal self-advancement or political causes. Instead, the scientist should embrace a value freedom and should act accordingly.

Communalism refers to the value of openly sharing the scientific practices and results of one's research. Researchers should present their work to others for evaluation and critique, and the researchers should embrace the open exchange of ideas and of criticisms. Researchers should reciprocate in kind.

242

Lastly, organized skepticism is the value that calls upon the scientific researcher to remain skeptical of all research findings. The scientist should not blindly accept (or reject) any research as the definitive statement on objective realities. Instead, the researcher should endlessly question research findings and their implications. Moreover, scientists do so in organized settings – in conference presentations, in classrooms, etc.

In addition, structural functionalists also see the task for the sociologist studying science to look at those social forces outside of the laboratory which contribute to or which impede this march of knowledge, particularly as these forces might prevent the four normative values from being realized in practice. For example, the bureaucratic forms of organization within which science operates might be structured in ways that allow for science to effectively work, or alternatively bureaucratic mechanisms may impede this work. If science operates for example in a context of a profit-making company, the bureaucratic demands of the organization might propel scientists to distort their research to conform to the desires of their bosses, e.g. to make a profit. In a similar way, Galileo was attacked by the religious authorities of the day – the leaders of the Roman Catholic church – because his scientific research on the movement of the planets challenged the authority of the Church, which claimed the geo-centric theory to be true. Similarly, when science becomes politicized, its effectiveness is deeply harmed. A classic case of this is the Lysenko affair in the Soviet Union. Lysenko was a government official in-charged of agricultural policy in the communist regime of the Soviet Union from the 1920s through the 1950s, when Stalin was ruling the country. Lysenko subscribed to a biological theory that conformed to the orthodox Marxist theory that was embraced by the rulers of the country. The rulers dictated that Marx's theory applied not only to political matters but to all matters related to the production of knowledge. Marxism was seen as a totalizing philosophy that could explain everything, not just political matters. Part of the Marxist doctrine was the concept of dialectics, which means that reality consists of contradictions, opposing forces. Reality is seen as dynamic and ever-changing. This is in contrast to the traditional view of the Western world which says that reality does not consist of contradictions, but instead consists of almost countless individual items and forces interacting with each other. Lysenko embraced the Marxist dialectical model and applied it to plant genetics. In other words, building upon the orthodox beliefs of the communist state, he scientifically claimed he could improve the genetics of plants, of corn, wheat, etc. through changing the environment within which the plants were raised. In short, he subscribed to a version of the "inheritance of acquired characteristics" (a model of genetics not unlike that developed by Jean-Baptiste Lamarck (1744-1829), a theory which has long since been debunked.). Thus, if you wish to improve the size of the wheat stalk, Lysenko said you could do so by changing the genetics of the wheat, and to do this one needs to change the environmental conditions in which the wheat is grown. That would produce better wheat genes and more and more wheat could be grown on an acre of land. He forced much of Soviet agriculture across the country to adapt this theory, and it was a disaster. Famine resulted. The theory was completely wrong. One cannot alter the genetic composition of a plant by subjecting the plant to one or another environmental condition. The theory is in opposition to the true theory of Darwin, which says that genes are not changed by environment. It was a sad case. But perhaps sadder is the fact that we see such misplaced political manipulations of science today in America. A classic example of this was when Trump's regime was in power it championed the denial of global warming. There is a consensus in the scientific community that global warming is a real phenomenon. Yet the Trump regime actively prevented government scientists form saying this and are actively preventing scientists from doing research that might further provide evidence of this. Again, this reflects the harmful impact of external forces, in this case politics, on the scientific process. Sociologists studying science from Merton's perspective or other like-minded perspectives would look at how and why conditions arise that lead to such unfortunate happenings. In sum, this traditional approach looks to understand the social forces that allow or impede good science from happening.

One of the implications of this approach for the sociology of science – the traditional, Mertonian approach – is that if external forces are prevented from interfering with the work of the scientists, then science will make steady progress. Science will move steadily toward an ever increasing understanding of how the natural world works. But other more recent approaches to the sociology of science question this very assumption about science works.

A very different sociological approach began with the publication in 1962 of Thomas Kuhn's book *The Structure of Scientific Revolutions*. Kuhn was a philosopher and historian of science, but his theory was embraced by, or influenced many, sociologists over the last sixty years. Kuhn argued against the traditional view of the history of science which says that science marches on incrementally, building steadily upon the truths already discovered. As more and more scientific knowledge is discovered, we come closer and closer to the truth about the workings of the world, according to the traditional view. This latter view was one that was embraced by Merton and others using the traditional approach. Kuhn, in contrast, says that the history of science is one characterized by long periods of scientific stability and growth interrupted by bursts of abrupt and radical change in basic scientific understandings and assumptions about the world. He calls these ruptures **scientific revolutions**. Radical breaks and changes in the way scientists see the world occurs in history of science, says Kuhn. We saw one of these earlier when discussing Galileo and the shift from a geo-centric view of the solar system in which it was scientifically claimed that the earth was at its center to a helio-centric view in which the sun is at the center. Galileo's claims were revolutionary.

Kuhn describes a historical process by which scientists establish a set of basic assumptions about how the world works and then build theories and conduct research using these assumptions. The research findings are fit into the conceptual model built upon the assumptions. He calls the overall perspective and set of assumptions used by scientists a **paradigm**. For example, before Galileo the scientific paradigm of the solar system claimed that the sun and all the planets revolved around the earth. Paradigms are in effect a way of viewing the world. The scientists go about testing the accepted theories and assumptions to see if the workings of the world conform or refute these. He calls this **normal science**. But Kuhn notes that what repeatedly happens in history is that scientists find **anomalies**. These are facts produced by scientific observation or experiment which cannot be accounted for by the exiting theories, or which contradict these theories. They are findings that do not quite fit the paradigms. In normal science, the scientists try to explain the anomalies away using their existing theories or simply accept that they cannot be explained, and file them away, or put them to the side, as troublesome though not fundamental problems. However, according to Kuhn under some circumstances the paradigm is challenged. Political or cultural or other such forces may force the scientist to address rather than to dismiss the anomalies. Or it could be that too many anomalies accumulate or they become too significant in scope to be ignored any longer. These things may contribute to the questioning of the paradigm. Normal science is then threatened. What then happens, often and repeatedly in history, is that the entire framework of assumptions and theories, i.e. the paradigm, comes crashing down and is rejected. The basic assumptions underlying the normal science are questioned and rejected. Then an entirely new and different set of assumptions are created, and a new normal scientific process occurs. A scientific revolution occurs. This is a paradigm shift, and the whole process begins anew.

Kuhn gives many examples of this process. One of these concerns the scientific explanation for what makes things burn. What was the scientific theory used before the modern era that accounts for how and why things some things burn and others do not, before we knew about such things as oxygen, and the like? In the 1600s the phlogiston theory was the scientific explanation used to explain how things caught fire and burned. Phlogiston was a theorized (and unseen) substance on materials that was needed for the substance to burn. Thus, some things burned because they had phlogiston; others did not burn because they did not have phlogiston. Wood had phlogiston; water did not. This theory has now been utterly rejected and replaced by a different one. (The phlogiston theory existed before the discovery of existence and nature of oxygen by the French chemist Antoine-Laurent Lavoisier and British scientist Joseph Priestly. Both proved the role of oxygen, rather than phlogiston, was a key to explaining how fire occurs and how things burn.) In the 1600s scientists built a set of theoretical ideas on the assumption of the existence of phlogiston, and conducted research based upon this. Anomalies piled up – things that could not be scientifically explained – and the phlogiston paradigm had to become increasingly complicated as a result. Eventually, the phlogiston paradigm was overthrown and replaced with the that one we now use.

Sociologists following Kuhn's lead then sought to understand the social conditions and social factors which allowed one or another scientific paradigm to maintain itself, and they sought to understand the forces which led to the crash of the particular paradigms. But by the 1970s a group of scholars – mostly sociologists and philosophers, in Britain, in France, and in the United States -- began to challenge both the traditional approach to the sociology of science as well as Kuhn's theory of scientific revolutions. These scholars developed a new approach which was associated in one way or another with what we may call the sociology of scientific knowledge (SSK)(though technically there are various theories related to this). Some of the notable scholars associated with this new approach are David Bloor, Bruno Latour, Barry Barnes, Steven Shapin, Harry Collins, and others. One of the more well known, and provocative studies in this tradition is Bruno Latour's *Laboratory Life* (1986), which was an observational study of the Pasteur laboratory in France. At the heart of SSK lies the claim that traditional (Mertonian-type) approaches as well as Kuhn's made a number of faulty assumptions. One of these was that scientists acted in purely rational (instrumentally rational) objective ways throughout the entire scientific process. That is, these approaches assumed the scientists were very much like machines or robots in their thoughts and actions rather than like complex human beings with moralities, values, emotions, passions, prejudices, pre-conceptualizations, etc. Cool, calculating, objective reasoning was deemed to be the only criteria used by the scientists in their decision making. The assumption of these traditional approaches was that the scientist in his or her laboratory was special and different from other people in their ways of acting. SSK starts with the assumption that scientists are humans and are not robots, and that their actions in the laboratory should not be seen as robotic but instead should be seen as common everyday behavior like anyone would engage in on a daily basis. Science, this approach, is not a mechanical process, nor is it a mystical one. It is not a special process somehow different from the rest of the world. When the researcher assumes the scientist is somehow special, SSK says the actual work of the scientist, in the laboratory for example, becomes misunderstood because it is a faulty assumption.

In addition, the SSK approach calls upon the sociologist studying scientists to use the same framework of understanding that the scientists themselves proclaim to be using in their day to day work. That is, sociologists studying scientists are scientists themselves and they should use the same methods. The sociologist should not impose their personal views or perspectives upon those they are studying. As such, the sociologist should objectively and impartially observe the scientist's actions using the assumption that the scientist is an object of scientific study of the sociologist. When the sociologist treats the scientist being observed as he or she goes about her work, for example in the laboratory, using the objective criteria of conventional scientific research, then the sociologist views the scientist as just another object in the field being studied. It is not assumed the scientist is acting in a mechanical, value free, and rational way. SSK makes no assumptions at all about why the scientist is acting as he or she does. It simply observes the scientist in an objective and unbiased way. Much as the chemist is a scientist objectively looking at causal relations in chemicals in test tubes, so the SSK sociologist looks at the scientist as a thing. He is not the motivating force. The task is not to understand his motives, as this would be unscientific, nor is it to assume the scientist has one or another set of motives. Scientists observe empirical facts. The task would be to make objective claims about causal relations of objective, observable facts.

In effect, the SSK approach reject the assumptions used in earlier approaches that scientists when they did their scientific work were somehow different, or special, than other people doing their work, or other people engaging in daily activities. Scientists in the traditional view are not impacted by social issues, by social or political arrangements, by moral considerations. Their views of the world are not shaped by anything other than rationality. They are seen as robotic. SSK rejects this belief and starts with an assumption that scientists are just like anyone else. They are not special or different. Together, these two things – challenging the pure objectivity of scientists' actions and decision making and calling for a symmetry between the formulas of explanation used by the scientists and the sociologists studying them, produce a framework that focuses in effect upon the social construction of scientific knowledge. SSK begins by bracketing any assumptions that scientists produce "truths" because this assumption distorts the scientific study of science. Instead, if one wishes to understand sociologically and scientifically, for example, how scientists came to believe that the sun revolved around the earth (i.e., the geo-centric view in the pre-Galileo era), then one must not assume that the geo-centric perspective was factually wrong. Knowledge is produced, not discovered. SSK (at least versions of it) argue that the actions and beliefs of the scientists are not governed by objective facts, but instead by social processes which produce socially constructed claims about objective facts. The task for the sociologist then is to look at the imperfections of the scientists reasonings and actions and to see how these combine with the scientists' claims of embracing objectivity in producing claims about the workings of the world.

SSK research has demonstrated that scientists often produce new findings based not on the methodological and systematic work of the scientist but instead based upon things such as chance. Similarly, SSK research shows that scientists sometimes if not often stumble upon discoveries and then in retrospect seek to legitimate their discoveries as logically derived.

This approach has produced numerous ethnographic studies of scientists working in laboratories. SSK often demonstrates that the research practices and findings are not the systematic, rational endeavor believed by many. Instead, some SSK research demonstrates that scientists make discoveries by chance. Other SSK research shows that scientists often reject findings that are not consistent with their beliefs and assumptions even when these findings were produced using accepted scientific practices. SSK research sometimes shows that the scientists in their pursuit to confirm their scientific beliefs skip or manipulate steps in the research process in order to produce findings consistent with their beliefs. In short, the SSK research shows that contrary to the popular image of science and contrary to the beliefs of many scientists, the scientific research process is not a simple, mechanical process involving objective, rational scientists acting like machines.

SSK is a highly complicated and intellectually rich approach. It is also highly controversial both within sociology and more so within the non-sociological scientific community. It is often harshly criticized and rejected by mainstream scientists, the latter who wish to claim that they conduct themselves in purely objective ways while doing science. Mainstream scientists often challenge SSK's claims about the social constructed nature of science and instead assert the objectivity of the world and its independence from social forces.

Technology, the Internet, Social Media: The Impacts on Self and Society

What is the growth of technology in society, and specifically the rise of the internet and social media, doing to the self and to social order? Does the internet and social media pose a threat to the self and social order, or do these things aid or enhance the self and social order? Are they oppressing or liberating? Are they good things or bad things? One need only look at the movies to understand the long-standing and significant concern about technology in general getting out of control and dominating and oppressing humans. From Frankenstein to the Matrix, from Space Odyssey 2001 to the Terminator, Hollywood has used this theme over and over and over again. But what do sociologists say about such things? The answer is that there is no one universally accepted understanding among sociologists and social scientists about the effects of technology, the internet, and social media on the self and social order. Some say we should be concerned and warn about the harms being done by technology; others say that these things are either liberating or simply changing our worlds without necessarily negatively doing so. Here we briefly look at a few arguments on both sides of the issue.

Numerous scholars have expressed concerns about technology. Forty years ago, Neil Postman wrote a little book titled *Amusing Ourselves to Death*. The book was written well before the age of the internet, but the argument is applicable today. Postman was concerned about what technological changes – and specifically television -- were doing to democracy and to the **public sphere** – the domain of life in which people interact and discuss things of shared social, political, or moral importance with strangers, in places such as the town square or the café. (There are three main domains of social life – the public sphere, the economic sphere, and the political sphere. Scholars sometimes argue that a meaningful democracy requires the existence of a vibrant public sphere, which is distinct from the political sphere – such as the process of voting, and the like.) Genuine democracy, as many commentators have noted, depends upon having a vibrant public sphere, and Postman's book was a concern about what the changes in media technology was doing to, or would be doing to, democracy. He saw technological development in the form of television as a threat to democracy. It was a threat because of the way that it affects the individual's consciousness. This in turn affects social relations. Postman focuses mainly upon the eighteen and nineteen hundreds and the shift from an American culture which relied upon reading to one that relies upon watching television to get its information and news about the world. He argues that the changing form of the media is the key to understanding.

He argues that the print media of newspapers and the like which were the main media technologies of the eighteen hundreds required the reader to be actively engaged. One has to take an active and evaluative stance when reading, when reading anything. One has to be psychologically engaged. Reading is an active process. The reader has to decide psychological to be focused on what he or she is reading. The reader must concentrate. He or she must focus his or her attention. Postman notes that most Americans, contrary to some opinions, in the eighteen hundreds were literate. America was a literate society. They could read and write, and they actively did so, readings, newspapers, political pamphlets, books, etc. This fosters, he argues, a genuine and vibrant democratic sensibility. It creates individuals who are actively oriented, critical, and engaged, and, Postman notes, it creates a type of people who discuss the issues of the day, discuss what they have read, with others.

However, when television appeared, this changed. Television requires a passive and unquestioning form of engagement. When watching television the viewer can fall asleep. He can daydream. His thought can wander aimlessly. We passively sit back and are amused at what we watch, at the endless stream of colorful, moving images on the screen. Moreover, we are controlled. For example, with laugh tracks we are told what to laugh at. We have become mindless consumers of the media as a result of the development of the television media, and this is a threat to genuine democratic sensibilities. We are encouraged to passively sit back and not to think. Television nurtures an unquestioned complacency, a selfish and uncritical posture of consumption, an orientation that is opposed to democratic sensibilities.

One can only speculate here how this argument might be applied to the internet and social media. But the reader can perhaps see how it might relate. We may be "actively" posting on Twitter or Facebook, but what does this mean? Is technology and specifically the internet and social media fostering a greater or less democratic citizenry? If one thinks, for example, about the algorithms used by social media sites to make one thing rather than another appear on one's Twitter feed, or other social media site, one realizes that you are being presented with ideas and views and images which are in agreement with your own perspective, your own moral, personal, political views. It does not foster a self-critical perspective, but reinforces complacent acceptance. This hardly fosters democratic sensibilities, or does so in a limited and skewed way. (This is not even to mention the manipulations of social media by various political and economic agents to sway the viewers' opinions.) Moreover, it has increasingly been argued, in light of current conditions in America, that the internet is nurturing and encouraging people to reaffirm their own beliefs rather than to challenge them. This works to heighten political and cultural divisions in society. (One thinks here perhaps of the insanity of the QAnon phenomena, where the mythical online persona of QAnon spouted this crazy conservative theories with no basis in reality only to have his conservative readers lap it up and parrot the insanity.)

Equally as critical of technology, but from a different perspective, the sociologist Robert Putnam argued in his book *Bowling Alone* (2000) that there has been a sharp decline in the amount that Americans are participating in the public sphere in recent decades. Putnam's book is based upon his extensive research on changes in participation and membership rates in dozens and dozens of voluntary associations in America. **Voluntary associations** are civic groups, clubs and organizations that people voluntarily belong to. Examples include bowling leagues, the American Legion, the Elks Club, The Shriners, bowling leagues, little leagues, parent teacher associations, the Red Cross, Greenpeace, churches, and religious organizations, among thousands of others.

Voluntary associations are part of **civil society**, or the civil sphere. Many sociologists have argued that there are three main public component parts to democratic societies – the economic sphere, the political sphere, and the civil society. In the economic sphere, social actors engage with one another largely as consumers and producers. In the political sphere, social actors engage as citizens. In civil society, social actors engage with each other voluntarily or informally in and through public settings and organizations. It has long been argued that to have a meaningful and enduring democratic society, one needs to have a meaningful civil society. This provides the informal connectedness and social involvement that is arguably needed to have a meaningful democracy.

It has long been argued by scholars from Tocqueville in his important work *Democracy in America* to Durkheim, that voluntary associations are a key component of the public sphere, and are vital and necessary to sustaining a meaningful democracy. Putnam shows through his research that there has been a sharp decline in participation in voluntary associations across the board from the 1960s through 2000. Membership and participation in civic organizations from bowling leagues to the Knights of Columbus, he argues, have declined precipitously. He attributes this decline at least in part to technological developments, and specifically to the mass media. His research was based on a time, not long ago, before the age of the internet and social media. But like Postman's argument noted above, one could readily apply the same logic toward an understanding of current circumstances: Technology may be contributing to a decline in civic engagement, and this could pose a threat to the maintenance of democracy.

Another argument that echoes the concerns of Postman and Putnam is that put forth by the scholars of what is called the **Frankfurt School**, which emerged in the 1920s and continued through the 1960s. The Frankfurt School is the informal name of the Institute for Social Research which began in Germany in the 1920s. (The Institute continues to exist today, but the theorizing advanced today is a far cry from what was advanced by the Frankfurt School itself.) While there were dozens of intellectuals associated with this school, the three most well-known are Theodor Adorno, Max Horkheimer, and Herbert Marcuse. Most of its members were Jewish and (loosely defined) Marxists intellectuals. All of these groups – Jews, intellectuals, Marxists – were hated by Hitler and the Nazis who came to power in Germany in the 1930s. As a result, the Frankfurt School members moved to the United States around the time of World War Two to flee Nazi persecution. Many remained in America after the war, though some returned to Germany. (The Institute reconstituted itself in Germany after the war and continues today.) In America the Frankfurt School members, notably, Marcuse, had a significant influence upon student protest leaders in the turbulent 1960s.

The Frankfurt School theorists developed a sociological theory which came to be called **critical theory**. Critical theory is a fusion of ideas found in Marx, Weber and Freud, the psychoanalyst. Members of the Frankfurt School saw the fusion of capitalism and rationality as a potent and extremely harmful force. It was harmful to the individual psychological well-being as humans; it was harmful to social relations; it was harmful to the planet. They were concerned about the growth of technology and its subservience to capitalism, and were concerned about what this was doing to individual's abilities to think critically about the world. Not unlike Postman, the Frankfurt School saw technology in the service of capitalism turning people into passive consumers rather than active citizens. In addition, they saw the fusion of technology in capitalism with the industrialization of consumer culture as also doing the same. Specifically, they were concerned about the **culture industry**. The culture industry refers to the production of popular culture, from music to movies to fashion, being fused with the logic of technological capitalism. Specifically, much like things are produced in factories, so to cultural products, like movies and music, are increasing being produced in factory-like settings, such as Hollywood. The whole project of the culture industry is to make the consumer happy and content. It is not oriented toward culturally enriching the human experience. The Frankfurt School argues that this serves to prevent people from being critical and from accurately seeing the harmful things that capitalism does.

It is harmful they say in many ways. One of these is what it is doing to the individual self. The focus in capitalism on instrumental rationality; on the emphasis of quantity over quality; on rampant consumerism; and the elevation of the exchange relation (e.g. buying and selling) as the dominant mode of interacting, all conspire to turn individuals into passive and happy, and mindless, consumers - machines of consumption. But this passiveness and happiness hides the harm that is actually occurring to the individual. Rational capitalism was negating humanity. The humanity of the individual is being drained as he or she is becoming more like a machine, a consuming machine, or a sheep, or a mechanical sheep. The individual in modern, rational capitalism, the Frankfurt School says, is losing his or her humanity, and this is a threat to the integrity of the individual (and also poses larger social problems, from environmental degradation to the possibilities of nuclear war). And it is not simply the individual that is said to be degraded by capitalism. So too social relations are equally harmed. Social relations, which should be based upon humanistic sentiments and values have largely been replaced by forms of relationships dictated by the market and exchange. We interact with others, whether in the market or in school or with friends in terms of "what's in it for me," just as one buys and sells things in the marketplace. Importantly, the Frankfurt School theorists argue that all of this harm is not readily seen by people because people are so immersed and happy in their consumption. So the harmful and destructive system of capitalism is allowed to continue unabated. The Frankfurt School theorists were writing well before the age of the internet. Yet their arguments could still be applied today.

Many other scholars take a very different view than those described above. Many see the advances in technology, and specifically the growth of the internet and social media, as enhancing the individual, social relations, and society in general. For example, Lee Raine and Barry Wellman in their book *Networked* (2014) present an overview of the current research on such things as they apply to social media and the internet, and they argue that the internet and social media have not harmed the self and social relations, as people following the arguments made by the Frankfurt School, Putman, Postman, and others claim. Instead, Raine and Wellman argue that we have a **new social operating system**, which changes the character of how selves are constituted and which changes the character of social relations, but does so in a way that is different or even better than that of earlier times. The new social operating system, anchored by social media, is one through which we now engage more in and through *networks* rather than in and through groups or organizations, which was the old forms of organized interaction. The new social operating system is fundamentally a network, and it has four characteristics. They write, "Like most computer operating systems and all mobile systems, the social network operating system is *personal* – the individual is at the autonomous center just as she is reaching out from her computer; *multiuser* – people are interacting with numerous diverse others; *multitasking* – people are doing several things; and *multithreaded* – they are doing them more or less simultaneously" (p. 7). Raine and Wellman argue that the individual self is not being degraded or isolated as the result of the internet and social media. We are not "bowling alone." Instead, they argue that a new form of individualism has arisen, a **networked individualism**, through which people maintain a network of connections with people near and far across social media. People draw upon these networks -- of people they know and do not know, for various things, from solving personal problems to discussions of things. In short, the nature of our social connectedness has fundamentally changed, but it has not diminished with these new technologies.

Others have argued that the internet and social media have, and will, fundamentally alter the nature of the public sphere for the better. Zeynep Tufekci, for example, in her study of recent social movement says a new **networked public sphere** has arisen, and this has altered the conditions of democracy and of protests. A networked public sphere is a new form of the public sphere. It is one whereby individuals can gather not only in public places such as coffee houses and churches to discuss important matters of the day, but they can also gather and discuss the same things in cyberspace, and this has important consequences. Clay Shirky (2008) in his book *Here Comes Everybody* says the new technologies foster greater, not less, democracy and participation. Shirky argues that the horizontalism of the internet and social media are more conducive and supportive of democracy and active citizen engagement than more traditional forms of engagement which tend to be through vertical or hierarchical organizations. Hierarchical organizations are top down. There is a leader or a boss, and there are people below him or her, and there are people below that person, etc. Horizontalism is the opposite. It is the idea of pure democracy, where everyone participating in some discussion or event or decision has an equal voice as everyone else. There are no leaders. If you a participating on Twitter, you can stop at any time. Shirky says this is empowering and is a strong democratic force. He specifically is optimistic that the internet and social media will foster social engagement, social (protest) movements and collective actions oriented toward a more democratic and equal political system. (Others have taken a different view about the role of the internet and social media in social movements. Turfekci in her book *Twitter and Tear Gas* (2017) shows how these things can aid movements while at the same time they can harm movements. She notes, for example, that the internet and social media facilitate rapid organization. One can create a protest almost overnight via Twitter. But such protests are fleeting because they have not laid the solid organizational forms needed to sustain them. Similarly, she notes that as much as the new technologies can facilitate social movements, they also have features that can impede them. The various technologies of the social media platforms are structured in different ways, and some of these may be more helpful to protests than others. In addition, Turfekci describes the ways that governments now have developed ways of using the internet and social media to defeat protests, for example by sending out disinformation.

Technology and Social Control

Echoing the likes of Putman and Postman, many scholars have expressed many other concerns about the growth of technology, and these concerns seem particularly relevant to the spread of the internet and social media. Many have noted with concern the present realities and future possibilities of large and powerful entities, whether these are governmental or private corporations, having great power to control individuals, groups, and the entire society, and many have expressed concerns that these entities are or will be oriented to furthering their own narrow, private interests rather than furthering the general welfare of the society. Social control through the use of the internet and social media happens in various ways with varying outcomes. The control might be on the individual and his or on her way of thinking or being, or it might be upon the community at large. Governments or corporations that believe themselves to be threatened by internal forces of opposition, for example by social movements, may employ tactics through the internet and social media to silence or eliminate these forces. Turfekci notes in *Twitter and Tear Gas* that authoritarian governments in places such as Egypt in 2011 had a relatively unsophisticated understanding of these things, and responded to their use by Egyptian protesters by attempting to shut down the internet in Egypt and elsewhere. But such crude attempts did not work, and governments and corporate entities have developed far more sophisticated mechanisms to silence, contain, manipulate, or eliminate oppositions movements. For example, the spread of disinformation and lies via Twitter or Facebook is a tactic used by powerful groups today. Some governments have agencies that activity work to send misinformation (or disinformation) and lies on social media to create confusion amongst the opposition. The intent is to sow confusion and to fragment the opposition, to render the opposition impotent.

Whether technologies, such as the internet and social media, are by their nature helpful or harmful to society is a matter of debate. At the most extreme side of the debate which sees technology as fundamental a harmful thing we find **luddites**. The term luddite refers to anyone who is opposed to technology and who sees it as the fundamental source of all major problems in the world. The term comes from followers of an early nineteenth century man Ned Ludd in England who saw the emergence and spread of factories (based upon technology) as ruining the social life of the then rural, farm-based populace. In response, the luddites tried to burn down the factories. On the other hand, many believe that these technologies are in themselves, by their nature, neither inherently good or bad, and that they can be used to further social life, and specifically they could potentially further democracy and the growth of a genuine public sphere. Jurgen Habermas, a student of the Frankfurt School, makes such an argument. He argues that capitalism and instrumental rationality have negatively affected the social world, but that technologies might be used, under the right conditions, i.e. under the conditions of genuine public control rather than under the control of capitalist agents, to foster what he calls **communicative action**, action which is based upon genuine interpersonal interactions, where the values of sincerity, truthfulness, and trust are embraced and championed. It is conceivable that the internet might foster such things and might be used to foster genuine democracy. It is conceivable that the internet might be restructured in ways to facilitate such things. It is questionable whether it is now structured in such a way.

Chapter Ten: Scientific Racism

In Chapter Two of this book, I argued that the concept of racism in public consciousness and in public behaviors today is very muddy, unclear, ambiguous. The concept as it is used in public consciousness and public behaviors today is problematic. It is problematic from a social scientific sense. It is problematic from a political and moral sense. It is problematic for no other reason than it obfuscates rather than clarifies. It is a distraction that does not readily allow for a genuine, democratic discussion of the issue. Two issues were discussed in that chapter. One concerns how the politically liberal use of the term, encased in concept of systemic racism, or some such term, wrongfully takes the concept from the sociological level – where it legitimately belongs – to the psychological, individual level – where it does not. This form of reasoning tends to lead to such things as "unconscious racism" to legitimate this formulation of racism. Yet as I noted earlier, once one enters the realm of the unconscious, one leaves scientific reasoning behind. Yet once one moves from the sociological to the psychological, one leaves reality behind. On the other hand, conservatives today often believe and often convince themselves they are not racist when mounds of empirical data suggest otherwise. There is a denial in their minds that they are racist, when it is arguably the case that many in fact are racist.

Underlying many conservative beliefs about race and racism lies the concept of scientific racism. While most conservatives who harbor racist beliefs undoubtedly are not very familiar with the details of scientific racism, and those that are have selectively ignored the wealth of criticisms raised against it, they nevertheless have some inkling that there is and was something called scientific racism that supports their beliefs. That is, they believe that races are biological distinct groups and some races are superior by genetics – in terms of intelligence, character, etc. – than others, and they believe that science supports their position.

In this chapter, we examine a bit more fully the concept of scientific racism -- its history and its problems. Racism is a belief that one racial group is somehow inferior to another. Racism can take two forms. One form is rooted in culture. This form claims that the culture – the traditions, beliefs, practices, moralities, etc. – of one group is inferior to the culture of another. As culture is malleable, it can and does change. This suggests that the problem or faults with a supposedly inferior group can be effectively addressed and changed by changing the culture of that group. If one can change the believes, values, etc. of a group, then the argument goes you can change the behaviors of the group that keep the group in an inferior position to address the issue of inequalities. This chapter is not concerned with that form of racism. The second form is more insidious and more vile. This second form has led the world into nightmares – most glaringly World War Two and the Nazis -- and has the capability of leading the world again into such situations. This second form believes that racial groups differ genetically, biologically, in terms of their intelligence, morality, or other personal attributes. One race is said to be smarter, more moral than another due to its genetic composition. In the classic form in the Western tradition it would be that white people see black people as having less intelligence and as having faulty character structures by nature, by biology, by genetics than whites. In the last two hundred years science has been used by some to advance and to legitimate the claim that one race is biologically inferior to another. This second form of scientific racism, rooted in biology, is the subject of this essay. When I use the term scientific racism through the following pages, I am here referring to the biological form. Scientific racism is the use of science (and pseudo-science) to claim that races differ in their socially significant genetic composition such that one race is genetically superior to another. As I argue below, scientific racism is a morally repugnant position. But what is a sociologist – a social *scientist* -- today to do with such claims? How should or can a sociologist today understand scientific racism?

This matter was addressed at least in part in Chapter Two. Here we focus specifically on the history of scientific racism. This essay presents a brief overview of the history of scientific racism and hopes to show that it is not possible to disentangle the moral and political from the scientific on this matter, and that the evidence used by scientific racists to claim that one race is biologically superior to another is not persuasive from a scientific perspective, from a political perspective and from a moral perspective. As such, it is argued here that scientific racist claims that one or another race is biologically inferior, i.e. has less innate intelligence than another, necessarily are not scientific in the genuine sense of the word, but instead are really political and moral claims, and any claims that they are indeed scientific, in the authentic use of the term, must be questioned.

A major intellectual problem confronts those who wish to argue that race and specifically the supposed biological differences between races have no social significance, e.g. intelligence, character, etc., and that racist scientific studies of inequalities between races should not be allowed. That is, those arguing against scientific racist claims are confronted with conceptual problems they must address if their critical arguments are to be deemed legitimate. One problem is that a supposedly basic and universal value of the modern world is that there is and should be free and unfettered inquiry on any and all matters. Science should be allowed to do its work no matter what the outcome, no matter where it leads. Scholars should be allowed, the argument goes, to study anything they wish to, as long as they are committed to the shared values of conventional science (e.g. objectivity, making assessments of causal relations based upon observations of empirical facts, etc.). As such, if a racist scientist wishes to conduct scientific studies related to the supposed biological differences between races – and specifically on such social impactful characteristics as intelligence (e.g., IQ – Intelligence Quotient) and morality, then he should be allowed to do so, at least if one is to conform to the ethic of free scientific inquiry today.

On its surface, this seems eminently reasonable. Yet reality interferes with such a position time and again. Reality is more complex than such a simplistic perspective would like us to believe. It is not possible to extract this value commitment – free and open inquiry – from the horrors of racism, from the repugnant moral and political manipulations that have been done and continue to be done in the name of science to justify the oppression of one racial group by another. One cannot disentangle the moral and political from the scientific in this matter. This then leads to the question or problem: How is one to determine whether one or another topic is allowed to be studied scientifically? Who should decide such matters? Ideally, the universities are the place in which free and open scientific inquiry should occur, but a quick review of history shows that it never was and is not now such a place (see below). That is a goal, an aspiration. What is and what is not studied is determined by complex social, political, cultural, and moral contexts. Nevertheless, it could be argued that we should embrace the values of free and open scientific inquiry no matter where it leads, even if it leads to scientific racism. Such claims are wrongheaded, if not disingenuous. The reality is again that decision making about what is or is not appropriate to study is determined by the social, political, cultural, and moral context. I could not get a research grant, for example, from the federal government if I stated that I wished to conduct a Marxist study of something or other. I also could not get a grant from any of the private foundations (see below), such as the Ford Foundation or others, if I announced that I wished to conduct a Marxist study. (By Marxism I am not suggesting doing a study that is not objective and scientific. I am suggesting the opposite. The point is, however, that certain forms of scholarship are allowed, and others are not allowed. It is a political and economic decision. Similarly, I have little doubt that I would experience great resistance, and likely would simply be denied outright, if I wished to study the psychopathology (mental illness) of greed -- the sickness of billionaires -- with the assumption that billionaires and Wall Street stock traders are morally evil, or mentally ill, or suffer fundamental character flaws by birth. Is there something wrong with Wall Street stock traders? Is this a legitimate inquiry? One might also ask whether a critical scholar, perhaps a Marxist but not necessarily so, wished to study the inner workings of a large corporation, say Facebook, or the U.S. military, or the educational processes at West Point, or prisons, would be allowed to do such studies. Clearly, the answer is that such a scholar would not be allowed to conduct these studies. History is filled with examples of powerful forces dictating and shaping scientific inquiry, molding it to their liking. These are simply just a very few examples of how political and economic considerations necessarily impact social science research. To pretend that factors like these do not significantly impact social science is fanciful. As such, for those claiming that scholars should be allowed to conduct scientific racist studies, I would propose that laws and policies be put into place to allow scholars to do some of the other studies suggested above before we even consider allowing scientific racist studies.

One last point bears noting here: As we see below the scientists who have conducted scientific racist studies both in history and in the contemporary era have almost all been members of the dominant groups in society, most notably almost all in the United States have been members of the WASP – White Anglo-Saxon Protestant group. (Today, we see some white ethnics as well as some Jews also embracing scientific racism. Not coincidentally, as noted in Chapters One and Two, the dominant group in America has transformed from WASPs to whites.) If one wishes to allow scientific racist studies to be conducted one will also have to address the various problems, discussed below, attendant with allowing members of the dominant group to conduct scientific research designed to convince people of their legitimate right to be dominant (see below).

None of this negates the value of the commitment to free and open inquiry. It does however say that anyone participating in such discussions should recognize the complexities involved in the debate. This opens up the possibility of endless relativism and a deep distrust of all science, at least all science pertaining to anything social. We should vociferously reject any and all roads that lead down the road to absolute relativism and to a distrust of science (whether this relates to global warming, COVID-19, or any other scientific topic). The task at hand is to balance a commitment to objective, free scientific inquiry and a recognition of the social influences upon science, at least at some times. (The task at hand in practical terms is to build institutions that are the least influenced by biased interests of money, politics, etc. Privately funded think tanks, for example, which have been so central to the production of scientific racism, are funded by wealthy patrons to produce findings that accord with these patrons' sensibilities.) To claim that scientific racism – either the legitimacy of its findings or its legitimacy as a scientific enterprise -- can or should be understood without recognizing the social context in which these claims are raised, upon review, is untenable. (And indeed, this is one of the themes of this book (see Chapter Two): America has reached a point of irresolvable paradoxes related to all of this that must be confronted.)

Perhaps one of the strongest oppositions to the claims of scientific racism, e.g. that one race is genetically superior to another, lies in a review of the historical record of this type of research, and in the recent research challenging on logical and scientific grounds the claims made by the scientific racists.

To understand this, we should take a brief look at this history of scientific racism. To begin we need to recognize the incredible complexities in defining the basic terms used in any effort to study racial differences and racial inequalities from a scientific perspective. After all, one cannot legitimately study something unless one has clear definitions of what it is he or she is studying. One cannot study gravity scientifically unless one clearly defines what gravity is. Yet the very concepts used in scientific racism are riddled with fundamental conceptual problems of definition. Two key concepts are race and intelligence (IQ). These two problematic concepts lie at the heart of some if not much of contemporary scientific racism. At first glance the concept of race might seem quite obvious, but it is not. It is riddled with ambiguities and contradictions, and its meaning changes in history. We might wish to say that race is a group that shares a long-standing genetic heritage. Thus, if your ancestors are from Europe, historically speaking, you might wish to say you are white or "Caucasian." So using this definition, how many races are there? Are there five or six? Fewer or more? Problems abound with clearly defining race. What race are people from Arab countries in north Africa, places like Algeria and Egypt? Are they "negro" or white? Are they a race that is different from either? Then if we look at the current, popular notions of race, more problems arise. What race are people from Southern Italy? Of course, most would say white, but why is it appropriate to put them in the same racial category as people from Sweden or Norway – light skinned, blond hair blue eyed people? Aren't people from Southern Italy more similar biologically to people from the

Arab countries in north Africa; they are Mediterranean. (Scientific racists of the late 1800s and early 1900s knew this problem quite well, and as a result many of them developed a racial typology that had several distinct racial groups within Europe, e.g. the Germanic northern – blond haired, blue eyed -- Europeans, the Latins from the south, the "Alpine" people from Austria and Switzerland, the Slavic people from Eastern Europe, etc. But this opens up a whole new set of problems. For example, couldn't one make even more local races using this model? Moreover, in light of the earlier claims that there are several distinct races within Europe, we should ask how and why did this idea change? Today, we generally do not think of people from Austria and Switzerland as being from a different race than people from Norway or Spain, but in the early 1900s, it was not uncommon for scientific racist to make such claims. So why did this change? Why do we no longer think this way? Was the change due to changes in scientific understandings? No. The change was due to historical, political, and cultural changes.)

The problems of defining race clearly and unequivocally abound. What physical features should one use to determine race? Should we use eye color or skin color? Or the curliness of hair? Height? Shape of head? One logical issue or problem that is sometimes raised against the scientific concept of race is the reality that there is more diversity within any one race than there is between races. The logical legitimacy of a concept requires the opposite. If one goes from east to west Africa, people look different. If one goes from north to south Europe, people look different. Conceptually, this renders the validity of the concept false.

When one looks at the science of genetics one also finds that human beings of all races share almost all of the same genetic makeup. This was one of the claims made by the prominent evolutionary geneticist R.C. Lewontin (1984) in his critique of scientific racism. Lewontin criticized scientific racist claims for a whole host of scientific reasons, ultimately showing that scientific racism from a scientific perspective is deeply flawed. Among other things, Lewontin shows that the genetic composition of all humans is almost identical. That is members of different races share almost all of the same genetics. In sum, the differences in genetic makeup between races is tiny. And these differences are unrelated to putatively, socially significant factors such as intelligence. Lewontin also argues, as many other have, that the differences in genetic makeup within any one race is significantly greater than the differences in genetic makeup between races, thus calling into question the basis of scientific racist claims.

The concept of intelligence, a cornerstone of scientific racism in the contemporary era, is even more fraught with difficulties than is the concept of race. Below I will cover the historical evolution of scientific racism, and I will say more there about measuring intelligence. Here a few brief words can be said. The scientific concept of intelligence and the measuring of intelligence is a uniquely modern thing. It has only been around for less than two hundred years, and it has only been since the late 1800s that some scientists have sought to capture intelligence through science. But any discussion of the science of intelligence and the scientific measurement of intelligence must answer many questions, questions like: What is intelligence? Is it fixed by biology and genetics, or can and does it change in one's lifetime? Is one born with a level of intelligence that fundamentally does not change throughout one's life, or can intelligence be affected by the social (or natural) environment? Is intelligence knowing facts, or is it the ability or capacity to manipulate abstract concepts in sophisticated ways? Is there one type of intelligence or more? How can we measure it? Can we use one number to indicate intelligence? Does it make sense to do so? The very definition of intelligence is problematic and ambiguous. If we define intelligence, for example, as the ability to use abstract reasoning to solve problems, then is a person who is brilliant at math – for example, Sheldon Cooper (from the television show The Big Bang Theory) who is incapable of understanding sarcasm or the nuances of social interactions intelligent or even capable of navigating the demands of daily life on one's own? The definition I just gave itself is fraught with problems. For example, the definition just given of intelligence involves problem solving, but what is a "problem"? Are we discussing practical problem solving such as fixing a car or winning a football game, or are we talking about solving the problems of understanding the origins of the universe, or the limits of the universe, or why evil and suffering exist? What is "abstract reasoning"? Did the great jazz saxophonist Charlie Parker – the originator of the Bebop style of jazz -- use abstract reasoning when he put together his amazing, and sophisticated, be-bop jazz riffs? What about the problem of the meaning of life? What is the meaning of life? If you "know" the answer and I do not, are you more intelligent than I am? This leads to the question or problem of whether there are one or more types of intelligence. The psychologist Howard Gardner many decades ago argued that there are many distinct types of intelligence (e.g. emotional, kinesthetic, logical, etc.). Some have argued there are even hundreds of forms of intelligence. And what about the fixity of intelligence? Is one born smart or dumb, and is this condition permanent or it is subject to change because of one's environment? Is biology destiny? (Scientific racist such as Charles Murray – see below – argue that intelligence is largely fixed and cannot be changed after a child becomes seven years old or so. The person's IQ, it is argued, stays about the same from age seven until death. This contradicts many pieces of research which show otherwise. For example, the average IQ score of African Americans has risen significantly in the last sixty years. How is it possible for this group's IQ to change over decades if it is fixed by genetics? We return to this below.) The measurement of intelligence is also a major problem. Is it possible to place one number, as the standard IQ (intelligence tests) tests do, on intelligence? Is intelligence no different than height? We can put a number on height, but does it make the same sense to do so for intelligence? The problems go on and on.

Most if not all of these issues related to the conceptual problems revolving around intelligence are largely recognized by recent scientific racists. For example, a prominent example of scientific racism is the book *The Bell Curve* (1994) written by Charles Murray and Richard Herrnstein. The authors respond to most of the problems noted above, though their responses, at least to this writer, are less than persuasive. In *The Bell Curve*, for example, they rely upon SAT scores (Scholastic Aptitude Test scores) as a proxy for IQ testing to make their argument about the biological or genetic intellectual inferiority of African Americans. But the SAT scores are not designed to measure intelligence. The SAT are clearly not a measure of innate intelligence. The company that puts out the SAT scores says the SATs are not designed to measure intelligence, particularly innate intelligence. The company that creates and administers the SAT says that the SAT only measures the likelihood of future success in college. (Much of the SAT is based upon what a student has learned. For example, there is a vocabulary section.) The vast majority of psychologists and scholars of mental measurement note that the SAT is designed not to measure intelligence. It is illegitimate to use these tests as somehow indicative of innate genetic potential. (For example, knowledge of vocabulary is certainly not innate, rather it is learned.) (The authors counter that it is legitimate to use the SAT as a proxy for IQ because the two are correlated.) In a similar way, the authors dismiss the claims that there are many different types of intelligence by claiming that these differences are highly correlated, thus rendering the differences mute. For example, they suggest that if one scores high on kinetic intelligence (control over one's body, e.g. athletics), then one will likely score high on mathematical intelligence. But the differences are not as highly correlated to legitimately dismiss them as meaningful or legitimate.

In short, neither the concept of race nor the concept of intelligence, particularly as a fixed biological entity, is sufficiently unambiguous to allow scientists to draw scientific conclusions about them, and certainly are not sufficiently unambiguous to draw conclusions about the relations of race and intelligence. (As we discuss below, Herrnstein and Murray do not argue that IQ is completely inherited. They say that approximately 60 percent of intelligence is inherited, the rest is shaped by environment.)

History

Scientific racism should be understood historically, and I argue here it must be understood historically if one wishes to honestly and truly understand its reality today. Ignoring history here massively misunderstands this concept. When we look at history, it seems rather clear that the social context has greatly influenced the production and reception of scientific racism. We can identify several distinct periods of scientific racism in the Western world, and in the United States in particular. The first period was during the Enlightenment (also known as The Age of Reason, which lasted roughly from 1600 through 1800 in Western Europe). The second period spans the nineteenth century. The third covers the late 1800s through the 1920s, what historians often refer to as the Progressive Era. The fourth period emerged in the 1960s and1970s and has expanded into the present. We discuss each of these in turn.

The first period in which modern scientific racism begins to emerge was in the Enlightenment. The

Enlightenment was a period of the birth of the modern ways of thinking. Philosophers through Europe challenged the then accepted understandings of the way the world worked. This accepted understanding –prior to the Enlightenment -- was that things such as tradition and religion governed one's understanding of what was true and proper – in the scientific world, in the political world, in the social world, in the economic world. Adherence to the dictates of the Church and the aristocracy, and their traditions and religious sensibilities governed people's sense of what was true and proper. Scientists in the Middle Ages, for example, said the sun revolved around the earth; the earth was the center of the universe. This claim was advocated by the Roman Catholic Church, which was dominant at the time. All of this changed with the Enlightenment. Enlightenment scholars rejected, on logical grounds, basing economics, politics, science on tradition and religion, and instead sought to elevate Reason (really rationality) to the prominent place. Objective, unbiased applications of reason would reveal the hidden secrets of nature and would make the world a better place. Reason should be the guiding light of science, of politics, etc., and not tradition or religion. And modern science is rooted deeply in an embrace of Reason over tradition, of Reason over religion. Modern science was born out of this sensibility and has grown enormously ever since.

Something else of equal importance was occurring during the 1600 and 1700s. This was the period of mass colonization, following the age of exploration, which began at that time but continued and spread through the subsequent centuries (until the decolonization in the twentieth century, and the accompanying growth of imperialism). The European powers – first Great Britain, Spain, and France, and then France and Great Britain, but also many others – set out with their boats and guns (and germs) and conquered much of the world. Spain conquered Latin America; Great Britain conquered most of North America; France and Great

Britain divided up much of Africa; Great Britain eventually (and later) conquered China and India. (The scope and rapidity by which this occurred was striking – from a handful of Spaniards conquering the Mexican (Aztec) empire in the early 1500s to the British conquering the far, far larger Chinese society in the twentieth century.) The reasons why Europeans were able to conquer so much of the world are complex and cannot be enumerated here. Suffice to say it was in partly related to the fruits of the Enlightenment. The Europeans had the advantages of science and technology on their side. But how were they able to legitimate to themselves and to others these conquests and how could they convince themselves of the rightfulness – moral or otherwise -- of world domination. Religion – particularly Christianity (and specifically Roman Catholicism) -- was used toward that end in the earlier years of colonization, in the 1500 and 1600s. But religion could only serve this end to a limited extent. In the age of reason, in the age of science and technology, of increasing change, the dominant Europeans were led toward science to morally justify their dominance. The dominants were compelled to justify – to others and to themselves – the rightful position as dominants. Scientific racism was one of the tools or techniques employed toward that end. But during this period, it remained more of a theoretical stance than an empirical practice. We do not see scientist to any great extent engaging in research to prove their racist ideas until the 1800s.

It was in the 1800s that scientists and others in Europe and America expounded upon the ideas of scientific racism. These writings spanned the period prior to the acceptance of Darwinian evolutionary theory, i.e. prior to the 1860s, and into the decades after Darwin's theorizing began to be accepted, i.e. in the late 1800s and early 1900s. I briefly describe here just a few of the more well-known scientific racists of the 1800s. Some of these were scientists, others were writers who popularized the science. One of the more influential scientific racist of the time was Louis Agassiz (1807-1873). Agassiz was a Swiss-born medical doctor and scientist who spent his career doing research on various aspects of natural history, including evolutionary biology. He immigrated to the United States where he taught at Harvard and elsewhere. One of his theoretical ideas associated with early forms of racism was polygenism. This was a pre-Darwinian idea of evolution (see Chapters One and Two for more discussion of the impact of pre-Darwinian ideas and Darwinian ideas.) Polygenism is the idea that all humans did not descent from the same group of first humans, but instead the different races descended independently from different origins. (To use the religious metaphor, polygenism says there was not one Adam and one Eve, but the different races each had their own Adams and Eves.) In keeping with his views of natural history, Agassiz said the different races (i.e. European, African, and Asian) evolved differently and independently, and the evolution occurred in relation to the actual physical or natural environments of the different races. For example, the black race in Africa evolved as it did due to climate and environmental conditions of Africa, and the white race in Europe evolved as it did due to the climate and environmental conditions of Europe. Ultimately, he concluded that the Europeans were a superior race. (Some scholars disagree with this assessment and claim that his Christian sensibility actually viewed all races of equal value under God. But his writings themselves belie a deep racism (see Gould 1981). Samuel George Morton (1799-1851) was another highly influential scientific racist. Morton was a Philadelphia medical doctor who conducted numerous studies on the size of skulls and the brain capacity of the skulls. He compared the cranium of different races with the intent on demonstrating the natural and legitimate superiority of Europeans and the natural and legitimate inferiority of other races, most notably Africans. He collected hundreds of skulls and tried to measure the brain capacities and size of the brain by filling the empty skulls with pellets and the like. He tabulated his results. He also embraced and championed polygenism. He routinely found that Europeans had larger skulls than other races, from Chinese to Africans. However, upon review, one finds major problems with his research. Gould (1981) went back and re-examined Morton's data and found that Morton research was driven by a priori conclusions. When Morton's research findings ran counter to his assumptions of racial inequalities, Morton rejected them. Gould concluded, "In short, and to put it bluntly, Morton's summaries are a patchwork of fudging and finagling in the clear interest of controlling a priori convictions" (1981, p. 54). (More recently, a study which re-examined Gould's examination of Morton's work concluded that at least some of Gould's claims are not correct.)

Another important and influential scientific racist was Paul Broca (1824-1880), an American medical doctor and physical anthropologist. Broca rejected the theory of polygenism of some of the other earlier scientists and instead embraced a monogenism, i.e. the claim that all races descended from the same group (i.e., Adam and Eve). He conducted numerous studies measuring the skeletons and craniums of dead people from various races. Gould analyzed Broca's work much as he did Morton's and found similar flaws. Gould writes,

> I spent a month reading all of Broca's major work, concentrating on his statistical procedures. I found a definite pattern in his methods. He traversed the gap between fact and conclusion by what may be the usual route – predominantly in reverse. Conclusions came first and Broca's conclusions were the shared assumptions of most successful white males during his time – themselves on top by the good fortune of nature, and women, blacks, and poor people below. His facts were reliable (unlike Morton's), but they were

gathered selectively and then manipulated unconsciously in the service of prior conclusions. By this route, the conclusions achieved not only the blessing of science, but the prestige of numbers. Broca and his school used facts as illustrations, not as constraining documents. They began with conclusions, peered through their facts, and came back in a circle to same conclusion. (Gould 1981, p. 85)

That conclusion was that whites were genetically superior to other races, specifically to blacks. As with Morton, though with more precision, Broca found that the skull capacity of whites was large than other races. Broca also ties this directly to intelligence, though IQ (intelligence tests) were not available at the time. But Gould found that Broca repeatedly produced findings that did not fit with his beliefs and instead of changing the beliefs he dismissed his findings. For example, in attempting to demonstrate the evolutionary superiority of the white race, he focused in one set of research on the length of the arm bones. Gould summarizes his analysis:

Broca began his search for "meaningful" [biological/genetic] characteristics – those that would display the established ranks [i.e. white genetic superiority]. In 1862, for example, he tried the ratio of radius (lower arm bone) to humerus (upper arm bone), reasoning that a higher ratio marks a longer forearm – a characteristic of apes. All began well: blacks yielded a ratio of .794, whites .739. But then Broca ran into trouble. An Eskimo skeleton yielded .703, and Australian aborigine .709 while the Hottentot Venus [a skeleton of a South African black person], Cuvier's near ape (her skeleton had been preserved in Paris), measured a mere .703. Broca now had two choices. He could either admit that, on this criterion, whites ranked lower than several dark-skinned groups, or he could abandon the criterion. Since he knew that Hottentots, Eskimos, and Australian aborigines ranked below most blacks, he chose the second course. [Broca writes]: "After this, it seems difficult to me to continue to say that elongation of the forearm is a characteristic of degeneration or inferiority, because on this account, the European occupies a place between the Negroes on the one hand, and Hottentots, Australians, and Eskimos on the other. (Gould 1981, p. 87)

Rather than rejecting his assumptions, as the research findings related to the arm bones says he should do – if one was to adhere to conventional scientific principles, Broca simply rejected the findings and continued to embrace his assumptions. Gould presents numerous examples of this form of practice by Broca and others through his book.

Broca and others did numerous other studies along the same lines. For example, Broca studied the location of the foramen magnum of different races. The foramen magnum is the hole at the base of the skull. Using Darwinian theory, in mammals the hole of the most evolutionary advanced animals is more forward than the least evolutionary advanced. For example, the foramen magnum of a horse or dog is toward the back of the skull, whereas for humans it is more toward the center. Scientific racists claimed the location differed not only between animals, but between races of humans. Broca and others claimed that the location of foramen magnum in black skulls was further in the back than it was for whites, i.e. they were less evolved. Yet when he actually studied this by systematically analyzing hundreds of skulls, he found that the results where the opposite. The foramen magnum of black skulls was actually closer to the front of the skull than it was for white skulls. But rather than accepting these results, he looked further and introduced new variables until he found the results he was looking for (see Gould 1981, pp. 101-102).

In the next period of scientific racism – 1890-1945 – the focus changed somewhat. Where earlier approaches focused on the physiology of different races, e.g. brain sizes, arm lengths, the location of the foramen magnum, etc. the focus now turned more to mental measurement. It was not that scientific racists stopped their studies of anatomy to prove inequalities amongst races during this period, but mental measurement tools were increasingly becoming prominent amongst scientific racists. Specifically, scholars were focused on such things as IQ tests and other psychological tests to demonstrate differences between races.

The third major period of scientific racism occurred between 1890 and 1935-40, the beginnings of the Second World War. This was a period of massive change in Western societies. It was a period of massive economic growth. It was a period of massive urbanization – more and more people were living in or near bigger and bigger cities instead of rural farmlands. It was a period of rapid industrialization. Manufacturing and factories become the dominant part of the economic system. And importantly, this was a period, in America, of massive immigration. There was a massive immigration stream coming into America from 1890 through 1920. This immigration stream was largely comprised of Southern and Eastern Europeans, of Roman Catholics and Jews, of people who were different from the WASPs who were already there. The immigrants flooded into New York and Philadelphia, into Chicago and Boston. It was a very, very large immigration. The people coming into the country were seen as very different, as very distinct from the people already in the United States, i.e. the WASPS. It was estimated that in 1900 one out of every four New Yorkers could not speak English. This illustrates the enormity of the scale of immigration at the time.

All of these changes alarmed the WASP (White Anglo-Saxon Protestants – people who were Protestant and came from Great Britain) elites who largely dominated and controlled American society since its founding, going back to the Pilgrims at Plymouth Plantation in Massachusetts in the early 1600s. America was dominated by WASPs from its founding through this period. The early 1900s was a time when the dominant WASPs felt threatened and felt that the good order in society was breaking down as the result of all of the changes happening. And the WASPs focused on the immigrants to explain (or blame) the threatening dangers of massive social change occurring at the time. (The period from 1890 to 1920 is often called by historians the Progressive Era because it was a time in which the WASPS sought to use social science to address, manage and control the various social problems arising with all of the changes occurring. This was the period of the birth of modern social work and modern psychology and modern sociology.) The alien races invading the United States were seen by some if not by many to be an existential threat to America, to what it means to be an American.

This was also the period of the beginning of the creation and use of modern mental measurements, including such things as intelligence tests, personality tests, tests for psychopathology (mental illness), etc. (Indeed, the government employed psychiatrists and mental health workers at the ports of entry, such as Ellis Island in New York City, to assess the mental statuses of the millions of immigrants flooding in to determine if they were healthy and whole, psychologically. If they were deemed unfit, they were not allowed into the country.) Psychologists and psychiatrists developed a range of such tests and set about using them – in schools, in the army, and elsewhere. One of the most influential of these tests was the IQ test. One of the earliest and influential IQ tests was created by Alfred Binet, a French psychologist. Of note, Binet created the IQ test as an instrument that would allow him to sort students in French schools. He wished to use the test to assign the brighter students to one classroom and the less bright to another. He was quite clear that he did not believe the IQ measured any sort of innate abilities. Binet's test was then appropriated by Lewis Terman, a psychologist at Stanford University, and his colleagues. Terman created the Stanford-Binet IQ test, which became widely used in America in the early and mid-1900s, and versions of it continued to be widely used today. Importantly, Terman rejected Binet's assumptions about what the test actually measures. Terman claimed it measured innate intelligence rather than learned knowledge, and this innate intelligence he said did not change much at all after six years old or so. (Terman also warmly embrace eugenics – the science of selective breeding to improve a race -- and his IQ tests supported his eugenic ideas.)

The Stanford-Binet IQ test is supposedly a measure of raw intelligence, with a score of 100 being the norm. (There are several components of IQ according to Terman. The test measures all of them and combines them into one IQ score.) Thus, if you have a score of 120 you are thought to be more naturally intelligent than someone with a score of 100, and if you have a score of 90 you are said to be less intelligent than most people. (The tests and the score also take into consideration of age. It is computed in a way to account for age. Thus, a person eight years old with an IQ score of 100 is normal, and a person fifty-eight years old with a score of 100 is normal. As such, the idea is that intelligence does not increase with age, after the age of seven or so.) Intelligence is fixed at birth.

In the United States, in the early 1900s mental measurement, including the use of the Stanford-Binet IQ tests, was embraced widely by scientists in psychology and in other fields. The Stanford-Binet IQ test and others similar types of mental measurement tests were widely used by scientific racists – largely WASPs – seeking to respond to the massive social changes afoot in the country. Immigration particularly was a focus of concern. Scientific racists set about measuring the IQs, and other psychological attributes, of the various ethnic groups flooding into America. They routinely proclaimed that the northern Europeans – particularly the British, but also the Germans, and Scandinavians – tested higher on the IQ tests than did the Southern and Eastern Europeans – Russians, Italians, Polish, etc. They often created a hierarchy of races in this regard, with people descending from the British on top, and those from Southern and Eastern European – Italians, Polish at the bottom, at least within the white race. The British were smarter than the Italians, Polish, Russian, etc., by nature, by genetics, by evolution. (The scientists of the time using the intelligence tests tended to focus as much if not more on understanding differences between different white races than between white people and black people.) Importantly, they took Binet's test and significantly changed its assumptions and meaning. These WASP scientists proclaimed that IQ was fixed and inherited, in contrast to Binet who made no such claims, and it differed from one race to another.

We see all of these ideas reflected clearly and unequivocally in the writings of Carl Brigham (1890-1943), another scientific racist, who spent his career as a psychology professor at Princeton University. Brigham was one of the more influential psychologists specializing in mental measurement. In his essay, "A Study of American Intelligence" (1923), he captures many of the ideas noted above. As was common for the time, Brigham viewed Europeans not as being of one race but of several. There were: the Nordic race (e.g. Scandinavia), the Alpine race (e.g. Swiss and Austrian), the Mediterranean race (e.g. Italy, Spain, Southern France, etc.). He conducted studies on the intelligence of the different groups and found that "the intellectual superiority of our Nordic group over the Alpine, Mediterranean, and negro groups has been demonstrated"

(1995, p. 575). In short, people from Italy are dumber by nature, by genetics, than people from Norway. Again, he writes, "Our own data from the Army tests indicate clearly the intellectual superiority of the Nordic race group" (ibid., p. 579). In keeping with his eugenic beliefs, he was also greatly concerned that the American gene pool was being greatly harmed as the result of recent immigration from Southern and Eastern Europe: "There can be no doubt that recent history has shown a movement of inferior peoples or inferior representation of peoples to this country" (ibid., p. 577). It was not only the Southern Europeans and black people that were inferior, but it was also the Jews, who Brigham argued had lower IQs than others. He writes, "Our figures, then, would rather tend to disprove the popular belief that the Jew is highly intelligent. Immigrants examined in the army who report their birthplace as Russia, had an average intelligence below those from all other countries except Poland and Italy. ... If we assume that the Jewish immigrants have a low average intelligence, but a higher variability than other nativity groups, this would reconcile our figures with popular belief" (Ibid., p. 573).

Scientific racists gave the dominant, wealthy, and powerful WASP group intellectual ammunition to push for social policy changes, specifically with regard to immigration. Many WASPs, fueled by the scientific racists' finding that America was being biologically, genetically threatened by inferior people immigrating into the country – from Italy, Poland, Russia, etc., warned about the future of America. The future of America was being threatened, as Brigham clearly argued, because the genetic pool of America would be weakened by the intermingling of the genes of the inferior races with those of the superior race, the WASP. Too many Italians, for example, were immigrating and these would eventually marry Americans of British descent, and this would be bad for America. It would make America less intelligent, less evolutionary advanced, or so this eugenics argument went. Alarms were raised by scholars and political pundits and others in the 1910s about this. One such concern was the widely referenced book *The Passing of the Great Race* (1916) by Madison Grant, in which the author expressed alarm at the changing racial composition of America. Grant's book is a classic racist work, built upon the claims of scientific racism. The great race – those descending from Britain (really the Nordic race) – is threatened by the new races in the immigration stream. Grant insisted that all immigration should stop immediately, and that America should enact policies – from eugenics to immigration -- to ensure that the pure and healthy British WASP genes should be enabled to maintain the dominance of the WASP group in America. (In Germany one finds a similar tale in Oswald Spengler's *The Decline of the West* (1918). Both books were widely embraced by Hitler and his followers a few years later.)

The door to immigration was closed in 1921 when Congress passed the National Origins Formula (Act), which severely curbed the number of immigrations allowed into the country. In testimony leading up to the law, scientific racists were called before Congress. They conveyed a sense of concern, urgency really, based upon their research, about the immigrants' effect on the genetic composition of America, and about the threats to the IQ and character of Americans it posed. Their testimony contributed to Congress' decision to close the door on immigration.

The United States was not the only place where scientific racism grew in the early 1900s. Scientific racism rose its ugly head in Europe at the same time. It was at the heart of the fascist German Nazi regime of Adolf Hitler and his followers. Hitler fully embraced the scientific racism of his day, and this fueled his insane behaviors that led to World War Two and the Holocaust – the murder of six million Jews, the murder of six million others in the death camps – as well as the insane slaughter of fifty million people – combatants and civilians on the battle fields, cities, and countryside of Europe (and elsewhere). (Fascists love war! Life is a struggle. The strong should be praised! The strong are good. The weak should be conquered or extinguished. Such is the thinking of fascists.) Hitler saw the "Aryan" race, i.e. the Germanic people, as genetically superior to all other European (and other) races. He sought to purify or cleanse Germany of all inferior racist stock, most notably Jews and the Roma people ("gypsies"). In addition, he relied upon the claims of scientific racism to kill millions of others – homosexuals, the mentally ill, the intellectually and physically disabled, etc. as part of his eugenic quest. In sum, scientific racism was used and supported by the evil German Nazi regime, and this use contributed to the great nightmare that was World War Two.

In the United States, beginning in the 1930s scholars and others were increasingly rejecting the scientific racism produced in America in previous decades and were increasingly rejecting the scientific racism promoted by Hitler's regime. Scientific racism became out of favor in America from the 1930s through the 1960s or 1970s in the American academy and to a lesser extent in the American public. (As we see below, it has arisen once again in the last few decades in America.) Two of the main factors that lead to American scientific rejection of scientific racism, beginning in the 1930s, are 1) the use of scientific racism by Hitler and the Nazis and 2) the demographic changes that occurred as the result of the immigration stream into America from 1890 through 1920. (This was noted above.) We can briefly look at each of these. The first – the use of scientific racism by the Nazis – made it less tenable for good, upstanding Americans to embrace scientific racism because Hitler and the Nazis were America's evil enemy and at the heart of their ideology was scientific racism. How could America proclaim its goodness in a war with the Nazis if Americans were to have embraced the same ideologies about race as the Nazis? That is, America had to view the Nazis as bad and evil, and they had to view themselves as good and pure. How could one be good and pure if one embraces the evil ideologies of the enemy – scientific racism. As such, scientific racism became highly disfavored in America, at least in mainstream circles. There is a second factor here. That is, the immigration stream of 1890 through 1920 of Italians, Jews, Poles, etc. led to the immigrants and their children becoming part of mainstream American society in the following decades, including becoming students and scholars at universities. As members of these immigrant groups became scholars, intellectuals, and researchers at American universities in the 1930s – as scholarship was no longer the exclusive provenance of WASPs, there came a push to reject scientific racist claims. Afterall, it would seem harder for many Italian or Jewish American scholars to argue that Italians or Jews are genetically inferior, genetically less intelligent, than their WASP colleagues. Together, these two things led to the large-scale rejection of scientific racism until the 1960s or 1970s.

Scientific racism lay dormant through the 1940s and 1950s. It began to raise its ugly head in small steps in the 1960s and it has expanded (considerably in some circles) since then. This fourth wave of scientific racism has gained much steam in the popular consciousness in the last few years, particularly with the regime of Trump and the New Republican Party, some of whom openly champion "Christian Nationalism" or white nationalist ideas. The first significant work of scientific racism during this period was that of Arthur Jensen, a psychologist at the University of California at Berkeley. Jensen published what came to be a notorious example of scientific racism in a 1969 article in the academic journal the Harvard Educational Review. The article, titled "How Much Can We Boost IQ and Scholastic Achievement," was not a work of original research, but was a review of existing research. Jensen's article was focused on whether programs such as Head Start actually can and do work. Head Start programs are designed to provide intellectual enhancement to young, pre-school children from poor and minority backgrounds with the intent, among other things, of raising their intelligence and as such enabling them to succeed more in life. Jensen concluded that such programs do not work largely because, he argued, intelligence was mostly inherited and cannot be changed through educational activities. It was innate and fixed. He also claimed that the average IQ of racial groups differed from one another. Some groups are by nature smarter than others. Of course, whites were smarter than blacks by nature, he argued. (The latter claim was made by Jensen perhaps more forcefully in his 1998 book, *The g Factor*.)(Of note, while his arguments are little different from those of people like Brigham forty years earlier, his racial groups changed. No longer was the focus on different racial groups within Europe. Now, these groups are lumped together as whites.)

Another notorious example of scientific racism to have arisen in this current wave of scientific racism is the book *The Bell Curve: Intelligence and the Class Structure* (1994) by Charles Murray and Richard Herrnstein. Richard Herrnstein was a psychology professor at Harvard University. Charles Murray is a conservative journalist and pop scholar (as opposed to a recognized, legitimate scholar, though he does have a recognized Ph.D. in political science). He has spent much of his life working for conservative "think tanks" (i.e. propaganda mills) such as the Manhattan Institute. (More recently he worked at another conservative think tank, the American Enterprise Institute – the latter which has become accepted by the mainstream media as a mainstream think tank, rather than as a radical right wing think tank.) Prior to *The Bell Curve* (1994), Murray was perhaps best known for influencing the changes to federal welfare policies during the Reagan administration, ending "welfare as we knew it". Murray at the time wrote a book titled *Losing Ground* (1984) in which he argued that liberal welfare policies that were initiated in the 1960s, during Johnson's Great Society programs, actually caused poverty rather than alleviate poverty; the policies did not work. They were actually creating more problems for the poor, he argued, than they solved. They supposedly caused poverty by encouraging a psychological orientation of dependency on the part of the poor, one that encouraged them to remain poor and to remain on welfare. Murray argued that the liberal welfare policies incentivized people to remain on poverty rather than incentivizing them to get off welfare.

Published in 1994, *The Bell Curve* claims to be a scientific study of intelligence and inequality in America. It basically argues that America is a meritocracy, a society in which the wealthiest in American society are the most intelligent and the poorest are the least intelligent. Ostensibly, it was written as a concern or warning that a meritocratic society produces threats to democracy and threats to social stability. The authors championed a meritocratic America and warned of the threats to it. This was not however the part of the book that caused so much controversy. The controversy was about the racist claims made. Arguably a major subtext of the entire book is that intelligence varies by race. (Murray has insisted, in classic propaganda style, that race was only a very small part of the overall argument of the book.) Some races are naturally smarter than others, the authors say, and this explains economic inequalities between the races. Whites, the authors say, are smarter than blacks, and this explains why whites as a group are wealthier than blacks. They write:

> The difference in [intelligence] test scores between African-Americans and European-Americans as measured in dozens of reputable studies has converged on approximately a one standard deviation difference

for several decades. Translated into centiles, this means that the average white person tests higher than about 84 percent of the population of blacks and that the average black person test higher than about 16 percent of the population of whites. (1994, p. 269)

The authors go on to note that there are differences, anchored solidly in genetics, in a whole host of personality and behavioral characteristics between races, from crime to accident proneness, to divorce.

It is crucial to understand here the details of their understanding of intelligence. They argue that intelligence is largely inherited. It is also largely fixed by nature and cannot be changed through education or learning or through changing any aspect of the social or economic context. After the age of six or so, the authors claim, the intelligence of a person does not change. That is, the raw natural intellectual capability of a person does not and cannot change in any significant way. Intelligence, they say, is inherited and, they say, varies by race. The authors argue that whites are more intelligent than blacks by nature.

Another recent example of scientific racism is the work of the Canadian psychologist J. Phillippe Rushton (1943-2012). Rushton builds on a theory of evolution to claim that some races are more advanced on the evolutionary scale, i.e. more superior, than others. Whites are said to be superior to, i.e. more evolutionarily advanced than, blacks. Rushton builds his evolutionary theory on the claim that there are fundamentally two distinct types of reproductive strategies taken by animals, what he calls the r-K life history theory. (He attributes the founding of this theory to the sociobiologist E.O. Wilson.) He writes, "the r-strategy means being very sexually active and having many offspring. The K-strategy means having fewer offspring, but with both mother and father giving them more care" (1999, p. 73). The r-strategy is used by insects and clams and less evolved species. In this strategy the mother animal produce thousands of offspring, with the recognition that most will not survive. In the species that rely upon this strategy there is no family unit and the parent animals do not care for their children. The K-strategy on the other hand – on the opposite side of the spectrum -- is that of some human groups. Here the mother animal has few children with the expectation that most will survive. In this strategy, the family is important, and the mother animal closely nurtures and protects the individual babies. Animals can be located on the spectrum between the two strategies, with the most primitive, less evolutionarily advanced nearer to the r-strategy and the more developed evolutionary species more toward the K-strategy other. Thus, for example, mammals, like horses, have fewer offspring than ants. Mammals care for their offspring; ants do not. So far so good. But it is the next step in Rushton's argument that becomes incredibly debatable – and to this author quite bizarre and really odd -- and really a classic in scientific racism. His theory of reproduction, he says, applies not only to different species, but it applies within species, and specifically within the human species. Different human races rely upon different reproductive strategies. Blacks, he says, are less evolutionarily advanced and therefore rely more upon the evolutionary strategies of clams and ants, i.e. the r-strategy, while whites are the opposite, i.e. draw upon the K-strategy. Blacks, he says, produce more children and care for them less than whites. (In light of the fact that some white groups, such as the Mormons in Utah, today have far more children than black Americans, I often wonder what Rushton would say about the genetics of Mormons?) On its surface, this theory is bizarre and does not accord with the facts of the world, that is, if one looks at the facts objectively. The number of children a group has and the family structures a group has is clearly the result of history and of social factors. Of this there cannot be any reasonable doubt when one looks at the facts.) (On a very simplistic level, this pseudo-intellectual argument has appeal, much as any propaganda does. It should perhaps be noted that Rushton goes on to make even more bizarre claims about racial differences. For example, he tried to study the length of the penises of blacks and whites, as well as the strength of the ejaculation stream, with the goal of making an argument to support his overall claims that the races rely upon different reproductive strategies.)

Rushton elaborates on the r-K theory. He claims that the differences are not merely in terms of number of children and the care given by parents to the offspring, but the differences are associated with a whole host of social behaviors and traits. For example, he writes regarding intelligence: "The r-type biological strategy involves higher levels of reproduction, while the K-strategy requires parental care and use of mental attributes. Since larger brains need more time to be built up all the stages of development are slowed down..." (ibid., p. 75) and this requires more nurturing parents and lengthy nurturing periods. In short, he provides an explanation that ties in parenting styles with evolutionary intelligence. Rushton goes on to argue that whites have larger brains than blacks. This produces, he claims, higher intelligence, and this is due to the evolutionary strategies of the two races.

As is rather common in many recent versions of scientific racism, Rushton says that whites are not the most advanced, most evolved of the human races. Rushton, as well as Herrnstein and Murray, say that the Asian race is the most evolutionarily advanced and the black race is least advanced, with the white race in between.

In his book, Rushton provides numerous studies (many or most of which are of dubious merit from fellow scientific racists) supporting his argument regarding the r-K strategy theory. He summarizes his bizarre conclusions about "race differences and r-K strategies" by presenting a list of 16 general findings, based ostensibly on research. He writes,

"Orientals are the most K. Blacks are the most r, and Whites fall in between. The signs of being more r are [among other things]: 1) Shorter gestation periods; 2) Earlier physical maturation ... 3) Earlier puberty [including first intercourse and first pregnancy]; 4) More developed primary sexual characteristics [including size of penis]; 5) More biological than social control of behaviors; 6) Higher level of individuality (lower law abidingness); 6) More permissive sexual attitudes; 7) Higher intercourse frequencies; 8) Weaker pair bonds; 9) More siblings; 10) Higher rates of child neglect and abandonment..." (ibid., p.80-81).

Rushton's theory is not accepted by mainstream scientists or mainstream scholars, though he sometimes gets the direct or indirect moral or intellectual support of prominent scholars. For example, the influential evolutionary biologist and Harvard professor E.O. Wilson defended Rushton on numerous occasions. (Wilson is not generally identified as a scientific racist, though a review of his theory of sociobiology clearly shows that it can easily elide with little effort into a full-blown racist theory.) Other recent scientific racists have generally been accepted by the mainstream academic community. One only need to look at the university affiliations of some of the more prominent scientific racists to recognize their acceptance. Herrnstein who co-authored The Bell Curve was a psychology professor at Harvard.

Perhaps the most mainstream of the recent and contemporary scientific racists is James Q. Wilson (1931-2012), who was a professor of political science and public policy at Harvard and at the University of California. (Some if not many readers might argue that Wilson should not be considered a racist. I fundamentally disagree. Despite his nuanced writings, his position is clear, as stated below.) Wilson was a very conservative scholar who wrote a great deal on crime and crime control and his ideas on such matters were highly influential on public policies regarding policing and criminal justice. His ideas contributed to the get-tough approach to crime that was seen in the late 1900s and was associated with the belief that the best policy option – really, he argued the only rational option -- to address the problem of rising crime was to incarcerate more and more people. The prison population and the entire criminal justice population grew tremendously in the closing decades of the twentieth century. (Almost six million Americans were in prison, on probation, or on parole by 2000. This is a staggering amount which no other advanced democratic society comes close to matching.) (Though it bears noting, that the crime rate also rose dramatically as well during this period.) His ideas also contributed to the new policing strategy that relied upon the "broken-window hypothesis," which argued that the best way to prevent or reduce urban, street crime was for the law-abiding people in the neighborhoods to take pride in their communities. If the community members had pride in their neighborhood, they would create a normative and moral community sensibility that would ward off crime. Toward that end, the broken window policing approach called upon the police to focus on controlling and arresting people who committed minor or petty street crimes, e.g. drinking in public, littering, selling illegal cigarettes, arresting the homeless, etc. By doing so, the law abiding community members could feel a sense of pride and ownership over their public spaces and this, the theory goes, would reduce crime.

Though Wilson is careful to frame his arguments about the causes of crime in the most intellectually nuanced way such that he could avoid charges of being called a racist, his writings nevertheless are clear. We see his beliefs clearly in *Crime and Human Nature* (1985) which he co-authored with Richard Herrnstein. The authors present a systematic argument complete with detailed discussions of the possible biological and psychological causes of crime (curiously they devote scant attention – as is so common amongst conservative and racist scholars -- to the wealth of sociological research on the topic). They argue that the cause of crime consists of an interaction of biological, psychological, and situational factors. Here we are interested in their assessment of the biological (e.g. "human nature"). While they are careful to say that individuals are "not born criminal," they go on to note that criminals are constitutionally (e.g. genetically) different than non-criminals. One of the key differences is in intelligence. They present evidence that shows that criminals have appreciably lower IQs than non-criminals. They note that they believe IQ is not completely inherited. Rather, they say that approximately sixty percent of IQ is inherited (i.e. genetic), and the rest is due to such things as the social environment and early natal and pre-natal factors. Then in echoing the same claims made by Murray and Herrnstein in the *Bell Curve*, they note that black people tend to score appreciably lower than white people on IQ tests. (In their ever-nuanced structuring of their argument, they are careful to state that one in fact cannot make blanket claims about race and IQ. They write: "Though the evidence strongly supports the existence of racial differences in measured intelligence, it does not allow us to say much about the degree, if any, to which these differences are heritable. The variation among individuals in IQ is to a large degree (probably on the order of .6) the result of inheritance, but this says little or nothing about the extent to which differences between groups are heritable. The social conditions in which two racial groups find themselves may differ so greatly and so persistently that the average difference between the two groups will be caused almost entirely by these conditions, while differences amongst individuals within one racial group will reflect a large genetic component. To the extent that the economic cultural, and geographic position of blacks imposes long-term disadvantages on them, average IQ scores may differ between blacks and whites for reasons having little to do with heritability" (1995, p. 471). Despite such statements found throughout their book, the authors routinely return to the claims of the legitimacy of the argument that says constitutional factor (genetics, IQ, etc.) are related to race and crime and constitutional factors cane explain differing crime rates. One can marvel at the sleight of hand of the authors, but one cannot ignore or dismiss their fundamental racist claims. The implied logic is clear: Black people are more prone to commit crime because they are born less intelligent than white people, and less intelligent people commit more crime than more intelligent people. They write: "If lower measured intelligence is associated with crime independently of socioeconomic status, and if blacks, on the average, have lower such scores, than these facts may help explain some of the black-white differences in crime rates" (1995, p. 471). Again, despite the endless qualifications in their argument this is their argument.

But IQ is not the only constitutional factor they offer to explain the higher crime rates amongst black people. They also draw upon the odd research of William Sheldon, which focuses on the physiognomy or body type or shape of people. In the 1940s and 1950s, William Sheldon, echoing earlier biologically based arguments from the late 1800s and early 1900s, created a somatotype theory to account for different personality types amongst humans, and he claimed that different personality types are associated with different types of social behaviors. He argued there are three basic physiognomies, i.e. body types or body shapes: ectomorphs, mesomorphs, and endomorphs. Ectomorphs are skinny; endomorphs are round; and mesomorphs are muscular. Sheldon argued the body types are associated with different personality types. Ectomorphs are quiet and restrained; endomorphs are relaxed, social, peaceful. Mesomorphs are active, assertive, dominant, competitive. (It perhaps should be noted that by the 1990s, Sheldon's theory and research was widely rejected by mainstream scientists, who demonstrated that the claims simply did not fit the evidence.) Wilson and Herrnstein present research that shows that criminals tend to be mesomorphs, and black people are disproportionately mesomorphs. One only needs to put the various individual statements presented by Wilson and Herrnstein together by logic to see what they are saying: Black people are constitutionally configured to engage in more crime than white people in part because of their inherited physiognomies. The racist is clear.

The Current Social Context of the Ideological Production of Scientific Racism

Unlike the second and third historical eras of scientific racism, noted above, this third period produced a massive wave of criticisms against scientific racist arguments. The criticisms have been leveled by mainstream biological and social scientists, and they roundly attacked and ultimately rejected almost all aspects of the scientific racist arguments, whether the arguments were rooted in the guise of intelligence, a la *The Bell Curve*, or in terms of biology, as in Rushton's work. One of the most interesting and popular criticisms of scientific racism to arise during this third wave is the book *The Mismeasure of Man* (1981) by the American paleontologist Stephen Jay Gould (1941-2002), which was briefly referred to earlier. Gould was a professor at Harvard. In this brilliant book, Gould systematically examines in great detail the biological scientific racists of the first three periods discussed here – in the 1800s and early 1900s. He systematically shows how the scientific arguments and conclusions are fatally flawed and erroneous. He critically evaluates the actual scientific work done by these researchers and demonstrates their essential flaws. The examples I gave about the foreman magnum and the size of the skulls, for example, come from Gould's book. Basically, he shows how the scientific racists had preconceived beliefs and assumptions about the natural inequality of the races and their research set about to try to confirm these pre-set beliefs. When their research results conflicted with their preconceived beliefs, they violated the normal practices of science and rejected the research findings rather than their preconceived beliefs.

Another well-known book which criticizes scientific racism is *Not In Our Genes* (1984) co-authored by the evolutionary biologist Richard Lewontin, the neurobiologist Steven Rose, and the psychologist Leon Kamin. The book harshly and systematically criticizes claims by scientific racist that intelligence is inherited and that the average intelligence of one race is higher than that of another race. The authors specifically focus on the science of genetics and show how the scientific understanding of genetics and biology does not support claims made by the scientific racists. The authors, for example, argue that the amount of genetic variability between races is so tiny when one considers the entire human genome, and the amount of identical genetic composition shared by all people is so great that it is scientifically meaningless to claim there are any differences on a genetic level of any consequence between the races. (This is not to mention the obvious fact that no one has ever discovered – and most would likely say no one ever will discover -- an individual "intelligence" gene.)

These are simply two of the many scientific criticisms that have been raised against the scientific racist arguments in recent decades. There are many, many other political, moral, and sociological arguments that have also been leveled at scientific racism in the last thirty years or so.

I have argued here that it is necessary to understand the social context within which scientific racism emerges and operates if one is to truly understand it, particularly if one wishes to understand it from a sociological perspective. We can turn now to describe a few of the sociological factors that may help to account for the rise of this fourth wave of scientific racism. Many of these echo the factors we saw in play in the early 1900s which spawned the scientific racism of that time. One of the changes that has occurred in America since the 1960s is another immigration wave. Much as there was a massive immigration in the early 1900s into America, so too today there is a massive immigration into America. The character of the immigration however is different in some respects. The massive immigration now is largely from Latin America, and particularly from Mexico, as well as from Asia. The immigrants are non-white, and often Roman Catholic and/or non-Christian. (One might wish to note that many of the immigrants today have arrived illegally, largely from Mexico and Central and South America. There are estimated to be up to ten million persons illegally in the United States today. But the fact of illegality has nothing to do with the argument being presented in this chapter.)

One could think of the recent revival of scientific racism sociologically as an instance of a symbolic crusade. The sociologist Joseph Gusfield used the concept of symbolic crusade in his study of the temperance movement (anti-alcohol movement) of the 1860s. He focused on Chicago and argued that the attempts to make alcohol illegal – it was finally made illegal in the United States during the Prohibition Era of the 1920s – was made by the WASP leaders of the time as a symbolic vehicle to combat the perceived threats to their status positions by Catholic immigrations – Irish and German flooding into America at the time. Catholics drank alcohol, the conservative WASPs did not. The WASPS saw the immigrations as a threat to their dominant status and used the issue of alcohol (unknowingly) as a symbolic vehicle to reassert their dominant status in society. In the same way it could be argued sociologically that the current wave of scientific racism is a symbolic crusade by the dominant groups – which now is not only the WASPS, but the Catholic, white ethnics and Jews who have assimilated into the power structures of society. Whites arguable are feeling culturally threatened at a time of massive uncertainty and change.

The current stream of immigration has made America far more ethnically and racially diverse than it has ever been. When we also consider the massive internal emigration of American blacks from the rural South to the urban north over a hundred years ago and the assertion of their political power – however limited -- from the Civil Rights era to the present, then we get a more complete picture of the social context within which the recent scientific racism has emerged.

A sociological explanation needs to go beyond this to understand more fully the rise of the current wave of scientific racism. One needs to consider politics. It is beyond the scope of this paper to present an extended description of the political and economic context (see Chapters One and Two for greater detail). Suffice to say that the history of America coupled with a two-party system that disproportionately advantages rural, white states over diverse, urban, and large states has conspired institutionally to elevate the more conservative elements of American society and simultaneously to disempower the more liberal elements. There has been a coalescence of increasingly conservative political power in America over the last thirty years. There are several dimensions to the economic context which also need to be appreciated. First, the economy of today is distinct from the economy of the early and mid-1900s. Specifically, the earlier period was characterized by a growing manufacturing economy. Factories and industrial production were the cornerstone of the economy. But from the 1960s into the present, the economy has fundamentally changed. We now have a post-industrial economy. The largest sectors of the economy are no longer manufacturing, but service and information -- software engineering and working at McDonalds, and the like. In addition, we now have a consumer-based economy rather than a manufacturing-based economy. Altogether, the economy of today has produced far greater inequalities in America in the last twenty years or so, compared to, for example, the 1940s. (The inequalities today approximate the inequalities of the 1920s.) The top ten percent of Americans have done exceptionally well economically. The bottom sixty have done worse, and the rest have at best remained the same. But rising inequality is only one aspect of this new economy. Another is the increasingly rapid change that lies at its heart. Everything changes, and changes faster and faster. These two issues – increased inequalities and increasing change – combined with the new immigration stream – have fueled the rise of scientific racism today.

They have done so in part because of the increasing insecurities produced by this new economy, and by the increased concentration of wealth and power in the hands of a small group of people. This increasing concentration of wealth and power fuels the growth of scientific racism for two reasons – 1) politics and 2) the control over intellectual production. Politics was briefly mentioned above, and will again be addressed below. Here I wish to call attention to the role of rich people (and private corporations) and their funding of highly conservative, right wing "think tanks." This is an important issue that cannot be ignored if one wishes to understand the current wave of scientific racism. What are think tanks? Think tanks are private foundations tasked with producing research, presenting their findings, and influencing social policies. They hire people with advance degrees to work at their institutes to do research and to produce papers and books and policy statements that support the political agendas and ideological perspectives of the funders of the think tanks. These institutes include such places as the American Enterprise Institute, the Cato

Institute, the Manhattan Institute, the Pioneer Fund, ALEC, and many more. The clear majority of private think tanks are conservative, which makes sense as the rich fund them and they are more likely to support institutes that support them. To repeat: Think tanks are designed in ways not for the promotion of the free exchange of ideas, but for the promotion of particular ideological positions. In effect, they are largely institutes of propaganda. (Of note, think tanks are a form of private foundation. Private foundations in the history of the United States often are not directed toward one or another specific political orientation. Historically, most private foundations sought to avoid political ideologies together. Foundations in the early 1900s, for example, like the Rockefeller Foundation, were largely oriented not toward the advancement of political positions (at least not directly) but instead were devoted toward funding projects for human betterment, such as medical research and education. The Gates Foundation today, created by Bill Gates, the founder of Microsoft, and his wife, Melinda, operates on the same principles of eschewing politics. However, today, it appears that more foundations, specifically more think tanks, are created and designed to be political tools to advance the interests of conservatives. This is a new and troubling trend.) (Conservatives might wish to argue that think tanks are needed today to counter-balance the "liberal" orientations found in universities today. Leaving aside a debate about whether the assumption of such an argument has merit, one needs to recognize that the nature of universities compared to think tanks is very different. Universities are not created and designed to produce any particular form of knowledge. They are not designed to be propaganda mills whereas think tanks are designed to do just that.)

When one looks at the scientific racism that has been produced in this current wave, one finds that it is funded in part, if not largely, by think tanks and private foundations. For example, Charles Murray worked at the Manhattan

Institute and the American Enterprise Institute. (The former institute funded his research for *The Bell Curve*.) Similarly, Rushton repeatedly used research and scientific findings produced by scholars funded by the Pioneer Fund to support his racist claims. (The Pioneer Fund is one of the more blatantly racist private foundations in America.) (These scientific findings produced by scholars working at this institute have been roundly if not unanimously rejected by mainstream scientists.) This is not to suggest that all recent scientific racism is produced in and by conservative think tanks or is funded by similarly oriented foundations. Some of it emerges from within the universities. As we saw above, Jensen worked at the University of California, Herrnstein and Wilson worked at Harvard, and Rushton himself worked at a public university in Canada. Nevertheless, one cannot deny the significant role played by private think tanks and foundations – with explicit political agendas – in propagating the new wave of scientific racism.

The second issue – politics – is reflected in the successful coalescence of the far right wing political dominance over America, reflected most recently with the installation of the Trump regime and the possible re-installation of Trump in the 2024 election. This arch conservative dominance, led by an authoritarian (some might say fascist), gives opportunity and voice to the radical right wing scientific racism.

Together these forces propel, much as they did in the second wave of scientific racism, scientific racism forward as a way of maintaining the increasing fantasy of an endless WASP, and now a white (Protestant, Catholics, and Jews), dominant society. But demographics are not on the side of this group. America is changing. America is becoming far, far more diverse ethnically and racially, and by some estimates there will be more minorities being born in this country than whites in the near future. America will soon be a majority minority country. Scientific racism is a frightening response to the changes in the social world; it is something that must be understood and challenged. Lest one think that fascism – in Hitler's version rooted deeply in scientific racism – cannot happen here, be aware of the old adage: History has a tendency to repeat itself.

The Artfulness of Ideological Production in the Propaganda Mill

Whatever one may think of recent and contemporary scientific racism, one might admire the artfulness of the ideological production coming out of the radical right wing propaganda mill. The ways in which scholars such as Wilson and pseudo-scholars such as Murray shape their arguments to appear intellectually rigorous and morally palatable is impressive. We have seen some examples of this earlier in this chapter. Let me end this chapter by noting a few other techniques used. A few of these have previously been mentioned.

One classic way in which this is done is in the use of IQ scores to put forth racist ideas. Recall, that in recent and contemporary racist accounts we see that scholars from Murray to Herrnstein to Wilson argue that different races have different average IQ scores and that there are social correlates to these differences. Moreover, these scholars say that IQ is largely inherited. The qualifier largely is important here. As noted earlier, these scholars like to say that around sixty percent of IQ is inherited, the rest is subject to change due to life experiences. This is important for their arguments because it allows them to say whenever confronted with uncomfortable facts that they are not denying that IQ scores can change if social environments change. This claim allows them to refute their critics while continuing to embrace their ideology. For example, the average IQ for black Americans has risen steadily from the 1960s through 2000. How would one explain this if IQ is fundamentally genetic? The scientific racists say that the rise is due to changing environmental factors, but they also say this does not refute their overall argument. Thus, their racist arguments are allowed to stand, at least in their own heads.

Another example of the massaging rhetoric used by recent and contemporary scientific racists is the often claimed contemporary argument that Chinese have average IQs which are higher than white peoples' and that white peoples' IQ are higher than black peoples'. We saw this above with Murray and Herrnstein (as well as with Rushton). This allows the scientific racists to proclaim themselves not to be white supremacists – after all the Chinese are superior to the whites! It gives the scientific racists a patina of scientific legitimacy. After all, if they were truly bent on advancing a racist ideology, wouldn't they claim that whites are inherently superior not only to blacks but to Chinese as well? It gives the appearance of scientific objectivity. It also allows them to maintain their racist arguments regarding black people. (It is interesting to note here that the scientific racists of the third era – in the early 1900s – consistently found that Chinese IQs were actually lower than whites. Whites were deemed by nature, by destiny, to be the smartest race. How and why did this change?)

We see such rhetorical strategies time and again with those scientific racists who are anchored in reputable institutions and who desire to impact culture and policy. Authors like Wilson and Murray are quite careful in their rhetorical strategies to appear to be objective and unbiased scientists. It is striking how well polished, seemingly well-schooled, the rhetorical styles are. On the other hand, the more blatant racists show little concern about the reception of their ideas. For example, Rushton shows little interest in massaging his claims, or in dressing them up to appear respectable and acceptable to mainstream society. These scientific racists make bold and stark racist claims and do not water down their ideas in pleasing and sophisticated rhetorical strategies.

Another element to the style of persuasion employed by recent and contemporary scientific racists is in the ways they use the research findings of others to support their arguments. The use of references and citations of other researchers who produce scientific racist findings give a patina of legitimacy both to the arguments of those citing this research and to the research itself. Yet when one looks more closely at the research often cited by scientific racists, one finds that these are often less than mainstream forms of research. The research is often produced by the same coterie of scientific racists funded by the same sources. For example, Herrnstein and Murray on a number of occasions cite research funded by the Pioneer Fund – a blatantly racist ideological foundation – in *The Bell Curve* to support their claims and they do so in ways that suggest the research is mainstream when it is not. This gives a false sense of legitimacy both to Herrnstein and Murray and to the original research.

The focus on self-consciously producing knowledge for political ends and the social crises this produces are themes we have encountered numerous times in this book. It has been argued that one of the elements of the current crisis in America is precisely the rise in this form of thinking and this form of practice. Sociology today would be wise to focus its attention today on how the institutional arrangements that nurture and support this distorted way of producing knowledge have arisen.

Chapter Eleven: Power, Political Sociology, and Political Economy

It seems like everywhere we turn the concept of power appears. It appears in relationships between parents and children and between bosses and workers. It appears between teachers and students and between countries. It appears between men and women, and white people and black people. Power is a rather ubiquitous concept, and it is one that is central to sociology. Afterall, can we really understand much about the patterns and patternings of the social world without examining power. This chapter gives an overview of several important, interrelated ideas and fields of study within sociology: power, political sociology, and political economy.

Power

Sociologists have many different ways of understanding power. In the following pages, we describe several of these. We begin with the widely used understanding developed by Max Weber. Then we discuss the three dimensional model of power created by Steven Lukes. This is followed by a brief discussion of the concept of the panopticon.

A classic sociological definition of **power**, first developed by Max Weber, is that it is the ability to get what you want from someone even if that other person resists. Thus, if a robber holds a gun to someone's head and demands they give him money, the robber has power over the other person. But of course power does not have to rely upon brute force. There can be power without such force. If my mother, who is elderly and lives three hundred miles away, asks me to visit her this weekend, even though I would very much not like to do so because the traveling is quite burdensome, but I go to see her anyway, then she has power over me. She is not holding a gun to my head. She cannot take away my allowance if I do not visit her. (Indeed, I of course do not have such an allowance; I am now providing her with money.) But I comply with her request. The point is that there are many versions of power. Weber distinguishes between power (macht, in German) and dominance or authority (herrschaft – in German which could refer to either dominance or authority; it could also refer to "leadership"). There are basically two forms of power: coercion and authority. Coercion is based upon force or threats of force. The power of the military or the police, for example, illustrates this form of power. The robber holding a gun to someone's head also is an example. Authority is basically anchored in legitimacy. It is legitimate power. That is, the person being requested to do something does it because he or she believes the one making the request has a legitimate right to make it.

Weber identifies three types of authority. **Traditional authority** is when someone follows the commands of another because the first person believes the second person's request is based upon the ways things have always been done, i.e. on tradition. In the Middle Ages in Europe, for example, the common practice was to have the first born son of a king become the next king. If one were to ask a peasant during this period, what he or she thought of this practice, what might the peasant say? Many would likely say the son of the king should be the next king, that it is the right and good thing, and that the peasant will recognize the legitimacy of this new king because that is the system they always had. This is traditional authority. The example offered earlier about my mother asking me to visit is also an example. I would comply with my mother's request because this is what I image a good son to do. It is based in tradition.

A second type of authority is **charismatic authority**. Charismatic authority is rooted in the personality of a leader. The leader has charisma, an indefinable attribute that some people have that causes others to follow them. It is a special, even magical quality a leader may have that causes others to be attracted to him or her and to do what he or she says. It is anchored in the personal character of the leader. Cult leaders often times have had charismatic authority. Some political leaders also can be said to have it. Some U.S. presidents, such as Barak Obama or John Fitzgerald Kennedy, could be said to have charisma. Martin Luther King, the great civil rights leader, also had charisma. But charisma need not only be found in what would generally be seen as positive leaders. Above I noted that cult leaders often have charismatic authority, and most would see these not as positive leaders. Adolf Hitler also had charismatic authority, and of course was not, and should not be seen as, a positive leader. To appreciate the power of charismatic leadership one might look at some old videos of Martin Luther King giving awe inspiring speeches, or of Hitler giving his ranting speeches. (The charisma of Hitler is infamously captured in one of the most famous propaganda movies ever made, *Triumph of the Will*, released in 1935. The movie was about Hitler's speech he gave in Nuremberg to an adoring audience of the Hitler Youth. The director Leni Riefenstahl used various cutting-edge directorial techniques in the movie to seduce the viewers into experiencing the magic, the wonder and awe of Hitler. It is a vile movie, particularly the original, unedited version, which is riddled with disgusting antisemitic imagery. Nevertheless, one can see clearly the understanding of charismatic authority in this film.) Of course, while Hitler rose to power on the back of charismatic authority, once he gained power he relied upon other forms of power, most notably coercion to maintain his control.

Rational legal authority is the third form identified by Weber. This is the type of authority that is based upon some abstract, typically written, code or set of rules that one is supposed to follow. It is based upon the belief that the code is legitimate in itself and as such should be followed. As the name suggests it is typically based upon some sort of rational code, based in law. But we should take this rather loosely. One can find examples of rational legal authority all over the place in the contemporary world. The modern political systems of democracy, for example, are based upon this form of authority. The U.S. Constitution is the basis for most Americans for deciding what they can do. Importantly, if one sees the Constitution as a legitimate basis of action, then is becomes the basis of rational legal authority. If a policeman pulls me over for driving eighty miles an hour on a highway where the speed limit is fifty five and then asks for my license and registration, I would comply. Why? One perhaps might say that I do so out of fear that if I did not then the officer would likely arrest me. This would be coercion rather than rational legal authority. And indeed coercion is likely present. But I would also likely comply because I know the policeman is following the law, following the rules, and I recognize the authority of the laws – related to speeding. Rational legal authority was present. If a boss asks an employee to do one thing or another at work, which conform to the normative expectations, and the employee complies, this too would likely be an example of rational legal authority. The worker recognizes the boss has a right to make the request; the request presumably is in accord with the rules of the organization. Similarly, if a teacher requests that students read certain things, take exams at certain times, etc. and the students comply, this too would likely reflect rational legal authority. The student believes the teacher has a right to make such requests and that the request conforms to the rules of the school. (Of course, students in college might comply because of traditional authority or even coercion. For example, students have been taught for over a dozen years to do as the teacher or professor says. It is tradition that may compel compliance.) One can also find rational authority in the field of science and in the acceptance of its findings by the public. Perhaps the most prominent setting in which one readily finds rational legal authority is in bureaucracies, large formal organization. Whether it is in private corporations, religions, or governmental agencies – from the IRS to the military, one finds rational legal authority as a dominant form of power.

Weber understood these types of authority as "ideal types." Ideal types are an importance conceptual device developed and used by Weber and by many sociologists. By ideal types he means abstract models of social phenomena that are to be used to understand actual social realities. They are not in themselves accurate descriptions of how the world works. Rather, one develops ideal types then compares the actual reality to these. This he says helps to understand how the world really works. It is important to understand that when he says ideal types, he does not mean the best type, or the type that should be realized in social practices. Rather, ideal types are more like pure types – types that capture the essential features of this or that social phenomena. Again, he is not saying that ideal types describe social realities; they are tools to be used by sociologists to compare to social realities. In the case of authority, we can see how any one situation may or may not have more than one type of authority or coercion present. People comply, for example, with directions often because of a combination of things like coercion, rational legal authority, and traditional authority. It is only through a concrete analysis of actual social realities can one actually understand which is and which is not present.

One can look at the ideal types of authority historically. That is, one can imagine life one thousand years ago during the Middle Ages in Europe and ask what types of authority were more dominant and which types were less dominant. This was an era dominated by the Roman Catholic church and the aristocracy. While both drew upon forms of coercion to maintain their powers, one could see how traditional authority was likely a dominant form of authority in daily life. The poor peasant likely complied with the demands of the king and pope and their local governmental representatives because the peasant believed the authority was legitimate because of tradition. "We have always done it this way," one might imagine the peasant saying. Traditional authority historically was long lasting.

In contrast, charismatic authority by its very nature is short lived. When the charismatic leader dies so too does the charismatic authority. Weber notes that sometimes the forms of authority put in place by charismatic authority remain after the leader has died. That is, the charismatic leader may create a set of rules or legal codes during his life which remain in effect after he or she dies. The form of authority changes, necessarily. This is the **routinization of charisma** – the turning of charismatic authority into traditional authority or more importantly into rational legal authority.

If traditional authority was dominant in the Middle Ages, rational legal authority has become dominant in the modern and contemporary worlds. As we noted above, we can see this form of authority every where we turn today – from corporations, to government, to scientific institutions. Weber also expresses concerns about what this may lead to. As we discuss in Chapter Nine, he was concerned about the historical process of rationalization and where it could lead. Rational legal authority fits hand in glove with rationalization. In a world dominated by rationalization, and by large institutions, bureaucracies, etc., people become disenchanted (see Chapter Nine). Part of this process involves the growing loss of meaning or the growing loss of a basis of meaning in a population. One of the possible consequences of this is that a rudderless, aimless population produced by rationalization and rational legal authority might look to someone to give them meaning and direction; they might look to someone to give them purpose, to make them great again! A charismatic leader, a leader who draws at least at first upon charismatic authority might be such a person. Indeed, within ten years of Weber's death, we see the rise of Adolf Hitler, a charismatic leader, and the rest was history. We perhaps see similar dynamics today in America with the fanatic cult followers of Donald Trump.

Lukes' Three Dimensions of Power

The British sociologist Steven Lukes, who has spent many years in the United States as a professor at New York University, has developed a different understanding of power. Lukes says there are three dimensions of power. Much like there are three dimensions of space, he says there are three dimensions of power which often if not typically operate at the same time. The **first dimension of power** revolved around the control of behavior. This is power that is observable. Tanks on the streets is an example of the first dimension of power in the political arena. One can see the raw power in action, through the behaviors of the government, i.e. through its use of tanks. The **second dimension of power** is about the control over agendas or arenas. This dimension involves observable and non-observable forms of power. It is often more subtle than the first dimension. An example of this could be potholes on my street. I am a citizen of a small town and I have potholes on my street that I would like to have fixed by the city government. I complain to my representative on the city council about this. I then go to the next city council meeting expecting my representative to present the issue at the meeting, and to get my potholes fixed. But my representative does not raise the issue. No one raises the issue. The potholes do not get fixed. If someone who did not know I made the request was at this meeting and observed what was going on in the meeting, he or she would not see that my issue was not raised at the meeting. There would be no indication that the issue existed. There would be no indication that issues related to power were present. Yet for me the issue was real. In reality, the issue was real, even if it was not observable – at least in the meeting. It was just ignored. This is an example of the second dimension of power. My representative and the city council at large had the power to ignore my request. I was powerless. But one could observe matters related to power in this example if one witnessed my earlier interactions and pleas with my city councilman. As such, power in the second dimension is observable and non-observable. Perhaps the easiest example of the second dimension of power concerns the editors of newspapers and newscasts. When you read a newspaper or watch a newscast, you do not see the decision making (power) that went on behind the curtain. The editor decides which stories to allow to be written about and which stories are not written about. But the person reading the newspaper does not see this decision making. He or she only sees what is in the newspaper. But what is seen is determined by the editors. Like our previous example, if you were an observer in the editorial room where the decisions are made to publish or not to publish one or another story, then you would see power in action. You would see the editor say, "we will not publish this story," or "we will publish this story." The editor has a great deal of power here. He gets to control the agenda; he gets to control what the readers see (and how they see it). This is the second dimension of power. It is observable and hidden.

The **third dimension of power** is about the control of ideas itself. This is largely the realm of ideology. In this dimension, behaviors are not controlled; agendas are not controlled, but thoughts are controlled. Ideologies are shared belief system. (A conflict theory perspective would take this further and say that ideologies are false, shared belief systems that serve to maintain a system of inequality.) One can think of Marx here. Marx once said, "the ruling ideas of any society are the ideas of the ruling class" By which he meant the beliefs and thoughts of a people do not naturally percolate up from social realities. Instead, the ideas of the rich and the powerful are those that are deemed right and good, and by implication those that are not rich and powerful are to unreflectively belief these are in fact right and good. Think of how we define what is good art? The art in the museums we are told is fine art. It is art we should admire. But who decides what art goes into the museum? Whose tastes are represented in these museums? Is it the taste of the working class or the poor? Or is it the tastes of the rich and the powerful? It is the latter. But more: Everyone is told to admire the art that is found in the museums. This is deemed to be good art and is should be admired by all.

Marx also famously said, "religion is the opium of the people," which is another quote that illustrates this idea of ideology and the third dimension of power. Marx says that religion serves the interest of the rich people by convincing the poorer classes that they should accept their place. They should not challenge the existing system of inequality because it goes against their religion. I think here of women in conservative Islamic societies such as Afghanistan or Saudi Arabia. Women are forced to wear burkas and are denied equal rights. In Afghanistan, women are denied access to education and other basic things. If one were to ask the women in these societies if they believe their country's rules are legitimate and right, what would they say? Perhaps some would say they are oppressed and would like to change the system. But possibly if not likely many women would say the system of inequality that is in place is good as it is. It is based on Islam, or so they may say. This is a clear example of power in the third dimension.

A more relevant, more immediate, and more concerning example of the third dimension in action concerns the influence of right-wing think tanks in America today. (The number of such think tanks are large. Here are just a few of them: The Cato Institute, The Manhattan Institute, The American Enterprise Institute; The Federalist Society, etc.). Think tanks are private, non-profit organizations funded to produce research and knowledge about one or another thing, in line with the formal charter or mission of the think tank. In effect, they are like research universities with political agendas, designed to produce "knowledge" that advances particular political agendas.. There are "conservative" and "liberal" think tanks. But there are far, far more conservative than liberal think tanks. And the number of these have grown in size and in number and in influence over the last fifty or sixty years. They are largely funded by rich individuals and corporations and their task is to produce and disseminate "knowledge" that supports the interest of the rich and of the corporations. (In contrast, traditional universities have as their mission the advancement of truth, not the advancement of one or another interest. Today, of course, one of the foci of the right wing think tanks is a criticism of the university. This of course reflects how these think tanks work.) If one looks at the intellectual claims and pseudo-intellectual claims propagated by the radical right today and disseminated to the public via right wing news programs and social media, one can often find that these are based upon the works being generated by these right wing think tanks. They have influenced and shaped policies and debates, elections, and public opinion – all with the intent of manipulating the ideas of people to further the interests of those funding these agendas. This is a clear example of the third dimension of power in action.

(One might be inclined, if one is swayed by the "knowledge" produced by these think tanks, that they are actually serving a useful counter-balance to the liberal knowledge produced at universities and colleges today. I cannot here explain in any detail how vacuous and erroneous this argument is. Suffice to say that it is. The organization of universities, particularly public universities, is radically different from that of right wing think tanks. Right wing think tanks are created to advance an ideological agenda. That is their mission. Universities are created to advance knowledge and the truths about the world. Their agendas are radically different from one another. One might say, echoing the ideological line of right wing think tanks, that while universities proclaim to be non-ideological, they are in reality liberal or radical. This is a fundamental misunderstanding of how universities are designed to work and how in fact they do work. Most importantly, such arguments further weaken democracies. See below.)

Importantly, power in this third dimension is not observable, like it is in the first two dimensions. It is hidden and it is largely unconscious. But it is real. And arguably as powerful if not more so than power in the first two dimensions.

The Panopticon

The term panopticon originally referred to an architectural design for a prison developed by the noted British philosophy Jeremy Bentham (1748-1832). In the late nineteen hundreds the concept was appropriated by the poststructuralist scholar Michel Foucault in his book on the history of modern criminal justice, *Discipline and Punish*. Bentham was writing at a time when modern sensibilities, anchored in the Enlightenment, sought to develop a systematic penal system based upon rationality. Bentham sought to design a prison that would be optimally efficient and effective. It would be optimally rational in organization. The prison design of the panopticon was a large circle, much like a wheel. The cells of the prison would line the circle and in the middle of the circle would be a courtyard. Each cell would have a window facing the courtyard. At the center of the courtyard would be a tall guard tower. At the top of the tower would be a guard post, but the guard in the tower could not be seen by the prisoners from their cells. The design was such that it would only take one guard to supervise the entire prison. More importantly, the guard in the tower could see into any and all of the prison cells. The guard could see what any prisoner was doing at any time. The prisoners knew this. They knew they may be watched, but because they could not see the guard in the tower, they never knew at any particular time whether they were in fact being watched.

The point of the design was that it was highly efficient, requiring only one guard. But more importantly, it maintained order by convincing the prisoners to police themselves. The prisoners, as noted, had to assume they were being watched all the time, but they never knew when they were actually being watched. As a result, the prisoners controlled themselves. The panopticon is a system in which the subjects police themselves to maintain order.

Foucault used the concept of the panopticon in his book describing the history of prisons in the modern era, but he also used it as a metaphor for the organization of modern society at large. The modern, contemporary era has become one of incessant, subtle control, under the guise of freedom and liberation. The modern society gets individuals – not prisoners, but people in the day to day world -- to police themselves without realizing they are doing so. He suggests that the large rational system impose a system of control and manipulations on people without their notice. It is personally oppressive and highly effective. It maintains order. The people, like in the panopticon, police themselves. Foucault was writing in the mid-nineteen hundreds before the internet era. He was writing before the massive deployment of video cameras arose. Today, whether online or walking down the street, one has to assume that one is being surveilled. But for Foucault the surveillance powers are more subtle than cameras and monitoring social media posts. The entire organization of society today, he suggests, is about control and discipline rational control and discipline, and this is harmful to the essence of being human.

Political Systems

Political systems are the formal, governmental institutions that have the power to make political decisions over a group of people, typically within a country. There are in the contemporary world two dominant types of political system: democratic and non-democratic. We discuss the meaning of democracy in Chapter Eleven. Here we describe some versions of democracy. The most basic distinction is between direct democracy and representative democracy. A system of direct democracy is one in which the people decide directly upon matters of governance. They do not rely upon elected representatives. Direct democracies do not exist, and many would say they can not exist in any large, complicated society. Not only would it be unfeasible, but it might be very unstable. The Founding Fathers, including James Madison, believed that a direct democracy would not work and instead argued for a "republican," i.e. a representative democracy. They believed that the passions of the mob, their irrational impulses, would need to be contained and controlled if a democracy was going to endure. Only cool, level-headed, rational representatives (i.e. members of the U.S. House of Representatives and the U.S. Senate) would be able to temper the passions of the mob, and only this system would allow for a stable democracy to exist. As such, they argued for the creation of system of elected representatives. (It is quite ironic today to see the elected Republican Representatives and Senators exhorting and fueling and not tempering the irrational passions of the masses – which is exactly the opposite of what Madison and other founding fathers envisioned.)

There are many versions of representative democracies. The two most notable examples are the multi-party parliamentary systems and the two party system. The United States has a two party system. (It bears noting that the Founding Fathers – from Washington to Madison – expressed great concerns about the possibilities of political parties emerging in America. They saw these as threats to the stability of the government. They wrote often expressing concerns of "factionalism" that political parties could embody.) Through laws and customs, America does not readily allow for the emergence of parties other than the two – Republican and Democratic. While it is theoretically possible for a meaningful third party to emerge, it is highly unlikely given the structural and legal impediments in doing so. A very different form of democracy can be seen in parliamentary democracies. Most European countries, as well as others, have this form. Parliamentary systems have multiple parties. The allocation of seats in the government (e.g., the senate or parliament) are determined by the percentage each party receives in general elections. Thus, if party A gets twelve percent of the vote and party B gets forty percent, then party A will have twelve percent of the seats in parliament and party B will have forty, and all the other parties would get their proportional amounts as well. Parliamentary democracies are also typically organized by having a president and a prime minister (the names of these offices vary from country to country). The president in most parliamentary democracies is designated as the head of state.

The prime minister is designated as the head of the government. This means that the president in most parliamentary democracies is far less powerful than the prime minister. The prime minister is tasked with managing the day to day operations of the government, of signing laws into effect, of working with parliament to pass laws, etc. The president, as head of state, is officially the person responsible for the overall stability of the country. In most parliamentary systems, these officers are selected by the elected representatives in parliament rather than through a general election. Thus, the party or coalition of parties having the majority can select who will be running the government and state.

Which of the two types of democracy – the two party system or the parliamentary system is better? Two issues stand out here: stability and the will of the people. Which is more stable? Until rather recently, many have pointed to the two party system in the United States as being more stable than parliamentary systems. The United States democracy, after all, has endured for over two hundred years. In contrast, one only need to look at Germany – and the rest of Europe -- in the 1920s, to see how the multi-party democracy there collapsed in the face of Hitler's fascism. Yet, as I argue in Chapters One, Eleven, and Twelve many scholars would say that recent happenings in America – most notably the rise of Trump – call into question the enduring stability of American democracy.

It is sometimes said that the two party system works in part by containing the excessive passions of the people. Thus, the system tends to reign in extreme political views. The nature of the two party system, it is said, forces the centrist ideas to become dominant, thus producing greater stability. Extremes are not given a voice in the two party system, or so this is the argument that has often been raised. In contrast, a multi-party system allows for the rise of extreme political parties and these could, as in Germany in the 1920s, lead to the destruction of democracies. But again, as I have noted on other chapters, the extremists who have taken over the Republican Party and their Republican Party supporters suggests that the above argument is not accurate.

This leads us to ask: which form of democracy better reflects the will of the people in policies, laws, and practices? It would appear that parliamentary systems better reflect the depth and breadth of the view of the public more so than two party systems, at least as the latter is reflected in American history.

There are many, many types of non-democratic political systems. For example, **oligarchies** are political systems in which a small group of people run the government and control society. This group could be a family, an organization (akin to organized crime), a group having shared interests (corporate or military leaders, or rich people, etc.). After the fall of the Soviet Union and the emergence of a fledging democracy in Russia in the 1990s, many noted that while the country was officially a democracy it was in reality an oligarchy. A number of people made enormous amounts of money in the transition to capitalism, once communism was abandoned. These people were called the oligarchs, reflecting their enormous power over society. (However, in the last twenty years or so, Vladimir Putin has coalesced his authoritarian control over society and has subjected the oligarchs to his control. As such, it would be more accurate to describe Russia today as an authoritarian regime, or perhaps an authoritarian democracy, than it would be to call it an oligarchy. We discuss authoritarianism below. A different form of non-democratic government is a theocracy. A **theocracy** is a society run by religious leaders. The laws and practices of the society are based upon the religious beliefs of the leaders, who typically are members of the religious orders. In a theocracy, there is no separation of church and state, as was the case in American history. The two are blended in a theocracy. The most noted theocracies today are in Iran, which is run by the leaders of the Shi'ite branch of Islam and Afghanistan, which is run by Sunni Islamists.

A major type of political system that is a direct odds with any form of democracy is authoritarianism. **Authoritarianism** is an anti-democratic form of government in which the will of the leader is the determinant factor in the laws, policies, and practices of a country. The authoritarian leader makes all of the major decision and opposition is not allowed, either in the government or by the people at large. Ultimately, an authoritarian government is one which sees the wishes and desires of the leader as paramount, and often sees the public as servants to his or her wishes or desires. This is in contrast to democracies, in which the government exists to serve the needs and interest of the people.

An authoritarian leader may believe he or she is acting at the behest of the people, or even of the majority of the people, and indeed some authoritarian leaders do in fact have the support of the majority of the people (see Chapter Eleven for an extended discussion of democracies). As such, some authoritarian leaders believe their will is nothing more than the will of the people. Some believe they are the embodiment of the will of the people. (Mussolini, the fascist dictator of Italy in the 1920s and 1930s, described his political philosophy and his political system as an "authoritarian democracy".)

There are two basic types of authoritarianism: Totalitarian and non-totalitarian. A non-totalitarian form of authoritarianism is a dictatorship where an individual or group rules a country without consideration of, or constraint by, the people. A dictator makes decisions by him or herself and for him or herself. He or she is not elected and is not accountable to the people or to any external force. A non-totalitarian dictator may or may not be oriented toward embodying some self-understanding of the will of the people, as fascist leaders do (see below). And this form of dictatorship is not necessarily oriented toward creating a regimented society in which the daily lives of the people are highly controlled and regulated. A non-totalitarian dictator will be focused on maintaining an order in society that benefits the leader. Whether this requires that the populace be surveilled and regimented or not is secondary. The only thing that matters is that the public does not resist or oppose the leader.

Totalitarian forms of authoritarianism are of a different sort. These are when the leaders, who are dictators, are driven to control and manage all aspects of the lives of people in the society. It is highly regimented and required endless surveillance. Totalitarian regimes tend to deny the possibility of any opposition in the country. Dissent is not allowed. Totalitarian leaders and their regimes tend to be ideologically based and tend to envision the possibilities of creating a "new man" in their image. A totalitarian leader often envisions him or herself as the embodiment of the will of the people. He or she is simply the purest representation of this will. He is the people. There is often a moral imperative driving such leaders, in contrast to other dictators who often are driven more by instrumental desires.

In the modern and contemporary worlds we have seen two versions of totalitarian systems -one at what we might call the far left of the traditional political spectrum and the other at what we may call the far right. One of these is communism, at least as it was (and is) practiced in many countries. Communism is a political system ostensibly based upon the ideas of the nineteenth century revolutionary philosopher Karl Marx, who saw capitalism as an oppressive and exploitive system that would one day collapse and eventually be replaced by communism. Communism traditionally is seen as the political system of the radical left of the political spectrum. In history, the first major communist regime was the Soviet Union, which emerge in Russia and nearby states as the result of the Russian

Revolution in 1917. Led by Vladimir Lenin, the communists took over Russia and imposed their version of communism on the country. The system lasted until 1989 when the Soviet Union and its satellite states (of Eastern Europe) collapsed. Communism in Eastern Europe died. By the 1920s and 1930s, The Soviet Union became, under communism, an oppressive totalitarian nightmare – most notably after Stalin became the leader. The state controlled everything, and dissent was not allowed. It was a harsh and brutal regime. The other major communist revolution of the twentieth century was in China. In the late 1940s, Mao Zedong led his communist revolutionaries to victory and took over the country. China formally remains a communist country today, but in reality its economic system is capitalist and its political system is more of a one party state, proclaiming to be communist. In addition to these countries, communist societies emerged in many countries in the twentieth century, mostly in non-industrial societies, from Viet Nam to Cambodia to Cuba and North Korea. North Korea today proclaims to be communist and is a very oppressive, closed, and poor society.

Karl Marx, the founder of communism, would undoubtedly have hated these societies. He would likely have hated what happened in his name. His belief was not that the future communist society would be one in which the government is massive and all-controlling. He did not want a totalitarian society. Indeed, arguably he envisioned a very different world, a world in which the state was either non-existent or had a less pervasive influence on society than it even has in capitalist societies. Marx once famously predicted that "the state would wither away" in communist society because it would have no reason to exist. He believed this because the existence of private property, i.e. the private ownership over the means of production, was the source of all problems, and private property was the only reason that the government exists. The government exists to serve the interest of the rich, i.e. those who own and control the most property. It exists to protect the interest and property of the rich. In communism, the leaders would abolish private property and thus there would be no reason for the state or government to exist. It would vanish. Ultimately, Marx's vision, at least according to some, was more similar to anarchy than it was to anything else. Anarchy is a political system without a state, without a government. (What exactly Marx envisioned communism to look like and what he meant by the state withering away has been debated endlessly. Some say Marx envisioned the continued existence of the state. It would just have a fundamentally different character than it does now.) In short, The totalitarian communist regimes over the last one hundred years are not the types of societies that Marx wanted. How and why his vision became so corrupted in practice is itself a very interesting topic, but one that must be left to discuss at another time.

The other major form of totalitarian political system to emerge in the modern era is fascism.

Fascism was discussed above in Chapter Eight: Sacralization. But a few more words can be said here. Fascism is on the radical right of the political spectrum. It is fundamentally opposed and contradictory to democracy. It is a political theory and practice which sees the state, and specifically the leader, as embodying the will of the people. The leader is worshipped as the embodiment of all that is good and pure in us. Dissent and opposition is not tolerated. Fascism tends to be characterized by an exaggerated masculinity. The values of toughness, resilience, relentlessness, violence, action for action sake, and all the other features a hyper-masculinity are found in this system. Conversely, the weak, the tolerant, the compassionate are despised, threatened or eliminated. Fascism also embraced a mythical notion of tradition and a mythical notion of "us." The us is morally and existentially threatened and fascism must defend it against the impure, immoral enemies, from within. (See Chapter Eight for more details.) The very nature of fascism is that it cannot endure. It implodes. The most famous and most horrendous forms of fascist societies were those of Adolf Hitler's Germany from 1933 to 1945 and Benito Mussolini's Italy. Mussolini ruled Italy from 1922 to 1945. During the early and mid-twentieth century, there were also fascist regimes or regimes highly influenced by fascism in many other countries in Europe, from Spain to Hungary. The fascist regimes of the 1920s and 1930s came crashing down in World War Two, which arguably could be seen as a war between three major political ideologies – democratic capitalism, "communism," and fascism.

Fascist sensibilities in Europe and America seemingly all but disappeared in the decades after the end of World War Two, in 1945. But in the last decade we have seen a rise in the power of radical right wing parties and authoritarian (and anti-democratic) leaders in many countries, from Donald Trump in America to Giorgia Meloni in Italy, from Jair Bolsonaro in Brazil to Viktor Urban in Hungary, from the growth of the AfD party in Germany to the growth of the Marin Le Pen's party in France. There is no question that these leaders embrace or are sympathetic to authoritarianism. Whether any or all of these could rightly be called fascist or whether any or all could be said to embody fascist elements or sensibilities is more of a debate. The term fascism is widely tossed about in public debates today, most often as an invective used by liberals against arch-conservatives. Its use is also widely criticized by many. Many say that the use of the term is at best imprecise to describe current realities or at worse simply wrong. Many say the term should not be so flippantly used as it distracts rather than clarifies the issues at hand.

I wish to argue here that there are indeed strong fascist elements in many of these radical right wing movements. Most of the current arch-conservatives championing authoritarian politics have significant elements of fascist sensibilities in their politics. Whether one wishes to say these elements are enough to rightly call such people fascist we could debate. But I think it would be wrong-headed to ignore or deny the fascist elements within these movements. Here let me briefly identify several elements of fascism that appear in some of the current right wing authoritarian leaders, and specifically that appear in Trump's movement. Fascist movements are characterized by cult-like followers, followers who adore their leader, and surrender their autonomous, rational decision making facilities, to the wishes of the leader. We see this, of course, in Trump's followers. The slavish surrender of reason and autonomy to the will of Trump is clear and is clearly a fascist sensibility, one found in Hitler's Germany and in Mussolini's Italy. In fascism, the impassioned, moral emotions fuel its followers, rather than detached and cool reason. And this is what we are seeing today in the supporters of these leaders. This is what we see these leaders championing in their mind-numbing rants. Umberto Eco (see Chapter Eight) lists "machismo" as one of the characteristics of fascism. This is clearly present today in fascist movements. Trump and the others seek to present a tough-guy image, one that is resolved, unwavering, one that embodies all of the stereo-typical features of a strong, masculine figure. Conversely, the feminine is degraded, seen as weak and indecisive. As Eco notes, fascism has contempt for the weak. This is obviously a feature of Hitler's Nazis and of Trump's Republicans. The strong are to be admired; the weak despised. Trump once favorably re-tweeted a quote from Mussolini that read something like the following: "It is better live one day as a lion, than a thousand days as a sheep." Hitler's horrendous eugenics programs where he slaughtered millions of mentally ill and physically disabled people, not to mention the Jews and other "inferior" racial groups reflects this sensibility. The cult of action for action sake is another feature identified by Eco. It is better to do something now, and think about it later. As such, it is better just to get things done than to follow any procedures in place. We see this in Trump's wall on the Mexico border. Reason would say that it is not the best solution to the problem of immigration. But passion says otherwise. The sociologist Michael Mann says ethnic and political cleansing are classic features of fascism. This too is clearly present in Trump's movement. His constant complaints about the dangers of immigrants ("They are rapists and thieves", "the country is going to hell…" etc.). So too does he endlessly proclaim that the U.S. Government is corrupt – the FBI, the judiciary, etc. We must cleanse them; he tells his followers. Another feature of fascism according to Eco is the use of "newspeak." Newspeak is a term used by George Orwell in his 1984 classic dystopian novel. It is a mechanism of social control that involves telling the public lies constantly and then changing the lies over and over again. If one confuses the public, they are more easily controlled. Is this not what Trump and his supporters are doing when they spew endless lies, for example, the lie that Trump actually won the 2020 election? We can mention one more feature of fascism here. This is Robert Paxson's claim that fascists seek "redemptive violence." Redemptive violence refers to a particular orientation toward violence as a political act. Specifically, it refers to the belief that violence is seen as morally right and morally necessary, for example to purify the nation. Violence becomes a moral imperative in fascism. As such, violence is at the heart of fascist regimes, and a particular form of violence is at its core. Thus, Hitler's action, either in his killing six million innocent Jews and six million other innocent people, was driven by a perverted moral compulsion. One wants to engage in violence as a good, just, morally necessary activity. There are clear elements of this sensibility in Trump's rhetoric and actions and in the rhetoric and actions of his followers. At no time in recent American history, have there been so many overt violent threats to people either opposed to Trump or who do not sufficiently support him by supporters of Trump. Trump's call for his supporters on January 6th to "take back our country" reflects this as well. In short, fascist sensibilities and actions are at direct odds with democracies and are direct threats to democracies. Fascists see democracy (and the rule of law) as weak and ineffective. Fascist are oriented toward the destruction of democracy. Of course, Trump supporters say and largely believe they are the champions of democracy, and they see "liberals" as the true fascists. Facts simply do not support such beliefs, and such beliefs reflect some of the features of fascism noted above, such as newspeak, the quest for purity, etc.

Economic Systems

There are many, many different types of economic systems that exist or that have existed, from hunting and gathering systems to capitalism, from feudalism to communism. (These can be described as command, market or culture-based economies. See Chapter Six). Here we describe various formations of two of the most well known types of economic systems in the modern era: capitalism and socialism. We have discussed capitalism in several earlier chapters (see Chapters One and Six). Here we describe it in greater detail. Capitalism is the dominant economic system in the world today. It is based upon the belief that the most effective and efficient way of allocating value – which is what economies do – is to rely on a free, open and competitive market. It is also based upon the existence of private property and its inviolate nature. The supply and demand of goods and services in a free, open and competitive marketplace will determine the price (e.g. the value) of those goods and services. The market will determine what is produced and what is not produced, and the value of what is produced. Competition will also produce innovation and expanded prosperity to all, or so the theory has it.

In reality, however, there are many forms of capitalism. One form is **laissez faire capitalism**. Laissez faire capitalism is an economic system in which the government or state takes a "hands-off" position regarding the economy. The state does not interfere or intervene in the economy at all. It does not create laws to control or regulate the economy or the economic actors. The government does not involve itself in the economy to manage the excesses of capitalism or to manage its failings. The assumption in this system is that the capitalist market self-regulates and state involvement will prevent the market from most effectively and efficiently doing so. In reality, there has not been in the modern era any examples of laissez faire capitalist systems. Perhaps one of the closest examples of this type of economy was in the United States in the late 1800s and perhaps early 1900s. the federal government largely was not involved in the economy. It started to become involved during the Progressive Era (1890-1920) and became heavily involved in the 1930s in the midst of the Great Depression when Franklin Roosevelt enacted the New Deal, which was comprised of numerous governmental actions oriented toward controlling and regulating the economy. Arguably, a pure laissez faire economy in the complex world of today would not work. It would lead, as it did over one hundred years ago, to crises and economic collapse. However, some if not many conservative economists today continue to champion this model as the one that should be realized in practice.

Another type is state capitalism. **State capitalism** is an economic system in which the state (or government) is highly involved in the regulation of the economy and of the economic actors, or when the state owns significant economic entities, such as corporations. Many, many capitalist systems today are of this type. European countries for much of the twentieth century, owned or had control over some of the largest corporations, from automobile companies such as Fiat and Renault to the European airline manufacturer Airbus. The economic regulations of European governments also reflect elements of state capitalism. The United States government similarly is highly involved in regulating the capitalist economy, though aside from the military does not own economic actors. Nevertheless, it can be seen as having a form of state capitalism. Likewise, China could also be seen as an example of state capitalism. While it proclaims itself to be communist, and not capitalist, in reality China has adopted the fundamentals of capitalism. And the government, through the communist party, owns or controls a number of corporations. In addition, the government directly or indirectly is involved in managing the economy.

A third form of capitalism is welfare capitalism. **Welfare capitalism**, as the name implies, is an economic system in which the health, education, and welfare is provided by the state. In contrast to laissez faire capitalism which would not have a state sector providing for education or health of its citizens, for example, as this would require taxes, and taxes would interfere with the natural workings of the market, welfare capitalism is an economic system that allows the market to function on economic principles but believes the government must provide with the needs of its citizens, specifically the health, education, and welfare needs. Thus, publicly funded education reflects this, as does a national health care system in which all are provided with health insurance. (Almost all developed capitalist societies have nationalized health care. The United States does not.)

These three types of capitalism are abstractions. In reality, one can see more than one element of these in most capitalist economies today. Thus, most European societies today have elements of both welfare capitalism and state capitalism. The United States, for all its pronouncements of embracing a laissez faire model, also has elements, albeit less than the European countries, of all three models. The United States health care system – with the Affordable Care Act (ACA) passed under the Obama Administration, for example, has elements of both laissez faire and welfare capitalism built into it.

A very different way of describing capitalism today comes out of the Marxist and conflict theory traditions of sociology. This is the concept of **monopoly capitalism**. Monopoly capitalism, theorized one hundred years ago by Vladimir Lenin, is the form of capitalism that arose in the twentieth century after laissez faire capitalism. Monopoly capitalism is a form of capitalism in which corporations have become so large and so powerful that they have in effect, whether self-conscious and intentional or not, control over the markets. Corporations even if they appear to be operating in competitive marketplaces, make decisions and influence the state to make decisions that will benefit their own self interests. The idea is that corporations are so powerful that they can control and manage or manipulate many or most of their environmental factors to serve their interests. Thus, while the auto industry has many companies, there are several that are so powerful that they dominate the industry and are able to dictate their wishes to governments. Governments in monopoly capitalism enact policies, laws and practices that favor the interests of the large corporate actors who dominate markets. In effect, capitalism is not governed now by market principles per se but by the needs and interests of large corporations that in one way or another assumed monopoly or monopoly like status.

Political Economies

We have described some political systems above, and we have described some economic systems elsewhere. But one might ask whether it is really possible to accurately describe either a political system or an economic system without recognizing that politics and economic are inextricably tied to one another. This, of course, was the position of Marx when he said one could not have a true democracy in capitalism, if for no other reason than the fact that the rich would control the decision making in any formal democracy, and as such would thwart the will of the people. But one does not have to be a Marxist to believe that one cannot understand a country's political system without understanding its economic system, and without understanding that the two systems are fundamentally tied to one another.

Some of the political systems noted above are in fact political economic systems. Notably, the extreme systems of communism and fascism are both built on the belief that the political and the economic are intertwined. But what about democracy and capitalism, are these inextricably intertwined? Does one need to have both or might it be the case that a society could be, for example, democratic and socialist – an economic system in which the state highly regulates, controls, or owns major economic entities? Conservative scholars sometimes claim that democracy and capitalism are linked and that you cannot have one without the other. The argument is often based upon the assumption that both are based on the belief that freedom is required for both. So if one denies freedom in one domain, for example, in the economic domain, then you will necessarily deny freedom in the political domain. (This form of reasoning was used by conservative scholars to foster greater economic integration with communist China, under the belief that the freedom required in capitalism – an economic system that China has largely adopted – would necessarily force changes in the authoritarian regime in China and would nurture the growth of democracy. This of course not happened.)

But is it true that democracy and capitalism are joined at the hip? Does one necessitate the other because of the role of freedom? To start, we can look at the above mentioned conservative claim that democracy and capitalism are necessarily supportive of one another. The claim is based on the belief that freedom is the cornerstone of both. But as we see in Chapter Twelve, there are different meanings to the word freedom. If by freedom one means freedom to, then one might see how the conservative argument has merit. Both capitalism and democracy require people to "free to". But if one draws upon the definition of freedom for – freedom as responsibility, then one reaches a different conclusion. Freedom as responsibility is necessary for democracy, but it is not necessary, and arguably antithetical, to capitalism. For example, the capitalist is forced to think and act in instrumentally rational ways (see Chapter Nine), without considering values in his or her actions. This leads to numerous, fundamental problems, from turning people into things to destroying the planet. Why is it today, for example, when most reasonable people recognize the seriously of climate change and global warming and most recognize that humans are destroying the planet, that nothing is being done to address the issue? Capitalism fails here.

But there are numerous other tensions or contradictions between capitalism and democracy. Perhaps the most obvious is that capitalism is based upon inequality and as capitalism advances there develops a concentration of wealth in the hands of a relatively small percentage of the population. This group then significantly influenced, if not outright controls, the political decision making in democracies, through its funding of politicians, funding of influential think tanks, etc. Its actions are oriented toward the advancement of its own interests, i.e. maintaining or expanding its wealth, and is not oriented toward the advancement of democracy.

A very different sort of political economy is **socialism**. The term socialism sadly in America today has been grossly manipulated and abused by the new right wing conservatives of the Republican party – particularly in public discourse. The perversions of language (see "newspeak") is a standard part of the conservative strategy today. Thus, these "conservatives" lump anything from the Nazis to Marxists to Franklin Delano Roosevelt into one camp called "socialist." From an academic perspective and from a reasoned perspective, this is absurd on many levels. First, it is absurd to call Roosevelt a socialist. Presumably he is called this because he favored the expansion of the federal government through such things as the creation of social security and the creation or expansion of Medicare and Medicaid. To be clear: it makes not logical sense to call Roosevelt a socialist. Doing so perverts the term to such a degree as to render it meaningless. A more significant egregiously erroneous part of this conservative rhetoric is to lump the fascists and the communists together under the one term "socialism."

One could speculate as the foundations of such claims. Perhaps some right wing conservatives make these absurd claims because while communism is legitimately associated with the word socialism (see below) calling the Nazis socialist is presumably based on the fact that the Nazi Party itself is self-recognized as socialist. That is, it is formally called the National Socialist Party. But of course, Hitler and the Nazis hated communism and hated socialism – at least as it is traditionally understood (see below). Using the logic of right wing conservatives in this usage of the word socialism, suggests that we should actually believe North Korea is a democracy, after all the official name of North Korea is the Democratic People's Republic. But it would be absurd to think just because it calls itself a democracy that it is one. Just like is absurd to call the Nazi's socialist just because they use the term in their name. Some conservatives who wrongly use the term socialism in this way, perhaps might be inspired by the writings of F. A. Hayek and his book *Road to Serfdom*, which argues that the radical left movements of communism and the radical right movements of fascism lead to the same place – and oppressive "socialist" totalitarian nightmare. But this is a topic for another time.

So what is socialism? There are three distinct meanings of the word. One meaning of socialism is the Marxist one. Here socialism is said to be a stage of history that was to follow the collapse of capitalism and was the come before the final stage of history – communism. According to Marx, the proletariat were going to lead a revolution that topples capitalism. The proletariat would take over the state and eliminate private property (or at least the private ownership over the means of production, e.g. corporations). This would be the period of socialism. Marx, by most accounts, did not foresee this to be a long period. He believed socialism would naturally evolve into a new form of society called communism, in which private property (over the means of production) no longer existed, classes no longer existed, and the state (at least as we know it) no longer existed. In real history, the Soviet Union proclaimed itself to be a "socialist" republic, using the Marxist sense of the word.

A second, radically opposed definition of socialism is that found in the radical right-wing movements of fascism. The Nazi Party in Germany, as noted above, proclaimed itself to be socialist – national socialist. Again, as noted above, Hitler and the Nazis despises communism and socialism, as it is defined in the first sense above. The fascist understanding of the word socialism refers to the belief that a fascist society, ruled by a strong leader – an authoritarian – would embody the spirit of the people. The actions of the government dictated by the leader would reflect the will of the people. A strong government, a strong military was at the heart of this. This meaning of socialism clearly is not a common intellectual understanding of the word today. Using socialism in this second sense either is disingenuous or wrong.

A third meaning of socialism refers to what is often called democratic socialism. (In Europe many of the socialist parties call themselves "social democrats.") In most democratic countries in the world today, with the notably exception of the United States, one of the major political parties is democratic socialist. The American Democratic Party is far more "conservative" than these. In the United States, members of the Democratic Part on the far "left" of the political spectrum, such as Senator Bernie Sanders from Vermont and the U.S. Representative from Bronx, New York Alexandria Ocasio Cortez are socialists in this third sense. Almost all other elected members of the Democratic Party today are not socialists. Socialism in this third sense is a belief that the capitalist market by its nature must be controlled and contained. Left on its own, it will create conditions favorable to the wealthy and unfavorable to everyone else. Socialists in this sense subscribe to either or both the models of state capitalism or welfare capitalism, noted earlier. They believe that government not only should regulate capitalism, but that the government should provide for the health, education, and welfare of its citizens. As such, socialists would support national health care systems, for example, and the robust funding of such things as public education and support for the poor, not to mention support for the protections of the environment.

Of note, all three forms of socialism embrace the belief that one should not understand the political as being autonomous from the economic. In their radically different ways, all three embrace the idea that one must understand the political and economic models as intrinsically connected. But they see these interconnections in radically different ways. The National Socialists (for example) fully supported capitalism and capitalist actors, as long as they acted in ways that conformed to Nazi ideology and policies. (At the same time, the Nazis also believed the government could be used to advance its economic agenda by owning or directing corporations to complete tasks assigned to it by the government.)

Chapter Twelve: Goodbye Democracy – Dimensions and Values of Democratic Societies

It is a strange experience watching the end of democracy in America. It is perhaps even stranger to witness and experience the blind denial of Americans just two years after the New Republican Party inflicted the most dramatic damage to American democracy since the Civil War with their attack on the U.S. Capitol building on January 6, 2020. This was done at the urging of Trump and his supporters and was based on the delusional lie that Trump won the presidential election when in fact Biden won. Now that it has recessed into the faint memories of so many, it is likely thought today that this was merely an aberration, that democracy stood firm against the forces seeking to overtly topple it, that all now is well with American democracy. All is not well with American democracy. Democracy is dying, in part due to the failure of Americans to recognize this reality or to care about it.

The January 6th insurrection was and is not the only indication of threats to democracy. Indeed, it arguably is just one of numerous forces, many longstanding, that has put American democracy on a trajectory to elimination. Democracy is dying in slow motion. I suspect in twenty or thirty years there will still be voting and America will still proclaim itself to be a democracy, but it will be a sham, a democracy in name only. Watching the demise of democracy in America is funny. It is so sad that it is funny. And we must make no mistake about one of the immediate causes:

The New Republican Party led by Trump and his delusional followers, with the active and passive support of non-Trump supporting Republicans, is killing democracy in America. The cause is clear. The delusional lies, the fervent passions driven by fear and mistrust, the abandonment of reason, of facts, all characterize this New Republican Party. But the forces as we see below that have laid the foundation for the destruction go well beyond the one event of January 6. There are many forces coalescing in America that contribute, as we discuss below.

As a sociologist who knows about such things I wish to watch in bemusement as if reading about the fall of one or another wondrous, distant civilization in history, but I cannot be bemused. I can only waffle between sadness and outrage. It is particularly sad for me as a sociologist to watch and to experience this slow destruction of democracy in America. Sociology, and the social sciences in general, are notoriously poor at prognostications. While they can provide rich analyses of past and present situations, their abilities to predict things is rather poor. And yet, there are times, such as these, when the evidence is so strong, so overwhelming, that the future is clear. Social science clearly tells us where America is headed, and it is not pretty. I think, for example, of how democracy disappeared in Germany in the 1930s, to be replaced by the insanity of Hitler's Nazi fascists. He rose to power through legal means. Democracy was destroyed from the inside and legally. (True, Hitler did engage in an illegal insurrection – the Beer Hall Putsch of the early 1920s, a failed revolution after which he was convicted and jailed for a short time. But after that, he adhered to the laws in his destruction of democracy. One might wish to claim that the night of the long knives, in which he arrested and killed numerous political threats to his regime, was illegal, but in fact it was legal.) Hitler rose with the support of the non-Nazi conservatives, much like Trump maintains power with the support of non-Trump Republicans today. This is just one practical parallel between then and now. But there are other social scientific claims that can be mentioned to support the argument that social science tells us that we are witnessing the death of democracy in America. For example, the elements of trust and the solidity of institutions are seen as two anchors of democracy. But both of these are eroded today in America. More on this below.

I am watching the end of democracy in America. Indeed, I would venture to say it has already ended. It will simply take some time for it to be realized by the intelligentsia. It is sad. I miss the highly imperfect democracy that America once had, in the mid to late nineteen hundreds. Before going further, I need to clarify a basic claim at the heart of my argument: A meaningful democracy is a system which is defined as a process rather than as an end state. A democracy is a political system and a society in which members strive endlessly to perfect the imperfect idea of democracy. Perhaps the most obvious indicator of the past democracy in this sense is the increasing enfranchisement of more and more people. At the founding of modern democracies, and particularly that of the United States, there was a concern by white, landed men about allowing women, black people, propertyless people, and others from voting. These groups were excluded. Women could not vote until the early 1900s and black Americans could not vote as white people could until the Civil Rights movement of the 1950s and 1960s bore at least some fruit, even if limited. Relatedly, at the founding of democracy in America, the founding fathers were very concerned about allowing citizens in general (notably white males) not to have too much direct say in governance. They were concerned about the possibilities of having a true or pure democracy.

They were concerned about the irrational and emotional impulses of the masses which if allowed to be realized in governance could quickly spell the end to the democratic experiment. Thus, we have Madison in *the Federalist Papers* arguing in support for the newly created Constitution, which was adopted, stating that "America is not a democracy," by which he meant precisely the above: He and the other founders believed that a direct democracy would not work due to the passion of the masses. A democratic republic, however, would work, he believed. That is ostensibly what the American system is. Madison and others believed that the elected representatives would have the temperament and judgement to decide things based upon cool rationality and would not simply follow or encourage the irrational passions of the masses. (It is rather ironic today that the Republican Senators and Congressmen are doing exactly the opposite of what Madison envisioned: Rather than tempering the irrational passions of the masses, these people are fueling these irrational passions, sometimes arguing that they, the Senators, are merely enacting the will of their constituents – again in opposition to Madison's views about how the system should work.)

The America in which you live, in which I live, is not the America in which I was raised. It is not the America of pre-1980s. It is not my America. I no longer recognize this country fleeing so wantonly from democracy. Before the 1980s, it was certainty not perfect. It was deeply imperfect. But it was also democratic in the sense noted above. It was a society committed to the essential principles and values of democracy. It was a society that embraced the belief that a democracy is a process toward the realization of these principles and values. To understand this strange new world, to understand how America is fleeing democracy, we should begin by understanding in more depth what democracy is.

Three Features of a Democracy

To have a truly meaningful democracy a society has to have three features. All three need to be present or at least all three need to be seen as goals toward which the society is advancing if it wishes to be called a meaningful democracy. We may think of these features also as forms of democracy, with some societies proclaiming to be democracies adhering to one or another of the three while not manifesting all simultaneously. The first feature is a formal system of voting in which the majority of those voting win and have their desires for representatives or laws or policies realized. Bit in itself, this does not make a democracy. Many societies have regular elections in which the results are respected or at least followed but which should not be considered meaningful democracies. Syria today, for example, is run by Bashad El-Asad, the president who routinely holds and wins elections, elections which most people would consider not free and not fair. Similarly, Russians have elected Putin time and again to rule their country. The elections perhaps are conducted in a "fair" way, at least in the sense that each vote cast is counted. Putin wins. Moreover, as we see in next dimension of democracy, the Russian people by most accounts support Putin. And yet he has killed and poisoned opponents and has intimidated those thinking of challenging him. A full and meaningful democracy, Russia is not today. One other example of note here: The United States, the "republican" structure of American democracy systematically gives rural (and predominantly white and Protestant) people a disproportionate say in federal elections. They vote counts more than the votes from people in large, urban states. This is due to such things as the electoral college used to elect the president which is based on the total number of U.S. Senators combined with the total number of U.S. Representatives. The latter is based upon population, with each seat representing roughly the same number of people as each other seat. But the Senate is based upon states. There are two Senators for each state, whether the State has less than a half a million people, such as Alaska or Wyoming, or thirty eight million like California. This skews the vote in favor of small, rural states. As a result, presidents can and have won the presidency by winning the electoral college while losing the popular votes. And in recent decades it is the Republican Party candidate that wins. Importantly, there is every reason to believe this distortion will continue and will be amplified due to demographic changes.

A second necessary feature of democracy is the manifestation of the will of the majority in laws, policies, and practices of government. The government should in its actions reflect the majority will. One might at first think this this is the same as the system of voting, but it is not. It is distinct. This criteria calls upon us to look at the law, policies, and practices of government. If they reflect the will of the majority, then this feature is realized. If they do not, then it is not realized. Of course, no meaningful democracy embodies this feature perfectly. It is not possible for the government to do every single thing that conforms to the majority will. But it is possible that the government does so as much as possible, and more often than not. When a government has systematic biases embedded within it that prevents the majority will from being realized, then this feature is lacking. It is increasingly lacking in America today. This is seen in the Republican Supreme Court actions. The current Court is ideologically driven, anchored in a perverted theory of law called originalism. It has steadily produced rulings that do not align with popular sentiment. The clearest example of this is the Court's overruling of Roe vs Wade. The Court said the Constitution does not guarantee a right to abortion and as a result individual states can and have outlawed abortion rights, more are expected to do so. In addition, the federal government may enact laws banning abortion in coming months or years. All of this is in stark contrast to polling which shows that Americans by a significant majority favor the legalization of abortion. The Courts' repeated assault on voting rights is another example. Many, many more could be given. And it is not simply the courts. Congress too often votes against the will of the majority, due in part to the legal construction of the Senate, which I have noted earlier favors small, rural, white states and disfavors the majority. The vote of a person from rural Kansas counts for more than a vote from someone from Los Angeles or New York City. We see this for example in federal law regarding marijuana. While individual states have legalized the possession and use of marijuana, the federal government has not. Marijuana possession and use is a federal crime. Moreover, marijuana is designated by the federal government as a class one drug, i.e. is deemed exceeding dangerous. Again, polling routinely shows Americans favor either the decriminalization or legalization of the drug.

The third feature of a meaningful democracy – in addition to the formal system of voting and the concept of majority will – is a society in which its citizens recognize, embrace, and live the concept of citizenship. This is the most conceptually sophisticated of the three features. It is the most philosophical and the most abstract. It is also arguably the most centrally important feature to have if one wishes to have a democratic society. It is also the feature most significantly lacking and the feature most relentlessly under attack in contemporary America.

The notion of citizenship in its most profound meaning goes well beyond legal membership in a nation state. It entails a way of being that is unique to democratic societies. The modern idea of citizenship burst onto the historical landscape at the culmination of the Enlightenment, in the great revolutions of the late eighteen century – the French and American revolutions. The revolutionaries put two hundred years of critical thinking which championed such things as Reason, the primacy of the individual, democracy, and equality, etc. into practice through their revolutions. In France we can see more clearly the commitment during the revolution, however bloody and chaotic it was, to the principles of citizenship as a new mode of being. In France, the revolutionaries sought to reject all elements of tradition -- anchored in the aristocracy -- and religion – specifically the Roman Catholic Church, believing that these forces enslaved the population. A new way of thinking and being was need, a new "Man" was needed to be born. This Man was the citizen.

A citizen is one who recognizes and embraced the view that he or she is responsible for self-governance. It is a view that embraces a concept of freedom that is anchored in responsibility (see below) – for the individual and for the management of the collective -- and is anchored in a concept of equity. A citizen in a democratic society recognizes and tolerates views opposed to his or her own. A citizen recognizes that his morality is not essentially superior to another's. Tolerance is an important feature of democracy. Importantly, this does not mean weakness or moral equivocation. Arguably, it means the opposite. A commitment to citizenship is a moral commitment and in a true democracy, citizens will vociferously demonstrate strength in defending it against the threats to it.

We will return to this important concept of citizen below. But before we do so, we need to describe some of the basic values at the heart of democracy, and when we do we can once again see the real threats to American democracy.

Some Meanings of Liberty

We can identify three types of liberty or freedom and three types of equality. Let us begin with freedom. There is 1) freedom from; 2) freedom to; and 3) freedom for (or freedom as responsibility). Freedom from refers to the freedom one has when one is released from the oppressive control of another. When a person breaks out of jail or is released from jail, then person is free from captivity. In the same way, if a dog breaks off its leash, the dog is free from the control of its master. Freedom to refers to the ability to make choices, to decide to do one thing or another. One is free to drink Coke or Pepsi. One is free to apply for a job at one place rather than another, and if hired, free to work at one place or another. A child and a dog are free in this sense. They can make choices; they can decide to do this or to do that. The third form of freedom – freedom for (or freedom as responsibility) is more conceptually involved. When one is truly free in this sense then one must assume responsibility for one's actions. Here freedom and responsibility are almost synonyms; they mostly refer to the same thing. A person is free in this sense when he recognizes that he is responsible for his actions. When a person denies his responsibility, then he is not free. When for example a person said he did something because someone or something made him do it, then the person is not free in this third sense.

A few more words need to be said about this third form of freedom. When we speak of freedom as responsibility, we could ask: responsible to, or for, what or whom? One might say that this understanding means that an individual is responsible only for him or herself and not for others and not for strangers or society itself. Or similarly, one might wish to argue, as some libertarians do, that a truly democratic society will emerge – to the benefits of most, most of the time – when people embrace this individualistic understanding of freedom as responsibility. When everyone embraces and lives a commitment to the idea that every individual is responsible for their individual selves and are not responsible for anyone or anything else, so the argument goes, a true and beauty democracy will arise. As such, in its most crass interpretation, someone embracing such a view would look at a homeless person and would not wish to give them aid believing that giving aid would negates the dignity – the essence of the human -- of the individual homeless person. If and when this homeless person recognizes that they are responsible (i.e. free) and that is the essence of their humanity, then it is their choice whether to remain homeless or not.

At the heart of this example lies the belief in whether the homeless person is homeless because of factors that are in his or her power to control, or whether they are outside of such things. If a person is schizophrenic or has a debilitating physical illness that prevents him from working, then one cannot reasonably say the homeless person is "responsible" for their situation. This raises countless conceptual problems for the radical libertarian position. One such problem is: how do we or can we determine with any meaningful precision whether an individual is responsible for his situation. What type or degree or kind of mental illness, for example, would be acceptable to allow one to say that a homeless person is not responsible for being homeless? This is simply one, albeit small, problem with the absolutist argument of libertarian concepts of freedom as responsibility. There are countless other problems. For example, when the stock market crashed in 1929 and the Great Depression began, the unemployment rate skyrocketed up to twenty five percent. If someone became unemployed and remained unemployed during this time, does it make meaningful sense to say it was their responsibility that they were unemployed. Clearly, no. the point here is that the notion of responsibility is far more complex than is imagined by people such as libertarians. When we speak of freedom for or freedom as responsibility, we are referring to the responsibility to self but also to others and to society itself. Moreover, we are responsible to the past and to the future, and to our objective worlds. To say that a polluter is not responsible for the destruction of the environment or for global warming, or other environmental disasters, is to negate the responsibility, the freedom, of the polluter. The denial of these realities negates the full meaning of this concept of freedom.

Importantly, dogs and chickens can be free in either of the first two senses of freedom – freedom from and freedom to – but only adult humans can be free in this third sense – freedom for. (Adults of course can be free in the first two senses as well.) In American popular culture today, and in the past, as well as in the pronouncements of politicians, we often times here the word freedom, as if it was a sacred foundation of American society. We have buildings named "liberty." We have "freedom fries". Freedom this, freedom that. If you listen closely to the implied meaning of freedom as it is used in popular culture and by politicians and if it is not completely empty pap, then one will likely hear one of the first two senses of freedom – to and from – being invoked while the third form – freedom for – is ignored; typically it is not considered.

However, a meaningful democracy, I argue, cannot exist unless it nurtures and realizes all three forms of freedom, specifically the third form. We will have much more to say about this below when we discuss some classic statements about democracy in America. Here we can turn our attention to the concept of equality.

Some Meanings of Equality

We can begin our brief description of three types of equality that lie within modern democratic sensibility by recalling something that was mentioned earlier – both in this chapter and in Chapter One of this book. I noted that Madison, one of the more influential founding fathers of America in *the Federalist Papers* proclaimed that America is not a democracy. His comments today are widely misused and abused today by arch-conservatives of the New Republican Party to diminish any truly democratic sensibilities. Madison, it will be recalled, was not opposed to democracy. He simply did not think that a direct democracy in which the will of the people could have direct voice through the democratic political process would work due to the passions of the mob. The masses are too emotional, too impassioned, too irrational to allow democracy to work. Instead, he argued for a republican or representative form of democracy in the belief that the representatives (i.e. senators and congressmen) would be able to maintain a cool, rational, and dispassionate view of whatever issue is to be decided. The stable and level-headed character of the representatives, Madison believed, would act to contain the possible passions of the mob. Moreover, the elevated character of people who are elected to be representatives is such that these member would be able to put their self-interests aside in making decisions that would be for the best for society. (Of course, in recent years we have seen that the arch-conservative New Republicans are acting in the exact opposite manner as Madison had hoped. They are leading and championing the irrational passions of the mob rather than attempting to contain these. This is but another reason that Americans need to reflect upon how perverted democracy has become.)

At the heart of his discussion implicitly lay the concept of equality. But of note, the term equality is mentioned very, very infrequently in the classic documents of the American revolution. From The Declaration of Independence to *the Federalist Papers* we hear a lot about freedom, even if it is not examined fully, but we hardly see the word equality. This has led some conservative thinkers to argue that equality is not a central value of modern democracies, or at least to American democracy. This is an absurd claim. One need only to read the classic Enlightenment philosophers to realize that equality as well as liberty was a central value of the democratic project. Similarly, the French revolutionaries explicitly identified it as such. The very motto of the revolution, "Liberte, Egalite, Fraternite," shows unequivocally the central position of the concept. In America, the concept of equality is indeed not explicit very much in the founding documents, but it is implicitly present throughout all of the thinking of the American revolutionaries. The issue then is not whether equality is a central value of American democracy, but what equality means in American democracy.

Much like there are three meanings of freedom, discussed above, there are three meanings of equality. The first meaning of equality is the equality of outcome. To understand equality of outcome, we can use the analogy of a foot race. Equality of outcome is a situation in which everyone finishes at the same time in the race; everyone crosses the finish line at the same time In terms of economic inequalities, it refers, for example in the purist instance, to a situation in which everyone is paid the same. Whether you are a medical doctor or a worker at McDonald's, you would be paid the same. A situation of equality of outcome is one in which everyone ends up with around the same amount of wealth (and power). This, of course, is anathema to American society. Equality of opportunity, on the other hand, is ideologically embraced by many Americans. Equality of opportunity is the position that everyone in society has an equal chance at getting ahead. Whether you are born rich or born poor, the argument goes, if you have equal access to those things, such as schooling, that may allow one to move up the system of inequality, then there is equality of opportunity. Using the foot race analogy, the idea is that everyone starts at the same starting line. Some people may be smarter or more motivated than others, and these will rise to the top. They will finish ahead of the others. It is important to note that equality of opportunity does not mean that everyone will have the same income. It does not deny inequality here. Indeed, it favors inequality of income. It does however say that individuals should be allowed to rise or fall in the system of inequality based upon their own merits and initiatives and that everyone should be provided with the same conditions (e.g. good schools) which would allow for this to happen.

Equity is a third understanding of equality. This concept is more philosophically complex and more subject to contradiction. A state of equity is one of fairness. That all people are treated fairly. Equity is a concept anchored in other concepts such as morality and justice. As such, the concept is far more difficult to capture definitively. After all, what is fairness, morality, justice? Is it fair that some people are rich and others are poor? Is it fair that some groups, such as white Americans, are disproportionately rich while other groups, such as black Americans, are disproportionately poor? The claims of equity either slide back into either the concepts of equality or opportunity or equality of outcomes, or they remain conceptually slippery. Perhaps the most centrally important feature of equity in this context is that it is a living concept. It is the notion that what is or is not deemed equal or fair is subject to continued discussion. This is quite different from the other forms of equality which can be determined beforehand.

There are tensions and contradictions that ripple through the values of equality and liberty. One might think that this suggests a limitation or problem with democracy, i.e. it is contradictory. But in fact this is the essence of democratic sensibilities: It is a living project that calls upon citizens to endlessly debate the meanings and realities of equality and liberty. These tensions and contradictions can be found within the values of equality and within the values of liberty, and they can be found between the values of equality and liberty. The recognition of these tensions and contradictions; the recognition that these are necessary elements of democracy; and the recognition that this means that democracy, in its meaningful sense, must be a living and dynamic practice rather than a staid, mechanical thing, all must be recognized when considering the concept. There are tensions, for example, between liberty and equality when it comes to such things as a neighbor blasting his music at all hours of the night. Everyone – equality – has the right to a peaceful night's sleep, but individuals also have a right to listen to music in their home. How one decides whether the neighbor should be allowed to blast his stereo or not hinges on how one understands the concepts of liberty and equality. Similarly, there are contradictions within the concepts. For example, if one were to embrace the concept of equality of opportunity, then one can envision that this could or would lead to a situation of inequality of outcome, which in term would lead to inequalities of opportunities as those that have succeeded, financially, etc., would likely provide their children with advantages, in schooling, culture, etc., that would perpetuate the inequalities, not because of merit or initiative, but because of background. These are just a few of the countless tensions and contradictions.

Some Classic Statements on American Democracy

One can find numerous sociologically informed analyses of American democracy and threats to it. Two of the classic analyses are Alexis de Tocqueville's *Democracy in America* (1835/1840) and Robert Bellah et al.'s *Habits of the Heart* (1985). We can look at each in turn. Alexis de Tocqueville (1805-1859) was born into a French aristocratic family soon after the beginnings of the French Revolution. The chaos of the French Revolution, the glorious expectations of democracy, of a new world, of the realization of the ideals of Enlightenment philosophers, served as the fertile soil upon which his critical intellect developed. On the one hand, he was from an aristocratic family; on the other, he loved the prospects of democracy, of equality, of liberty. But he wondered how the democratic revolution of the French

Revolution did not produce a stable, peaceful, and prosperous society. Instead, it was a nightmare; it wrought the Reign of Terror and then Napoleon, and then a restoration of the monarchy. Democracy did not arise smoothly in France. And yet he saw in America that the Americans were able to create a stable, peaceful, and prosperous democratic society. Tocqueville wondered why that was the case? What was it about America that allowed for it to do so? Desiring to know, he managed to get a grant from the French government to go to America. Ostensibly, the grant was to study the American penal system, but in reality Tocqueville used it to study American society – American political culture -- and how it was able to produce a stable, functioning democracy. Tocqueville came to America in 1831 and travelled all around the country. He spent nine months talking to countless people, observing Americans at work and at play. He then returned to France and compiled his astute insights in a two volume book titled *Democracy in America* (1969 [1835/1840]). The book remains a classic study of American democracy and American culture.

Among his many insightful observations are a number that directly relate to our earlier descriptions of democracy, and the democratic values of liberty and equality. For Tocqueville, liberty and equality are both essential for democracy but equality is more foundational. He nicely captures this sentiment in the following passage:

> There is indeed a manly and legitimate passion for equality which rouses in all men a desire to be strong and respected. This passion tends to elevate the little man to the rank of the great. But the human heart also nourishes a debased taste for equality, which lead the weak to want to drag down the strong to their level and which induces men to prefer equality in servitude to inequality in freedom. It is not that peoples with a

democratic social state naturally scorn freedom; on the contrary, they have an instinctive taste for it. But freedom is not the chief and continual object of their desires; it is equality, for which they feel an eternal love; they rush on freedom with quick and sudden impulses, but if they miss their mark, they resign themselves to their disappointment; but nothing will satisfy them without equality, and they would rather die than lose it. (1969, p. 57)

Later, in a section of the book titled, "Why Democratic Nations Show a More Ardent and Enduring Love for Equality than for Liberty" he noted that "it has been said a hundred times that our contemporaries love equality much more ardently and tenaciously than liberty" (ibid., p. 503). One of his concerns was that if not protected, democratic societies could rather easily go from ones that have equality and liberty to ones that have equality without liberty. "I think democratic peoples have a natural taste for liberty; left to themselves, they will seek it, cherish it, and be sad if it is taken from them. But their passion for equality is ardent, insatiable, eternal, and invincible. They want equality in freedom, and they cannot have that, they still want equality in slavery. They will put up with poverty, servitude, and barbarism, but they will not endure aristocracy" (ibid., p. 506). He notes these concerns time and again throughout his book.

In *Democracy in America*, it is clear that Tocqueville sees equality rather than liberty as being foundational to democracy. As he notes, "Freedom is found at different times and in different forms; it is not exclusively dependent on one social state, and one finds it elsewhere than in democracies. It cannot therefore be taken as the distinctive characteristic of democratic ages" (ibid., p. 504). But what does he mean by equality? Perhaps the best way to understand his meaning is to recall that he is comparing democracy to the aristocracy in France prior to the 1789 Revolution. In the aristocratic era – the pre-democratic era – there was no equality. The stratification system in place was anchored in what some have called an estate stratification. This is not unlike a caste system. In France, and throughout Europe, for over one thousand years, there was a system of inequality based upon the existence of different groups ("estates") having different rights, duties, and privileges based upon their birth and nothing else. Thus, if you were born into the nobility, say as a prince, then you would automatically be accorded certain rights, duties and privileges, and you would be given powers that others, in the non-nobility estates, such as the commoners, the serfs/peasants, and even the newly arising independent businessman or merchant do not have. There was no equality in this system. It was anchored in tradition and in religion.

The French Revolution, deeply influenced by Enlightenment thought rejected this entire system, and the democratic revolutionaries proclaimed that everyone is inherently equal and should be treated as such. This was a profound change in thinking and in organizing society. But in America, there was no such history of aristocracies. Even before the American Revolution, there were no caste-like groups, comparable to the serfs or the aristocracy. (Of course, America did have a system of slavery, which Tocqueville despised. He noted in the 1830s, that slavery could not and would not survive in a democratic society.) In America, there was a tradition of equality, at least in terms of a rejection of any semblance of an aristocracy. It was this that Tocqueville was responding to.

He saw equality as the fundamental feature of American democratic society. It shaped all aspects of society. But what exactly does he mean by equality? Does he mean equality of opportunity, or equality of outcome, or equity, as discussed earlier? In *Democracy in America*, Tocqueville lays out a different, fourth meaning of equality: "Equality of conditions" (sometimes he describes it as the "equality of social conditions").

There are several dimensions to his understanding of equality of conditions. One of these is a philosophical sense. He believed, based upon his observations and interactions with Americans in the 1830s, that Americans saw themselves as inherently equal to all other Americans. There was a belief that everyone has the same, universal value and worth, whether someone was a poor farmer or a rich banker. And people would interact with each other as essentially equals, in dramatic contrast with aristocracies which was based upon inherent inequalities.

Another dimension of this understanding of the equality of conditions is the claim by Tocqueville that social classes (economic classes), or estates, do not exist in America. There are no groups with different amounts of power, privilege, and resources. For him, classes do not exist in America, and the rich are not a coherent, self-interested group, acting in a coordinated way to advance their own class interests. (They are, he says, cowered into silence due to the power and weight of equality. It prevents them from asserting their potential power.)

The reason for this absence of classes lies in the open mobility he sees in America, brought about by the equality of conditions, and democracy. People are forever moving up and down the economic ladder. As a result, classes cannot solidify. (He does however warn of the possibility and prospect of the rich consolidating their power and in acting in ways to entrench their class position. He says if this occurs, democracy will be threatened.) In discussing the wealthy class, he notes: "The rich [in America] ... are scattered and powerless. They have no conspicuous privileges, and even their wealth, being no longer incorporated and bound up with the soil, is impalpable and, as it were, invisible. As there is no longer a race of poor men, so there is not a race of rich men; the rich daily rise out of the crowd and constantly return thither. Hence, they do not form a distinct class, easily identified and plundered...." (ibid., p. 636).

He also suggests, echoing the sentiments of the equality of outcome, that in America real economic inequality is not that great. He writes, "Men with equal rights, education, and wealth, that is to say men who are in just the same condition, must have very similar needs, habits, and tastes" (ibid., p. 641). Here, he seems rather clear: equality of conditions seems to be based upon equality of outcome.

In short, we can see that his concept of equality of conditions has elements of the concept of equality of opportunity noted above. But it also has elements of equality of outcome. It is not that he sees Americans as all having the same wealth. He recognizes that economic inequality is real. But he suggests at numerous times in his book that the actual amount of inequality in America is not very great, and because of the open mobility, he sees it is less significant than in other places such as France. There is also an element of equity in his concept of equality of conditions. That is, both concepts are anchored in the belief that all are and should be treated equally.

His analysis of democracy revolves around the mores, the "habits of the heart," the culture and forms of being produced by democracy, that shape the ways Americans think and act. There are numerous dimensions to the democratic way of being he found in America. One of these is the positive attitude toward work that Americans have. Americans held work "in high esteem." (He suggests this attitude can be traced to the Protestant founders of America who settled in New England. See Max Weber for comparison.) He says Americans were hard workers and were constantly seeking to improve their lot, to rise up the economic ladder. He also says there was an endless "agitation" in Americans. They were constantly on the move, constantly seeking out new opportunities to prosper.

Another feature of Americans was the embrace of individualism. He notes there are different forms of individualism. One form is egoism, which leads to selfishness and isolation, to a withdrawal of any concern with the social, with society. But there is another form of individualism, and this is the one taken by Americans. The form of individualism taken by Americans is not one of selfishness and isolation. Instead, he says it leads to social participation and engagement. Indeed, the form of individualism in America leads to Americans constantly participating in social affairs, helping others out, and the like. They do so, he says in part because this allows them as individuals to feel good about themselves. It elevates their self-esteem.

This orientation is related to an important concept raised by Tocqueville – voluntary associations. He sees these as an important factor in contributing to the success and stability of American democracy. America, he says, is a society of joiners: "Political associations are only a small part of the immense number of different types of associations found [in the United States]. Americans of all ages, all stations in life, and all types of dispositions are forever forming associations. There are not only commercial and industrial associations in which all take part, but others of a thousand different types – religious, moral, serious, futile, very general and very limited, immensely large and very minute" (ibid., p. 513). He contrasts this with European societies which lack such things, or more precisely which lack such sensibilities.

These voluntary associations, outside of the political and economic realms, are part of what social scientists call civil society, and many scholars from Tocqueville through the present, have argued that a vibrant civil society, e.g., a society with many voluntary associations, is needed for a meaningful and stable democracy to exist. Voluntary associations – from bowling leagues to the Knights of Columbus, from parent teacher groups to religious organizations -- call upon individuals to actively engage with others – with strangers and friends – who are not family and not intimates to advance the public good. It binds people together and it does so in a way that nurtures and requires citizens to have an active engagement, rather than a passive resignation, to social life, to their worlds, to their society. It is the glue that binds a truly democratic society together, or so this is what Tocqueville and other likeminded thinkers believe.

Tocqueville sees democracy in America as a wonderful thing. However, he also identifies numerous features of it that were less that complimentary. A number of features were less that positive. For example, he says that there is a leveling of the population in American democracy. The society does not produce great scholars, scientists, and artists. Instead, it produces a society of workers where the higher value lies in work and production than in intellectual engagements. It is a society of mediocre talent, though one of engaged, hard-workers.

He also complains about the lack of deep and enduring moral framework held by Americans. Democracy he says fosters a sensibility in which moral commitments are weakened and people can and do change their moral positioning readily.

Not only does he recognize some inherent limitations with democracy in America, he also identifies numerous dimensions that are contradictory, being seen as both positive and negative. For example, above we noted that individualism is a characteristic of American democracy. But Tocqueville also says that this individualism leads in America to a lack of independence of thought. He writes: "I know no country in which, speaking generally, there is less independence of mind and true freedom of discussion than in America" (1969, p. 254-55).

Perhaps the most well know, and often misunderstood, concept in his analysis of democracy in America is the tyranny of the majority. He warns of the prospect of the tyranny of the majority arising, and by implication he suggests this is a significant potential threat to democracy. In common usage, the tyranny of the majority refers to the real possibilities that a majority group might routinely manage to win in democratic practices. If this group constantly wins, it may routinely make decisions in its own particular interests rather than in the interest of society, and it may consolidate its political power, thus undermining democracy. If it wins, it may do things in its own interests and against the interest of the minority. Thus, if one defined group, say a racial group, constitutes fifty one percent of a population and this group routinely votes and participates in the democratic process to further its own interest rather than the interest of society or of minority groups, then this majority could become an anti-democratic tyranny. This would not be a democracy. (We have seen elements of this in the deep South in American history and into the present, as white southerners manipulate the political system to favor themselves and to disfavor or disenfranchise black southerners through for example gerrymandering.)

But Tocqueville meant something else or at least something in addition to the above when he uses the concept of the tyranny of the majority. For him, the tyranny of the majority is related to morality and is anchored in his belief, noted above, that democracy produces a population that does not have strong moral frameworks. In a democracy, he warns, people in the minority might come to believe the majority is not simply the group getting the most votes, but is the group that is morally right in its perspective. He writes, that in a democracy, "the majority is invested with both physical and moral authority, which acts as much upon the will as upon behavior and at the same moment prevents both the act and the desire to do it" (1969, p. 254). But it is not simply the minority that believes that the majority are morally right, because they are the majority, it is the majority as well who believes the same. This process corrodes the very foundation of democracy and can lead to the actual destruction of democratic systems. Simply because the majority has won an election does not mean that their position is the morally correct one. But Tocqueville says this is what people tend to believe and it produces a tyranny of a majority.

One set of more recent scholars largely embracing Tocqueville's ideas are the Americans Robert Bellah and his colleagues. In the 1980s, they published a widely read book, *Habits of the Heart: Individualism and Commitment in American Life.* (The very title of the book, Habits of the Heart, is a homage to Tocqueville. It is a line from *Democracy in America.*) The subtitle of the book captures the main theme: Bellah and his colleagues wished to understand American culture, from the founding of the country through the present, and specifically identified the idea of individualism as a common theme. "Individualism lies at the very core of American culture" (p.142). Americans "believe in dignity, indeed the sacredness, of the individual" (ibid.). But there are four distinct cultural traditions regarding individualism in American history. The book largely is focused on examining these four distinct traditions and it argues that there is a crisis in American society today related to these traditions.

The four traditions are 1) the biblical tradition, 2) the civic republican, 3) the utilitarian individualism, and 4) the expressive individualism. The focus of the first two traditions was on social connectedness, community, and ethical commitments. In the biblical tradition, there is a view that the individual is ethically responsible to care for the community and this orientation is anchored in the bible; the civic republican is focused on community and the responsibilities of individuals in their communities. Toward that end the republican tradition favors a decentralized government, a government that would nurture small communities and would nurture the involvement of individuals in these small communities. The second two traditions – utilitarianism and expressive individualism – eschew any impassioned or moral commitment to the community or to social connectedness and instead focuses purely on the self as the end-all in social life. The individual in each of these traditions becomes paramount; the community is secondary. Utilitarian individualism is captures in the phrase "enlightened self-interest." People are and should be encouraged to be self-interested, and when they are then we all benefit. This of course is a founding ethos of capitalism (whether it is accurate or not is another question). Expressive individualism also elevates the individual, and individual freedom, above all else, but it does so in a different way. Bellah uses Walt Whitman as a classic nineteenth century example of expressive individualism. "[F]or Whitman, the ultimate use of the American's independence was to cultivate and express the self and explore its vast social and cosmic identities" (p. 35).

Bellah is arguing that the expressive and utilitarian forms of individualism have become more prominent in the later decades of the twentieth century, and that biblical and civic republican traditions have receded. Moreover, there has been a substantial fragmentation of these forms of individualism in recent decades, whereas in the past they tended to glide into one another. The authors are expressing concern for the stability and future of American society if utilitarian and expressive forms of individualism remain dominant. As we saw, these forms of individualism devalue the community; they devalue social connectedness, and as such threat social cohesion.

We can also see how Bellah's analysis echoes some of the themes noted earlier regarding the democratic values of freedom and equality. Clearly, the biblical and republican traditions prioritize the values of equality while the utilitarian and expressive traditions prize the value of freedom. But which form of freedom and which form of equality are being referenced here? The biblical and civic republican traditions prioritize the third form of liberty – freedom for, freedom as responsibility – while also embracing the first two. These traditions also arguably embrace the third form of equality – equity – which also embracing the first two. In contrast, the utilitarian and expressive traditions prioritize the first two forms of freedom – freedom to and freedom from – and the biblical and civic republican traditions elevate equality of opportunity over equality of outcome and equity.

For Bellah, individualism not tempered by social orientations and by a focus on doing right for the community threatens American society, and American democracy. This argument echoes those others who have argued that there has been a decline in voluntary associations in recent decades and as such a decline in civil society (see Chapter Nine). If Bellah and Tocqueville are right in their claims about what is needed to have or to maintain democracy, then a look at America today should be of concern.

The Dying Democracy

It may be tempting to deny or ignore the significance of recent political events in American history. It may be tempting to see Trump becoming president and Trump spouting endless lies and enacting endless practices significantly threatening to the institutions of democracy and to the very concept of democracy as a blip on the historical landscape. One might be tempted to say that democracy works, the threats posed by Trump did not topple the edifice of democracy in America. It withstood the challenge. Similarly, one might wish to downplay or dismiss the events of January 6th, when a large mob of Trump supporters sought to topple the U.S. government. Again, one might say the system worked. Democracy prevailed. Or one might note that the most radical wing of the New Republican Party today repeatedly supports and spouts ideas and actions that are anti-democratic, but the system works. Some might say their very presence demonstrates the effectiveness of democracy as voices from all corners are allowed to be expressed.

It is a gross misunderstanding to think that these events and so many more in recent American history are not significant threats to American democracy, to the values of liberty and equality, fully understood. A very large section of the New Republican party today, and a sizable minority of Americans today do not subscribe in any meaningful way to democracy as a system in its full meaning or to the values of liberty and equality, fully understood. We can look at the three meanings of democracy noted earlier and see that the New Republican Party rejects all of them. The first meaning was a system of formal voting in which the majority vote getter is elected to office. The millions of Americans who embrace the delusional lies put forth by Trump and his followers that the losses suffered by Trump or by governors such as Kari Lake in Arizona or Doug Mastriano in Pennsylvania were actually victories attest to a rejection of the basic institutional meaning of democracy. This is on top of the reality that the national elections in the U.S. are structured to give rural (and white rural) votes disproportionate power in the Senate and in Presidential elections. This is a formal arrangement that is fundamentally anti-democratic, and arguably one that has in part contributed to the crises in which the New Republican Party believes it is not being democratically represented.

The second meaning of democracy is that the laws, policies, and practices of the government reflect the will of the majority. Of course, this could never happen always, as noted earlier. No government can ever reflect the majority will in all things. It is impossible. Nevertheless, it is assumed here that a meaningful democracy is one in which the government tends toward reflecting the will of the majority. But here too there is a long history of the U.S. Government doing things that run counter to the will of the people. Moreover, this has been compounded increasingly in recent decades and there is little reason to think the trend will be reversed anytime soon. At the very minimum, the same faulty arrangements noted earlier which give rural (and largely white) Americans a disproportionately greater voice – their vote counts for more – than others fuel this tendency. Thus, we have a Senate that reflects the will of a small percentage of Americans. But it is more than this, the current Republican Supreme Court consists of six New Republicans who have shown through their legal philosophies and actions a disdain for the popular will. Moreover, there are multiple social forces in America today that will lead to this trend being increased – from the concentration of wealth and power of a small economic class to demographic changes.

The third meaning of democracy – as a society of citizens – is also sorely lacking in American practices today. Oddly, the New Republicans, who in reality are fundamentally anti-democratic in sensibilities and practices, proclaim to be embracing and living this third form of democracy. For example, the terrorist supporters of Trump who assaulted the Capitol on January 6 did so out of self-deluded notions of democracy and citizenship. The point is that there is a difference between delusions and reality. This third meaning of democracy is based upon the idea that no one party, in a democracy, has the exclusion corner on truth. It is only through a pragmatic, open and tolerant engagement with others over the facts can democracy work. When millions deny realities, then democracy cannot work. When millions embrace ideas that are essentially anti-democratic cloaked as democratic, then democracy cannot work. James Madison was right to note that a modern democracy requires representatives to be in place to cool the passions of the mob.

But now we have representatives of a New Republican Party that have abandoned this principle and instead have embraced the irrational passions of the mob. All of this is fundamentally antithetical to democracy as a society of citizens.

If a meaningful democracy must have in practice the three meanings of the value of liberty as well as the three meanings of the value of equality, then again American democracy is failing. The trends here have been longstanding but have, as with the overall meaning of democracy, exasperated in recent years, particularly by the actions and commitments of the New Republican Party. The embrace of a simplistic and naïve understanding of liberty that sees it simply as the freedom to do this or that or the freedom from this or that without any consideration of the reality that freedom entail responsibility, and specifically responsibility for others, for society, that has been a long standing element of Republican Party sensibilities has been exaggerated by the New Republican Party. The simplistic moral mantra embraced by many that "you should be allowed to do anything you want as long as it does not hurt anyone else" embodies the moral sensibilities of the New Republican party – and importantly is embraced by millions of others who are not part of this party. But it is a deeply flawed and dangerous and unrealistic mantra – however simplistically seductive -- that often has as its implied follow-up: you should be allowed to do anything you want to as long as you do not hurt anyone else, and as such I am not responsible for you or for what happens to you.

Chapter Thirteen: The New Right and the Alto-Right

The Governor of New York, Andrew Cuomo, resigned from office on August 10, 2021 after several weeks of intensive criticisms over his behaviors toward women. He did not rape anyone. He did not attempt to rape anyone. He did not have sex with prostitutes or with underaged women or girls. He did not hit or attack anyone. The complaint: He made women whom he interacted with feel uncomfortable as the result of things like shaking hands with young women and holding their hands for too long, or hugging women, or "groping" women, though this term is used incredibly loosely. He also apparently spoke in ways that made women feel uncomfortable, though again he never clearly made offensive comments, though they have been interpreted as such by these women. Numerous women reported feeling uncomfortable with these actions. The political pressure on Cuomo was intense. Most major national and state Democratic Party leaders said he should resign. No one publicly stood up to support him. We curiously see equally bizarre things emanating from the supposed opposite political perspective. Trump and his followers continue to spew dangerous lies and delusions, as we have mentioned several times in this book. Some of these pertain to the rejection of science. The response to the COVID-19 vaccines is an example. His supporters have rallied around the anti-vax campaign, fighting against getting vaccinated against the COVID-19 virus and fighting against measures such as wearing masks that science demonstrates would be effective at mitigating the spread and mutations of the virus. One cannot know how many people have needlessly died because of these anti-vaxxers, but it is clear the pandemic has and will cost far more lives than it otherwise would have had these people not been so forceful in their denial of science.

These are just two examples of the seeming cultural polarization in America today. All of this is crazy. It is not normal. This is new in America culture. We find that the two dominant political camps in America have become detached from common sense, and arguably from reality. As I stress below, I am not somehow suggesting we strive to reach a middle ground between these two. After all, what is the middle ground between truth and fiction? That approach fundamentally misunderstands the social dynamics. I am suggesting we need to understand what is happening here. Instead of thinking of these two camps as being somehow opposite extremes, we should better think of them as having great similarities. It is the similarities that I will explore here. We should be examining the social forces that pattern American life to produce both sets of unreal beliefs.

In the last five to ten years a rather odd and dangerous political culture has emerged in America. On the political "right," we have the emergence of the New Republican Party. On the political "left", we have the politically correct crowd, who use such concepts and terms as "micro-aggressions," "privilege," and "systemic racism" and the like. It is important to note that the New Right, or the New Republicans, are fundamentally different from the Old Republicans. In the same way, it is important to note that the new political "left" is fundamentally different from the traditional political left in America. There are some other important points to make. One of these is the lack of political symmetry that exists between these two factions. We should not see these as polar opposites sitting on the extremes of a continuous line. There is not an equivalence between them. And for the sake of democracy, we should not somehow seek a compromise or happy medium between the two. That attempt fundamentally misconstrues the nature of the factions and fundamentally does not address the essential problems at hand. The most central point, however, is that there are fundamental thematic similarities between the New Right and the new political left, which I here call the Alto-Right. (As I describe below, the thematic basis of the politically correct "liberals" is actually anchored in a radical right, crypto-fascist formulation. I would use the term "alt-right" to describe this perspective, but that term has already been appropriated by some of the New Right to describe themselves. As such, I am here using the term Alto-Right to describe the new liberals.)

The New Republicans and the Alto-Right appear to be radically different. They appear to embrace two opposing world views. Superficially, this is true, but when one digs just a bit deeper one finds numerous unsettling commonalities in the structurings of the two world views. Many of these commonalities can be found in the elements of the forms of consciousness embodied by the two perspectives. We discuss a number of these here. The first is the relationship of truth to power. Both the New Republicans and the Alto-Right reject a basic epistemological position that have governed forms of thinking in the modern era. That is, the conventional, traditional, modern epistemological position, anchored in Kantian philosophy, claims that truth is or should be understood as distinct from power. Traditionally, if one thinks of science or of the production of knowledge more generally, it was believed that the way to ascertain truths about the world was in part to look at the world in an objective, value-free way. In this perspective truth is simply out there in the world and the task is to discover it through unbiased objective investigation. This was the dominant approach taken by members of the major public institutions in America through the mid-1900s, whether they were scientists, journalists, professors, medical doctors, or others. Power along with any other consideration should not be allowed to pollute this project. This is a basic cannon of modern science and was a basic epistemological position in general in the modern world.

But both the New Republicans and the Alto-Right reject this. The New Republicans, most classically manifested in Trump, and his followers, and in the New Right propaganda machine, reject this. Truth is of no concern for these people. They see the entire political project as the manipulation of "facts" to place them in accord with their own interests or passions. Thus, we have the New Republicans believing a wide array of blatant falsities. Some of these things have discussed on numerous occasions throughout this book. The entire Trump presidency was an almost endless series of efforts to let power dictate truth rather than to let truth stand on its own. The same theme appears, albeit in a different guise, with the words and actions of the Alto-Right. This is classically seen in "systemic racism" and associated concepts. At its heart, the claim is that people can be or can act in racist ways without knowing it. "We are all racists." In other words, what appears to be true is not true. If a white person does something negative or harmful to a black person, the white person might be charged with being racist even if he or she did not believe he or she was racist and/or did not intend to act in a discriminatory way. The point is that this removes the claim of racism from objectively determined facts, and locates it within the subjective perspective of others, either the recipient of the act or of others. To claim that an act reflects racism when there is no racist intent means that the determination is based not on objective facts but on the opinions of one or another group, in this case on the recipient or victim of the act or on his or her supporters. This necessarily means that the truth of the situation is now determined not by objective facts but by the relative power of the parties. In short, we find the same logic in both the Alto-Right and the New Right.

As noted elsewhere, this situation seems to negate my argument that scientism, rooted in and championed by capitalism, is a source of the decline of democracy in America. After all, both parties seem to be rejecting the basic claims of scientism here: the value of objectivity, etc. But in fact, their arguments emerge from the ironies of scientism. Scientism empties our worlds of meanings; scientism fosters a (particular) form of critical thinking that can bleed easily into cynicism; scientism, as the sociologist Max Weber noted, using different concepts, fosters disenchantment. It creates a society of sheep looking for meanings. This was all discussed in previous chapters.

A second theme in the forms of consciousness formed in contemporary democratic capitalism is the altered relationships between appearances and realities, also as discussed previously. We see this alteration in the above rejection of the possibilities of, or values in, ascertaining or trying to ascertain objectively truths in the world. This leads both the New Republicans and the Alto-Right to proclaim that their interpretations of appearances are all that matters in proclamations of truths. Any underlying realities are meaningless, as these deep truths become fused with the appearances, or more accurately as the truths become submerged in appearances. Thus, we now have a public political culture that repeatedly is based on falsities and fabrications rather than on a recognition that there is an objective reality that is separate from the pronouncements made by the different factions.

One might wish to argue that this is not new; that the manipulations of appearances and the ignoring or denying of facts has been a longstanding part of political culture. Politicians lie, one might say. (Though such an argument becomes a bit strained when one thinks of scientists, journalists, and professors – as it was historically seen that these professionals were not oriented toward manipulations but were oriented toward presenting truths about the world.) Politicians always have and always will lie. As such, the present argument that the decline of democracy is being fostered by recent events, such as the current workings of capitalism, is simply in error. It is true that politicians and their followers have lied since the founding of the republic. But the depth and seriousness of the lies and delusions one finds now is not merely of a different degree but of a different kind, of a different character, than that found earlier. How many earlier presidential candidates who lost elections decisively, in the most recent case by seven million popular votes and many electoral college votes, proclaimed the election to be rigged? How many times has an insurrectionist mob violently attached the U.S. Capitol, prior to Jan. 6, 2021? One could cite endless examples of the fundamental differences in the character of the falsities found today and those found earlier.

Arguably, one of the most important themes of the current forms of consciousness embodied in the two seemingly opposing political orientations – the Alto-Right and the New Right – revolves around the sacralization of the self (see Chapter Eight) and of the elevation of identity in forms and expressions of being. Many scholars – from the conservative philosopher Charles Taylor to Erich Fromm, the leftist psychodynamic scholar associated with the Frankfurt School – have correctly noted that the self is constituted and realized in the modern world in a way that is distinct from the way it was constituted and realized in the pre-modern world. In the pre-modern world, the self was embedded within the social fabric of life; it was stitched inextricably to local, lived circumstances – to family, religion, sexuality, etc. One did not ask or have to ask in the 1400s, "who am I?" or "what am I going to do with my life?" These questions would be unthinkable. Now, the self and identity have lost their moorings. We are required to ask such questions, endlessly, today. Am I gay or straight, a Christian or an atheist? The assumptions underlying such a situation is that there is some sort of essential self and identity that is to be found, and one must search for it. One must strive to find ones' authentic self; one must strive endlessly to answer the essential question: Who am I? Who am I, really?

This endless quest has proved to be a centrally important dynamic in the forms of consciousness in the contemporary era. Countless scholars have commented upon this. If we are too fully comprehend this and to fully appreciate the implications of this, we must understand the processes which led to this situation. And for that we can turn once again to the forms of consciousness nurtured and required by capitalism and by democracy. Both conspire together to produce this homeless self and identity. It is not merely that both nurture and require individualism. It is not merely as Durkheim warned one hundred years ago that the modern world has the potential to create a "cult of individualism". Rather, we must look to scientism to understand this phenomena. Scientism, as I noted earlier, fragments the world; it lifts the particulars out of the lived contexts and treats them as universal and timeless entities. It treats the world as if it consists of almost countless independent and discrete objects. All of these elements and more foster a particular way of seeing and of experiencing the self – the way that is see today. But of course the self and its identity are not like other objects. It is not like a rock or a chair. But our form of thinking makes it so, at least conceptually. And yet at the same time, one cannot escape the existential reality that we are by nature fundamentally, essentially different from the other things of this world. This tension fuels the crises of self and identity that pervade democratic capitalism today.

Self and identity have shifted historical for other reasons in addition to those suggested above. We can understand this by first noting three distinct forms of identity: personal, situated, and social. Personal identity is the unique identity one has. One has a unique and individual family. One grew up in a particular neighborhood, etc. Personal identity is rooted in biography. Each of us has a unique biographical situation. Situated identity is the identity associated with the concept of role. One might be a student, a barista at Starbucks, a college professor, a mother, etc. The role is largely enacted in particular times and places. One has typically many such identities. Situated identities change through one's life and one's circumstances. Social identity is one's connectedness and affiliation with a group. One might be a Latina or a black American, or a Christian, etc. Social identity is anchored in one's affiliation and identification with a larger social group. The forces of contemporary capitalism which are anchored, pushed by the likes of scientism here combine with the increasingly complicated social order, one with not only huge division of labor but also one in which networks are becoming more dominant than groups in individual's lives – the latter which traditionally were more dominant. These and other forces conspire to diminish the importance of roles in the formation and maintenance of situated identities. Thus we are in a world in which there is an increasing demand for the elevated place of self and identity in our experience, but we are left with only two forms of identity – personal and social – that continue to be the most vital and most salient.

What does this mean for contemporary identity? We see the elevation of the importance of personal and social identities both in the New Right and the Alto-Right today, though they appear in radically different guises in the two groups. The New Right is often called or is at least often associated with White Nationalism, a belief that America is foundational a "white" country, a country supposedly created by and for white people. The patriotism attached to this is clear. (The New Right today publicly proclaims itself to be nationalist. While it tries to avoid claiming to be white nationalists, its sentiments are clear. Some in the New Right are more comfortable in explicitly championing "Christian nationalism" instead – proclaiming American to be a

Christian nation.) In short, the New Right is deeply anchored in a social identity. But the New Right also embraces fervently (and however hollowly) the idea of "liberty" (however ill conceived), even if this embrace is more ideological than it is a reflection of actual, real commitments. (It is hard to reconcile a conservative embrace of liberty when the United States has a Supreme Court which is dominated by arch-conservatives who seek to remove numerous rights that emerged in history.) At the heart of their view of liberty – at least ideologically -- is the notion that the individual is paramount. The unique individual is the be all and end all of the world, at least from this view. This reflects the importance of personal identity. We find a parallel structure in the Alto-Right. The very claims of "systemic racism" reflect a deep commitment to the importance of social identity. It is one's membership with a group – in this case a racial group – that is a definitive aspect of identity. But the Alto-Right is also deeply committed to personal identity (however paradoxical). The idea for example that individuals have the right to be who they are – I am thinking specifically in terms of gender identities, but also others – is central to this orthodoxy. The entire focus on "micro-aggressions" and the associated concepts reflects an almost obsessive commitment to caring about how an individual is experiencing his or her world. This is centrally a focus on personal identity. In short, we see both the Alto-Right and the New Right fervently embracing personal and social identities.

Despite its origins, the term "cancel culture" which was originally fabricated in the elaborate right wing propaganda industry that has so corroded American democracy reflects nicely some of these themes of identity discussed above. Cancel culture refers to the recent and current trend to fire, terminate, silence, charge, or otherwise silence voices which are deemed to be offensive to the sensibilities of one or another group. Pressuring elected representatives to resign for sexual indiscretions or for too causally using words or phrases that are deemed insensitive racially or otherwise; tearing down statues of Confederate soldiers and generals (and Columbus!), are all reflective of this cancel culture. This is the way that the new conservatives see this concept. But cancel culture is equally if not more powerfully used by the New Right to silence opposing views. Whether it be in voter suppression laws or in laws banning the teaching of critical race theory in schools and universities, or in the banning of various rights for transexuals and others, one could cite numerous other examples of the New Right employing a similar drive to silence their opposition.

What is interesting about both sides of the cancel culture is that it reflects the demise of situated identities and the elevation personal and social identities. Cancel culture is a reflection of groups seeking to assert their answers to the question: Who are we? Of note, it is a self-conscious desire to do so.

Equally if not more important is the issue of morality and ethics. There is a particular ethical orientation attached to a self-produced identity in an embedded context compared to a self-produced identity in a disembedded context, as we have now. We can turn now to look at how the preceding discussion relates to the decline of democracy in America today, and specifically how it relates to the ideologies and practices of the New Right and the Alto-Right.

In addition to identity, another theme shared by the Alto-Right and the New Right concerns the present historical context which has produces a mind-set, a popular philosophy, of the relationship of appearance to reality which is starkly different from pre-modern understandings of such things. This is yet another topic discussed more fully in earlier chapters. Recall, that capitalism enhances the divide between appearance and reality. Think about advertising. Capitalism nurtures and ultimately requires participants in the system to recognize the difference, the gap, between appearance vs reality. If it looks too good to be true, then it probably is not good. This is the essence of the forms of being in capitalism, and is reflected in advertising, in sales, in marketing. It is also deeply reflected in popular culture where popular media starts work fervently to produce and maintain an image, an appearance. Putting on an act is central to public persona, but arguably this form of being has extended to more and more non-public peoples. Think for example of how one portrays oneself on social media. It is all image; it is all self-conscious designs meant to convey particular views of the individual.

This focus on appearance and the manipulation of images has always been around. A seller in the Roman Forum two thousand years ago likely tried to convince the prospective buyer that the seller is honest and is the buyer's friend, etc. The point here is that the focus on appearance vs reality is not new to the contemporary world. What is new is the structuring of the social settings through which this appears. Prior to the contemporary world and prior to modernity, the line dividing normatively accepted places whereby one could or should champion a distinction between appearance and reality was clear. The seller in the Roman Forum normatively was allowed to put on his act. But in the home, the wife and husband in Roman two thousand years ago, did not resort to putting on acts as such. The lines where it was and was not acceptable to maintain the cleavage between appearance and reality was clear. But now the line is fuzzy at best. And it has moved. It has increasingly encroached upon the personal and the private. This confusion combined with this encroachment produces social instabilities, which further a demand for anchoring identities, as discussed above. The relationship between appearances and reality and the self are central to understanding the conceptual symmetry between the Alto-Right and the New Right.

Concomitant to the rise and elevation of particular understandings of self and identity in the contemporary era, and concomitant to the elevated importance of appearance, is the decline of sociology and the social sciences. As psychology – a field conventionally focused on all things individual -- expands, sociology declines. The decline of sociological thinking and/or the disparagement of this form of thinking is symptomatic of the problems of the contemporary era, and reflects well the centrality of the themes emerging with democratic capitalism, including scientism and the elevation of self and identity as we just discussed. It is rather telling that in America today when one or another of the myriad of social problems are discussed – whether it is mass shootings, high crime and murder rates, terrorism, or any other of the many issues confronting America today – that public discuss inevitably relies upon a psychological understanding and a psychological form of response rather than on a sociological understanding or form of response. For example, when mass shootings happen, the response is to look at the psychopathology of the individuals committing the act and when no evident explanation can be found there, we hear that the shootings were "senseless". Similarly, when people talk in the public square about personal and social problems the conversations often turn to the topic of mental illness. The discussions of such factors rarely if ever ask, "what is it about the social organization of the society that might be producing such things" What is it about the social organization that might be producing massively high murder rates? What is it about the social that might be producing the mass killings? These are of course sociological rather than a psychological questions and are largely expunged from public discussions. This again reflects the elevation of self and identity. (It also reflects the tendencies discussed in Chapters One and Two produced by capitalism to think about reality as composed of discrete things rather than relationally connected things.)

As with our other themes, we find both the Alto-Right and the New Right ignoring or dismissing or disparaging sociological considerations. The form of consciousness produced by democratic capitalism and through scientism does not readily allow for sociological forms of thinking. We can define sociology here as the systematic (some might say scientific) study of the patternings of social life. There are patterns evident in social realities which are undeniable. Continued inequalities, for example, between blacks and whites in America is just one example. But sociologists do not simply wish to chronicle the facts related to such things. They also wish to develop explanations for the causes of such things. Often, sociologists seek to explain the cause of the patternings of social life by focusing not on psychology, but on social arrangements or cultural factors, such as the moral organization of a society. It is not hard to see how the organization of social arrangements produces patterns in social reality. One need only look at the Jim Crow South to understand how white Southerners created and implemented an elaborate system of rules, policies, customs, and practices to keep black Americans in a profoundly lesser state. But it is the question of morality and of culture more generally where the continuous issues arise with respect to attributing cause of one or another pattern of social life.

This is captured in the works of the important early French sociology Emile Durkheim. Durkheim sought to establish the legitimacy of sociology as a distinct scientific discipline – distinct most notably from psychology. In his book *Suicide* and elsewhere he sought to demonstrate that patterns of social behavior can be explained without the need to focus on psychology. Suicides and specifically suicide rates can be explained by looking at the systematic forces operating outside of the individual. Patterns can be explained by the systematic organization of a society. In *Suicide*, Durkheim argued that suicide rates in France went up and down depending upon the degree of social integration and moral regulation. We need not describe in detail his account (see Chapter Two for a fuller summary). Suffice to note that the cause of the changes in suicide rates lay outside of the individuals and in the patternings of social life. (Ironically, Durkheim also embraced a deep commitment to scientism – really positivism. The grafting of scientism on to a project of attributing the cause of social patterns to systematic forces outside of the individual is an essential contradiction, a contradiction that has animated much of sociology ever since.) In his other work, Durkheim argued that there was a moral force with a sui generis reality that transcends individuals and that forms the heart of any society. This "collective conscience" is distinct and different from the conscience of the individuals, and it operates under its own laws. In short, the social is real and distinct from the individual; sociology is real and distinct from psychology.

But the essence of his work lies in the paradoxical suturing of two opposing forces: the forces of scientism and the forces of this social reality called the collective conscience – a "group mind", an independent social force bearing down on individuals but not inside individuals. The logic of scientism, with its commitment to fragmentation and observation of facts, is contradicted by the realities of something like the social, or the collective conscience. One might wish to argue there is no such tension or contradiction: Much like a physicist cannot see gravity but only the effects of gravity, so too it might be said one cannot "see" the social or the collective conscience. One can only see its effects. But such reasoning is highly problematic for those embracing a scientistic approach. Science might say there are essential forces of nature, such as gravity, which cannot be seen, but such forces are timeless and transcendent, unlike any such thing as the social or the collective conscience. If such things can and do change, then it is not possible to make scientific claims about the workings of the world based upon them.

And yet this is precisely what Durkheim does in *Suicide*: Suicide rates vary, for example, with the degree of moral regulation present in a social context. Too much or too little regulation between expectations and outcomes produces higher rates of suicide. Does this resolve the problem at hand? Yes and no. It superficially appears to do so, but it also nurtures a religious commitment to scientism which when elevated ultimately, as noted earlier, leads to fragmented understandings and to a demand to "see" the realities in question. Either we are left with scientism and no social, or the social and no scientism.

Returning to the discussion of the New Right and the Alto-Right, one finds that each of these in their own way base their perspectives within the contexts of this contradiction. Superficially, it may appear that the New Right embraces scientism and rejects the realities of the social, and the Alto-Right may appear to reject scientism and embrace the realities of the social, but within each ideological formulation one finds numerous contradictions related to these themes. The point is that both are swimming in an ideological formulation whose parameters are those just noted. In short, the foundations of discourse here are such that both sides are led to confusions and paradoxes in their ideologies and practices because in part both are operating within this same framework.

Despite the thematic similarities which I have argued above that are similar in both the New Right and the Alto-Right today, there are numerous differences between these two groups. Here we introduce just two of these differences. The first concerns the concepts of symbolic politics and moral crusades. The second concerns the sophisticated propaganda and rhetoric employed by the New Right. Both the Alto-Right and the New-Right are in the business of symbolic politics and moral crusades (see Chapter Thirteen). By moral crusades I am referring to the process by which a group uses moral issues to advance its own political interests. Moral crusades typically focus explicitly on one issue but in realty are trying to advance another, hidden one. This is a symbolic crusade – an almost religious question to advance a group's interest by focusing on an issue superficially unrelated to the deeper issue. Moral crusades tend to nurture an emotionally charged response amongst the followers, one that nurtures an embrace of moral emotions and passions at the expense of cool, rational debate. Moral crusades are fundamentally political efforts to achieve a political advantage or interest of a group that is unrelated to morality by invoking morality to do so.

Arguably the Alto-Right and the New Right today are engaged in symbolic politics and in moral crusades. But there are important differences. Several stand out. One is the self-conscious rhetorical strategies used. The New Right is clearly more organized and self-conscious in the production of manipulative rhetoric. This manipulation is anchored in the right's news centers as well as the right's think tanks. The New Right's rhetorical strategy also employs a self-righteousness, as does the Alto-Right, but the self-righteousness of the New Right is not a symbolic crusade but a political technique. Whereas the Alto-Right produces rhetoric to feel good about itself, to proclaim its own righteousness as the result of its own suffering, its grievances, the New Right produces rhetoric not to feel a particular way, per se, but to foster political action. In short, the New Right is a far more dangerous threat to American democracy today than is the Alto-Right. As such, I dissect the rhetorical strategies of the former here and leave a discussion of the latter for another time.

The Rhetoric of the New Right

The rhetoric of the New Right has a clear structure to it. There are rules governing this structure. At the heart of this rhetorical structure lies the deep beliefs of intolerant righteousness and mistrust. The New Right believes it is in a battle between good and evil and it is good. Moral emotions serve as the bedrock of this belief. One cannot compromise with truth, goodness, and certainty. Compromise is seen as weakness, and as such as the anti-good. Alone this might not be such a threatening rhetoric, but when one fuses it with mistrust and fear it produces a powerful and dangerous orientation. We have seen earlier some of the issues related to embracing an orientation of mistrust and fear. At the least, democracy cannot survive in a world of people who are essentially mistrustful and fearful.

A number of central themes can be identified in the rhetoric of the New Right. Two of these are opposition and equivalence. Opposition is the formulation of an argument ostensibly on its polar difference with the opponents. It is an assumption used in rhetorical strategy and not a conclusion. One formulates a rhetorical position by assuming that the opponents' position is fundamentally wrong simply because it is the opponents' position, and then one creates a position supporting this belief. Equivalence is closely tied to this. Equivalence is the assumption that there are two sides – the New Right and the Democrats – and that the New Right believes that whatever the rhetorical argument it produces it can justify by claiming that the opponents, the Democrats, present arguments that are rhetorical and structurally the same. That is, this equivalence manipulates and fashions an understanding of the opponent's rhetoric to be a mirror image of its own, however warped and illogical. For example, when the New Right is confronted with the realities of the seriousness of the right's insurrection on the Capitol on January 6th, the New Right proclaims a grievance that people did not protest so vociferously when Black Lives Matter protesters engaged in violent riots a couple of years earlier. (The riots, however destructive, were not a real and direct threat to the American government, to American democracy. January 6th was.) The New Right is turning events which are fundamentally different into the same such that the New Right can maintain its rhetoric and maintain intolerant righteousness.

Related to the above, a central feature of the rhetoric of the New Right is the elevation of experience, of emotion, of passion, over logic and reason. While by definition the rhetoric of the New Right must superficially appeal to logic and reason, the reality is that the New Right's rhetoric is fundamentally animated by factors of non-logic and non-reason. We need not bother to repeat here the many elements of the New Right's rhetoric that defines logic and reason here. We have done so repeatedly throughout this book.

At the heart of the rhetorical strategy or the rhetorical styles used by the New Right is the concept of meme. The concept is defined in various ways. Here we define meme as an image or a symbol that takes on a life of its own after numerous repetitive uses, and whose basis of meaning changes as these uses continue. Specifically, the meaning of a symbol or image at first might be tied to the thing it represents. A picture of an elephant has the meaning of the animal the picture represents. But the meaning of a meme is different. The meaning of a meme is anchored not in the thing being represented, but in the immediate and visceral moral emotion that is raised upon the presentation of the meme. It is a precognitive understanding. (Hitler and Goebbels, his propaganda minister, knew the power of such things – though they did so well before the pervasive use of memes brought about in part as the result of the internet and social media.) Once a symbol or image has been transformed into a meme it assumes a life of its own, being maintained by repetitive usage conjuring up one or another moral emotion.

The New Right has become particularly effective in its employment of memes. But even before the rise of the New Right, we see conservatives using such things. The term liberal was effectively used in the closing decades of the last century to instill loathing and repulsion in anyone designates as such. Liberal politicians ran fast away from calling themselves liberal as a result. In recent decades, the New Right draws upon the creation of memes regularly to further its cause. Hillary Clinton arguably lost the presidential election of 2016 to Donald Trump at least in part because of the New Right's effective strategy of turning the very name Clinton into a meme. Memes are widely employed by the New Right today with great effect. For example, it is common for the New Right to use the term woke to disparage Democrats. The term woke original was used in some parts of the black community as a term of derision for white liberals who speak up on issues of racial injustice. Its original usage was meant to be insulting to white liberals for their phony or shallow commitment to racial justice. White liberals are seen to be woken to these injustices. The implication is that their commitment is not genuine or deep or longstanding, but rather more of a fad that comes and goes. The New Right has appropriated the term woke effectively to garner support amongst conservatives. They use the term regularly today to invoke righteous indignation at "liberals" for their shallow commitment to the fad of social justice. The use of the term effectively cases liberals as less than serious, less than committed, and less than thoughtfully reflective. And the term fosters amongst the New Right a sense of intolerant self-righteousness. Anther curious example: the use of the terms Democrat and Democrat Party rather than Democratic to describe members of the Democratic Party. This memetic device decenters the members of the Democratic Party. It negates ever so subtly the legitimacy of the members by calling into question the Democrats own understanding of themselves. But more important memetically speaking is that the use of the term Democrat effectively conveys to the users and the listeners membership in the New Right. Disparaging Democrats by calling them Democrat reinforces the group solidarity of us amongst the New Right. These are just a few of the almost endless and effective use of memes by the New Right today.

Relatedly, another rhetorical mechanism used is re-appropriation. Re-appropriation is taking a term or a symbol that has one meaning for one group and completely changing the meaning for another group with the ultimate goal of changing the meaning for all groups. We have seen a number of instances of re-appropriation above – woke, democrat, etc.

Closely related to the use of memes, is the use of tropes in the rhetorical project of the New Right. A trope is a turn in language. Metaphors and similes are tropes, so too are synecdoche and metonym. We use tropes constantly – "the pen is mightier than the sword," "Boston beat New York last night," .... When tropes are paired with memes powerful rhetorical devices are created. One of the classic tropes in politics concerns race. The Republican Party under Richard Nixon developed what politicians call "the Southern Strategy" to turn the South from a Democratic Party stronghold, which it was before the 1960s into a Republican Party stronghold, which it has become since then. The Southern strategy relied upon the vile use of race to get whites to move to the Republican Party. The strategy basically was to depict black people as bad, irresponsible, etc. – as all the negative stereotypes – and to lead white Southerners to the party that was opposed to black America. The strategy called for subtle uses of imagery associating black Americans with crime, poverty, etc. such that whites would out of fear gravity toward the opposing party. The Republican strategy worked.

Perhaps one of the most classic tropes – fused as a meme -- used by the New Right today is the creation of George Soros into an evil billionaire intent on destroying all the is good and pure in the Western world. George Soros is a centrist, Jewish Hungarian American billionaire. He made his money through investments and stock trading. He has also given much money to liberal and centrist political and social causes, often through the foundation he created called The Open Society Foundation. (Of note, The Open Society Foundation is named after a book titled the Open Society, by the conservative political philosopher Karl Popper.) Soros has been a favorite target of wrath by the New Right supporters. They depict him as an evil force bent on destroying America and Western societies. The antisemitic trop is clear here, and echoes loudly the similar tropes used by the Nazis in the 1920s and 1930s: Soros is a Jew. He is not one of us. Jews are not us. He is evil and must be stopped. Jews are evil and must be stopped. He is immoral and is pushing for the destruction of the Western world. Jews are immoral and are pushing for the destruction of the Western world.

Another rhetorical device sometimes used by the New Right is to latch on to some issue that creates even a slimmer of plausible doubt about the correctness of other's views and to relentlessly champion this doubt until it becomes a meme. We see this with the visceral reaction against the COVID-19 vaccine. We see this also in many of the speeches given by Trump. Recently, he gave a speech casting doubt on the reality that a bunch of New Right supporters created a plan to capture and execute Gretchen Whitmer, the Governor of Michigan. The plotters were arrested and will be on trial for this plot. Trump suggests they are not guilty.

A more blatant rhetorical technique is simply to deny reality, which as we have seen throughout this book, is a common practice of the New Right today. One example of this is in the statements of Marjorie Taylor Greene, the New Right, United States Representative from Georgia. Greene believes many things that are not true. One of these concerns the January 6th insurrection. Greene repeatedly claims the insurrectionists were not from the New Right but instead were members of antifa – a radical leftist group. (In fact, antifa stands for anti-fascist, and it is not a group but a set of tactics.) Antifa has been created as a meme amongst the New

Right. Greene clearly states that she believes the Jan. 6th insurrectionists were members of antifa. They were not. No one adhering to common sense and to truth would belief this. Yet she repeatedly champions this.

Lastly, fake news is a rhetorical technique of sorts to advance the political cause of the New Right. The term fake news is based upon the view that journalists, and for that matter any professional group, cannot be and are not impartial in their recounting of facts. The claim of fake news is built on the assumption, as we noted elsewhere, that all people – whether they are journalists or politicians – constantly lie and therefore cannot be trusted. As noted, the embrace of this ideology is very corrosive to the fabric of democracy, and yet it is vociferously championed by the New Right. Perhaps most startling is the parallel between the charges of fake news and comparable uses of comparable terms found elsewhere. Most notably, Hitler and the Nazis complained about the lugenpresse (the "lying press") repeatedly, until any semblance of a free press was eliminated by the regime. The concept of newspeak described by George Orwell in his classic book *1984* is another parallel example.

In short, when one combines all or many of the rhetorical elements described above, you get a population motivated and acting not based upon reasoned judgment but based upon impassioned emotions. The cognitive confusions sowed by this passion opens up a population to be more not less receptive to being led by someone whose intent and interest may not be in accord with what is best for the maintenance of a democratic society.

References

Aristotle. 1999. *Nicomachean Ethics*. Second Edition. Translated by Terrence Irwin. Indianapolis, Indiana: Hackett Publishing.

Bellah, Robert, Richard Madsen, William Sullivan, Ann Swidler, and Steven Tipton. 1985. *Habits of the Heart*. Berkeley, California: University of California Press.

Bloom, Allan. 1987. *The Closing of the American Mind: How Higher Education Has Failed Democracy and Impoverished the Souls of Today's Students*.

Brigham, Carl C. 1995 [1923]. "A Study of American Intelligence," in The Bell Curve Debate, edited by Russell Jacoby and Naomi Glauberman, pp. 571-582, New York, New York: Random House.

Durkheim, Emile. 1965 [1915]. *The Elementary Forms of the Religious Life*. New York, New York. The Free Press.

Goffman, Alice. 2014. *On the Run*. New York, New York: Picador Press.

Gould, Stephen Jay. 1981. *The Mismeasure of Man*. New York, New York: W.W. Norton.

Grant, Madison. 1916. *The Passing of the Great Race*. New York, New York: Charles Scribner and Sons.

Habermas, Jurgen. 1984. *The Theory of Communicative Action, Vol. 1 and 2*. Boston, Ma.: Beacon Press.

Herrnstein, Richard and Charles Murray. 1994. *The Bell Curve: Intelligence and Class Structure in American Life*. New York, New York: The Free Press.

Latour, Bruno. 1986. *Laboratory Life: The Construction of Scientific Facts*. Second Edition. Princeton, N.J.: Princeton University Press.

Lenski, Gerhard and Patrick Noland. 2014. *Human Societies: An Introduction to Macro-Sociology*. Oxford, England: Oxford University Press.

Lewontin, R.C., Steven Rose, and Leon Kamin. 1984. *Not In Our Genes*. New York, New York: Pantheon Press.

Locke, John. 2015. *Two Treatise of Government*. Digireads.com Publishing.

MacIntyre, Alasdair. 2007. *After Virtue: A Study in Moral Theory*. Third Edition. South Bend, Indiana: University of Notre Dame Press.

Mann, Michael. 2004. *Fascists*. Cambridge, England: Cambridge University Press.

McAdam, Doug. 1999. *Political Process and the Development of Black Insurgency*. Second Edition. Chicago, Ill.: University of Chicago Press.

Pager, Devah. 2019. "The Mark of a Criminal Record," in *Readings for Sociology*, Garth Massey and Timothy O'Brien, editors, pp. 34-43. New York, New York: W.W. Norton.

Paxton, Robert. 2005. *The Anatomy of Fascism*. New York, New York: Vintage Press.

Rainie, Lee and Barry Wellman. 2014. *Networked: The New Social Operating System*. Cambridge, Massachusetts: MIT Press.

Rushton, J. Phillippe. 1999. *Race, Evolution and Behavior*. Abridged Edition. Somerset, New Jersey: Transaction Publishers.

de Tocqueville. 1969. *Democracy in America*. Translated by George Lawrence. New York, New York: Harper Perennial.

Weber, Max. 1958 [1905]. *The Protestant Ethic and the Spirit of Capitalism*. Translated by Talcott Parsons. New York, New York: Charles Scribner's Sons.

Wilson, James Q. and Richard Herrnstein. 1985. *Crime and Human Nature*. New York, New York: Simon and Schuster.

Wilson E.O. 1999. *Consilience: The Unity of Knowledge*. New York, New York: Vintage Press.

Made in the USA
Middletown, DE
26 August 2024

59717850R00219